Ulster and the City of Belfast

Richard Hayward

Clachan
Publishing
3 Drumavoley Park, Ballycastle, BT54 6PE,
Glens of Antrim,

Clachan Publishing
3 Drumavoley Park, Ballycastle, BT54 6PE,
Glens of Antrim.

Email: info@clachanpublishing.com
Website: http://clachanpublishing-com.

ISBN - 978-1-909906-27-3

This edition published 2015

Original edition;
ARTHER BARKER Ltd.:
30 Museum Street. London W.C.1
First published 1950

Copyright © Clachan 2015

This book is sold under the condition that it is not sold, by way of trade or otherwise, be lent, resold, hired out or in otherwise circulated without the publisher's prior consent in any form of binding or cover other than that in which it is published and without similar condition, including this condition, being imposed on the subsequent purchaser.

Old Irish harper

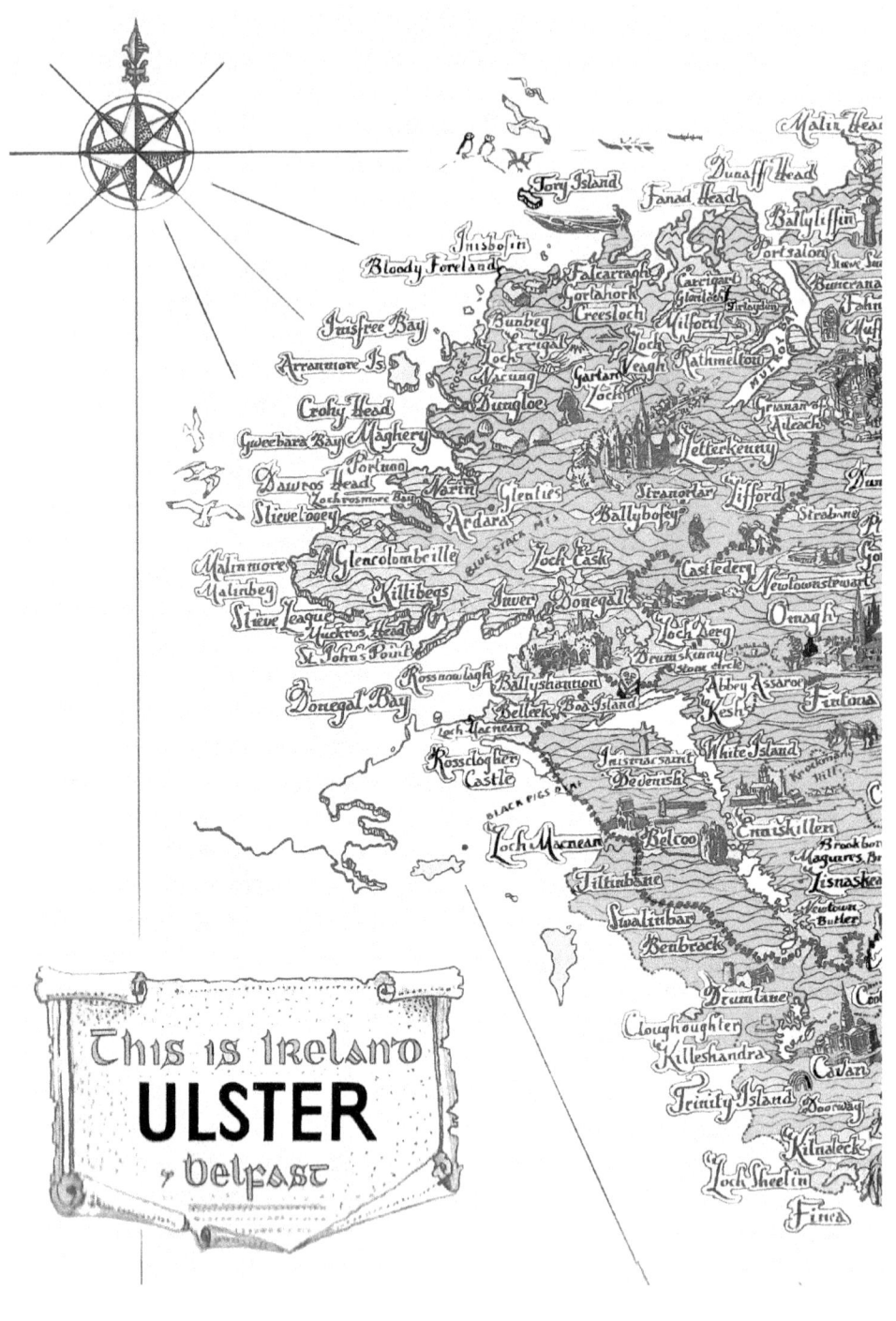

Acknowledgements

We wish to acknowledge the support given to this publication by the National Museums Northern Ireland, Cultra, Holywood, who, as holders of the Richard Hayward estate, gave Clachan Publications permission to republish this work.

We must also acknowledge the wholehearted support of Paul Clements who not only encouraged this project but also has done so much to reestablish the position of Richard Hayward in Ulster's cultural heritage.

Seán O'Halloran, EdD.,

Editor
May 2015

Richard Hayward biography

Richard Hayward was a pivotal cultural figure in the middle decades of twentieth-century Ireland. His distinctive presence and unique voice made him one of the most popular singers and actors of his generation. In his travel writing he explored aspects of Irish cultural history and was a broadcaster, folklorist and collector of Ulster dialect.
Born in Southport, Lancashire in 1892, Hayward grew up in Larne, Co. Antrim and tried to disguise his English background. He lived in Belfast and devoted his days to promoting Ireland.

Ulster and the City of Belfast was first published in 1950 and has long been out of print. A period piece of travel writing about a province that has changed beyond all recognition, this is the first time that the book has been republished. It will help retrieve the cultural legacy of Hayward and bring his work to a new generation.

Paul Clements biography

Paul Clements is a journalist, broadcaster and writer based in Belfast. He is the author of a trilogy of travel books about Ireland: *Irish Shores: A journey round the rim of Ireland* (1993), *The Height of Nonsense: The Ultimate Irish Road Trip* (2005), and *Burren Country: Travels through an Irish limestone landscape* (2011). He has written and edited two books on the travel writer and historian Jan Morris. His acclaimed biography of Richard Hayward, *Romancing Ireland*, was published in 2014 and adapted for BBC television. He is also a contributing writer to *Fodor's Ireland*, *Insight Guide Ireland* and *The Rough Guide to Ireland*. A former BBC journalist, he is a Fellow of Green Templeton College, Oxford.

Acknowledgements

Clachan Publishing is grateful to the National Museums Northern Ireland for permission to publish Richard Hayward's text. We are also grateful for the cooperation of Orion Publishing Group, present owners of the title rights of Arthur Barker Ltd publications.
We are willing to acknowledge permission from the owners of Raymond Piper's estate, should they respond to our previous requests.

Ulster and the City of Belfast
Introduction to republished edition

Sixty-five years on from its original publication in 1950, it is a pleasure to introduce to a new readership Richard Hayward's meandering journey through all nine counties so vividly recorded in *Ulster and the City of Belfast*.

This was Hayward's second Ulster book and came twelve years after the publication of *In Praise of Ulster* (1938), the first of many digressive quests around Ireland and a landmark book that helped establish his credentials as a travel writer. By 1950 he had already written and published three books of poetry, a play, a novel and five other travel books. Those on the Shannon, the Corrib, and Kerry were researched, written and published, largely during the years of the Second World War.

Ulster and the City of Belfast was the second in a series of regional topographical books called 'This is Ireland' which covered the whole country in five volumes. Hayward launched the series in 1949 with the publication of *Leinster and the City of Dublin*.

At the start of the Ulster book he describes himself as a 'confirmed wanderer and extreme individualist'. For those unfamiliar with his work, his books reflect his wide range of interests, including archaeology, geology, the built heritage, cultural history, music and folklore. A lover of rugged country and wild landscape, he was particularly drawn to mountainous regions such as the Mournes and Sperrins as well as Donegal which he awarded his 'prize as the greatest and most rewarding county in Ireland for those who take their pleasure afoot.' In fact, the county is afforded the longest chapter and is given twice the amount of space devoted to County Antrim. The book reflected changes that had taken place after the end of the war, and while it included stories from his previous Ulster book, it also contained fresh material.

To help illustrate his writing, Hayward collaborated with the artist Raymond Piper whom he had met through the Belfast Naturalists' Field Club. For his Ulster book he quartered all parts of the province in the company of Piper, stimulating his interest, not only in wild flowers, history and archaeology, but also stories and legends. As Hayward was making copious on-the-spot notes about everything they came across, Piper kept his gimlet eye peeled for the best angles for drawing. Sketchpad in hand, he zoomed in on time-worn historic monuments such as the Giant's Ring, Georgian houses in Armagh, or a narrow alleyway in Belfast, reproduced in soft dreamy shadow as a half-tone pencil drawing.

Piper's artistry and draughtsmanship are evident in the evocative sketches in the book which brought added value. They portray postwar town and country life, antiquities of the countryside, archaeological remains and mountain ranges. Many of the big architectural set pieces are here such as Queen's University, the City Hall and Clifton House in Belfast as well as the

Walls of Derry; the sketches also capture thatched cottages, the Kilgolagh horse-fair in Cavan, and a farmer with a turf-donkey in Donegal. Collectively, they are a valuable record of scenes of an Ulster long gone. The bright colour cover features the County Antrim coast road near Glenarm and shows that Piper had well and truly caught the spirit of the place.

In his writing Hayward took care to give the original Gaelic of the place names of all the towns and villages through which he passed – a testimony to the Irishness of every corner of the country. Originally Hayward rendered these in Gaelic script (*cló Gaelach*) which was generally replaced in the 1950s. For the benefit of the modern reader a Romanised version (*cló Rómhánach*) is used here. This concern for authentic placenames was something he had inhaled many years earlier from reading the work of George Borrow, a nineteenth-century English novelist and author of travel books. Borrow's interest in these names ignited Hayward's imagination, sending him off on a philological track that he wrote later yielded treasure to him.

When it came out in May 1950 the Ulster book was warmly received by the critics. *The Belfast Telegraph* said: 'Very largely this is Ulster by a writer with a predilection for its old-time Irish setting ... while the book is a general guide, it is distinctly not the stereotyped guide-book or a glorified transport timetable from which to learn when the last bus leaves for Glengormley or Stranmillis. In fact Hayward was more at home in recalling the derivation of such names.'

Three further books in the series, all illustrated by Piper, were published in the following years. *Connacht and the City of Galway* came out in 1952, *Mayo Sligo Leitrim & Roscommon* was published in 1955, and after a lengthy gap, the final book *Munster and the City of Cork* was released in 1964.

Hayward admitted that he indulged in some purple prose and in the flowery language of enthusiasm. But he succeeds in answering the two essential questions that constitute engaging travel writing: What is a land and its people who live in it really like? And secondly: How did they come to be as they are today? He effectively links the past to the present by time-switching, encapsulating the twin pillars of people and place. For anyone who wishes to know what Ulster, and the wider island of Ireland was like in the years after the war, then the five books in the series 'This is Ireland' are indispensable. They remain an important window into a country going through dramatic social and political change as it emerges into the modern era.

Apart from his travel writing, there were many other sides to Richard Hayward and his life touched many people. He was a singer, film star, stage actor, folklorist, dialect-collector, freelance journalist, broadcaster, and sales representative for Fox's Glacier Mints and Needler's Chocolates. He moved easily between the parallel worlds of filmmaking and the theatre, as well as singing, acting and speech-based programmes on the BBC, Ulster Television and Radio Éireann.

In the final years of his life he received awards including an honorary degree which was conferred on him by Lafayette College in Pennsylvania in

June 1959. The citation stated that his doctorate was awarded for 'distinguished services to Irish literature' and in recognition of his contribution to the development and spread of Irish literature. In June 1964 he was appointed OBE for his services to art and literature although the award was never formally conferred on him. His tragic death in a car accident near Ballymena on 13 October 1964, in which two other people were also killed, was widely reported in the press.

Richard Hayward was a man of boundless energy, fierce ambition, and infectious enthusiasm. Through his books and writing, his guided tours and films, he opened up the country to thousands of people. In a gesture of recognition in 2013, the Ulster History Circle erected a blue plaque at his house on the Antrim Road in Belfast where he lived for more than twenty years. The plaques commemorate men and women who have made a significant contribution to the history of Ulster and its development. A BBC Northern Ireland television documentary, *In Search of Richard Hayward*, broadcast in 2014 in the 'Groundbreakers' series, brought him to a wider audience while a Linen Hall Library symposium explored the legacy he has left us through his multifarious cultural activities.

The republishing of *Ulster and the City of Belfast*, long out of print, will help ensure that his work lives on. A new generation will be able to enjoy his writing, his knowledge of the country, its history and topography, his whimsical vignettes and of course his sparkling humour.

Paul Clements, Belfast 2015.
Author of *Romancing Ireland, Richard Hayward 1892-1964* published by the Lilliput Press, Dublin.

PREFACE TO THE FIRST EDITION

A BOOK about the whole of Ireland, similar to the several regional studies of the country which I have made in recent years, has been in my mind for a long time. I have pondered on a book which must remain light and entertaining enough to attract the average intelligent reader, but which must be free from those grosser errors, copied from writer to writer since pre-Victorian times, that beset the pages of nearly everything now available on the subject of Irish travel and topography. The lessons of geology, and the more recent discoveries of modern workers in the field of scientific archaeology, too often treated in a dry and ponderous way, must find a place in such a book, though they must be touched in with a light and colourful brush, revealing beauty and interest instead of inducing boredom and heaviness of spirit.

No country has suffered more than Ireland from the follies and inventions of the romantic antiquarian, but a book which must eschew those pleasant fancies, and inter, once and for all time, a multitude of muddle-headed though beloved sentimentalities, is difficult to shape and poise, especially if it is to remain ever mindful of the real charm of Ireland, and the endearing, colourful ways of its most imaginative people. But perhaps the biggest problem of all is the task of bringing such a large subject within the scope of a volume of modest size.

The device of writing four books instead of one, happy idea of my old friend and publisher, Arthur Barker, was the solution of that problem, and with the publication of the first of those four volumes: *Leinster and the City of Dublin*, I was at last launched upon my long-cherished enterprise of a book about Ireland as a whole. This present work carries me half-way through my formidable but most pleasant journeying, and leads me along highways and byways which have been familiar to me since childhood, and which are in very truth an intimate and close-knit part of my life and being.

Throughout my pages I have adopted the practice, which I introduced into all my other travel books, of giving the approximate Irish form and meaning of every place-name alongside its corrupt English equivalent. Those who have no taste for this sort of thing may ignore the Irish form and meaning, though not without loss, for there is a comeliness and significance about our Irish place-names that is too often smothered beneath the uncouth forms which the anglicisers of the seventeenth and eighteenth centuries put upon them with so heavy a hand. In their original forms these names have about them the pleasant sweet sound of a song, and often enough they light up with their meaning some association of local history or topography that might otherwise remain in obscurity. From all of which you will not be surprised that I use the correct form *loch*, instead of the unnecessarily transliterated *lough*, a corruption which our cousin the Scot never suffered to be visited upon him. Similarly, I have omitted the fussy and incorrect apostrophe from such personal names as O Connel and O Conor, for O or Ua means grandson, and then descendant, and the accent which appears in Irish over the prefix is there to show that it is a long vowel, and for no other purpose whatsoever. From a misunderstanding of this accent our anglicisers set it down as an apostrophe, thinking, perchance, that it was a contraction sign, such as occurs in man-o'-war, or maybe not thinking at all. The prefix *Mac* I also invariably use in its full and correct form, even when an insensitive usage has debased it into *Mc*, or worse still *M'*, and I make a plea for similar purification of our Anglo-Irish by all writers who care for historical and etymological rectitude and nicety.

I am well aware that the whole subject of place-names is obscure and complicated, and I have taken the best advice in each locality, added this to my own knowledge of the general problem, and given what I consider to be a fair suggestion of the likely Irish form. I am also aware that in many instances, save by second-hand, there is no Irish form, many place-names, and especially those of rivers and mountains, having come down to us from pre-Celtic tongues of which we have no present knowledge. But if my interpretations do no more than awaken, in the minds of some readers hitherto apathetic to such things of the past, an interest in this fascinating study, I shall be satisfied. In this subject there is no finality, and I claim nothing more for my suggestions than that they are reasonably intelligent and scholarly approximations to likelihood.

In the making of this book about my homeland I have none of the usual acknowledgements to set forth, for in writing about a countryside which is as familiar to me as the palms of my hands, I had to seek no assistance outside the bounds of my own memory, experience and deep affection; though I cannot fail, once again, to thank my nephew, Brendan Adams, for his helpful suggestions about Irish forms and derivations. Nor must I neglect to doff my hat to the Belfast Naturalists Field Club, with whose fellow-members I have spent so many rewarding hours in the fair fields of our beloved country. Archaeologists, botanists, zoologists and geologists, I thank them all for their happy comradeship.

My choice of the young Belfast artist, Raymond Piper, to illustrate these books, has turned out to be fortunate even beyond my high expectations, and I would like to place on record my warm regard for the cheerful manner in which this young man has ever sought to accomplish the tasks which I set him, as well as the deep satisfaction which the brilliance and integrity of his work has brought to me.

RICHARD HAYWARD

FOREWORD- First Edition

(To the Leinster Volume)

By MAURICE WALSH

RICHARD HAYWARD, my good Northern friend, has made his books on the Irish countryside uniquely and intimately his very own; and no one is better equipped than this son of Ulster to write about Ireland as a whole. For he loves all Ireland, and knows all Ireland, from the centre to the sea, better than any man I know—and I know a few. Richard has the rare gift of being able to make a living entity of it, so that his readers can see the contour and colour of the country, the queer shapes of the hills, the silken sheen of the lochs, the sparkle of water in the green valleys, and come to a knowledge of the way of thinking of the people who dwell amongst them. And he has two qualities that rarely go together: a geological and archaeological curiosity that is informed with an exact and scientific spirit, and a quite remarkable sense of atmosphere and colour. In telling us about those massive cairns and dolmens, those primitive beehive cells and sophisticated Hiberno-Romanesque churches, those earthen raths and Norman castles, Richard draws us on, so that we know, with him, the manner of men our forefathers were, saints and fighting-men, poets and singers, and sinners too; and in his descriptions of mountains and valleys, lochs and rivers, he reaches a level that is extraordinarily high because it is both intuitive and affectionate. His word-pictures of the marvellous colours of our countryside, ever-changing and fickle as any lovely woman, succeed where a painter must inevitably fail, and through and under the colour we see the shapes of our hills and their all-pervading mystery and loveliness.

I have watched and encouraged Richard in his regional studies of Ireland, ever since he produced that monumental book: *In Praise of Ulster,* which has now become a standard work; and I am more than happy to know that he is at last engaged in the task of writing an over-all work on Ireland as a whole, to come to the public in four separate provincial volumes. I have long been persuading him to do no less, and if the three books which are to follow this Leinster volume are of the same standard of writing and comprehension, Ireland will indeed be lucky in such an understanding, dignified and living presentation.

I am especially interested in Richard's description of the City of Dublin, which he approaches objectively as a Northerner, and yet with the deep affection and understanding of an unashamed lover. Once again his superb sense of colour nourishes his pen, and his intense regard for all that is best in Georgian architecture brings an infectious warmth to his page.

This is an intimate book, a gay, knowledgeable book, a grand, rambling book, and I shall be surprised if it does not capture its reader at once with its colourful charm, and hold him from first to last even as it held me. There is a power of thought and learning about it, a bigness of approach and a sureness of handling, that may all too easily pass unobserved because of that lighthearted bantering geniality which Richard possesses in such abounding measure. For in giving us Ireland, and the Irish people, Richard never falters nor blurs a line, but sets everything before us with a near-perfection which stems directly from his overflowing love of the country, and from his heart-warming gift of friendship which makes a complete stranger feel like an old friend of a warmly remembered youth.

I am looking forward keenly to the other volumes which are to complete this series, and I am sure that the already great value of this present book is much enhanced by the numerous lovely and delicate pencil drawings by Raymond Piper, a young Belfast artist who is just at the outset of his career. Author, illustrator and publisher have combined in a rare way to make this book a credit to Ireland.

MAURICE WALSH

CONTENTS

Richard Hayward biography. ii
Paul Clements biography. ii
Acknowledgements. ii
Introduction to republication of *Ulster and the City of Belfast* . iii
PREFACE TO THE FIRST EDITION . . . vii
FOREWORD *(To the Leinster Volume)* by Maurice Walsh . ix
CONTENTS xi
ILLUSTRATIONS xii

CHAPTERS

ULSTER 1
BELFAST. 19
COUNTY ANTRIM. 39
COUNTY DOWN. 57
COUNTY ARMAGH. 78
COUNTY TYRONE. 97
COUNTY FERMANAGH. 112
COUNTY DERRY. 123
COUNTY DONEGAL. 137
COUNTY MONAGHAN. 175
COUNTY CAVAN. 184
INDEX. 201

ILLUSTRATIONS

Old Irish Harper	*iv*
Map—Black Pig's Dyke and Spade Types	7
Map—Earth Foldings	9
Typical Ulster Gateposts	18
The Giant's Ring	20
The Cave Hill and MacArt's Fort, with Belfast below	21
Clifton House, Belfast	23
The Queen's University, Belfast	25
University and Malone Roads, Belfast	29
Donegall Place and City Hall, Belfast	31
Orange Procession, Belfast	33
Wilson's Court, Belfast	34
Parliament Buildings, Stormont, Belfast	35
Saint Mary's Church, at the end of Bank Street, Belfast	36
Crown Entry, Belfast	37
Carrickfergus Castle	38
Pogue's Entry in Antrim Town	41
The Home of the Arthur family, Dreen, Cullybackey, County Antrim	42
The Home of President MacKinley's forebears at Conagher, County Antrim	44
The Town of Antrim	47
The Antrim Coast Road, near Glenarm	48
Boneybefore, Co. Antrim, where President Andrew Jackson's parents lived	53
Fireplace of Dobbin's Castle, Dobbin's Castle Hotel, Carrickfergus, Co. Antrim	56
Saul Memorial Church, County Down	60
The Mountains of Mourne from Slidderyford dolmen County Down	65
Old Cottages of Flemish weavers, Waringstown	69
Waringstown House, from the yard	70
Waringstown Church, County Down	73
Priory Church, Newtownards, County Down	75
Holywood Priory, County Down	76
Mud-walled Cottage	77
Scotch Street, Armagh	79
The Observatory, Armagh	79
The City of Armagh, from the Cathedral Tower	81
Sheela-na-gig	83
Georgian Houses, The Mall, Armagh	87
Derrymore House, County Armagh	89
Clontygora Horned Cairn, County Armagh	93
Slieve Gullion, County Armagh	95
The Moyry Castle, Gap of the North, County Armagh	96
Georgian Doorway, Dungannon, County Tyrone	98
Stone Circles at Beaghmore, County Tyrone	101
Benburb, and the River Blackwater, County Tyrone	103
The One Horse-power Railway	107
Gray's Shop, Strabane, County Tyrone, with old Printing Press	109
Knockmany Cairn, County Tyrone	111

Enniskillen, County Fermanagh	116
Figure on Boa Island, County Fermanagh	118
Figures on White Island, County Fermanagh	119
Devenish, Loch Erne, County Fermanagh	120
Monea Castle, Fermanagh	122
Section of Wall and five London cannon City of Derry . . .	127
Kane's Rock, River Roe, near Limavady, County Derry . .	131
Benevenagh and Mouth of Loch Foyle, from Limavady Road, County Derry	133

THE BORDER

Carndonagh, County Donegal, with Saint Patrick's Cross . .	141
Horn Head, from Atlantic Drive, County Donegal . . .	147
Bloody Foreland, County Donegal, with Tory Island. out to sea .	151
Errigal, County Donegal	157
Loch Gartan, County Donegal	159
Doon Cashel, Loch Doon, County Donegal	161
Cross at Glen Columcille, County Donegal	162/3
Glen Head, County Donegal	165
Slieve League, County Donegal	169
Donegal Castle	171
Man and Turf-donkeys, Horn Head	175
The Monaghan Country	177
Dublin Street, Monaghan	181
The High Cross, Clones, County Monaghan	182
Tyrladen Village, County Donegal	184
Hiberno-Romanesque Doorway, Kilmore, County Cavan . .	187
Cloughoughter Castle, County Cavan	191
Drumlane, County Cavan	193
Kilgolagh Horse-fair, County Cavan	195
Mulroy Bay, County Donegal	197
General Phil Sheridan's birthplace, County Cavan . . .	201
Loch Sheelin, The Fairy Pool	201
Maghery, County Donegal, with sea-rods drying on the wall . .	202

HE Province of Ulster consists of nine counties and covers an area of 8566 square miles, as distinct from the political entity, made up of six counties comprising 5400 square miles, which is known as *Northern Ireland*. The population of the Province is in the region of 1,600,000, and since Northern Ireland holds all but 330,000 of this, we are with an easily remembered total of about a-million-and-a-quarter souls as the population of the Six-County area. It is with the ancient Province as a geographical whole that I shall deal in this book, but the three Ulster counties now administered by the Government of Eire, will, for the convenience of reader and author alike, be treated together at the end of the volume. In our Leinster journey we found the line of the Shannon a most convenient feature to distinguish that Province from Connacht, but no such demarcation offers itself in our Ulster wanderings. The hill barrier which separates Newry from Dundalk, and which gives us the *Gap of the North*, does indeed indicate in some degree part of our limits, but elsewhere the Provincial, as well as the political, boundary, is unmarked by any easily recognisable feature.

In the main, Ulster is a hilly but fertile area, and its only considerable tract of low, flat ground is that region which lies around Loch Neagh and then runs northwards, along the valley: the Lower Bann, to the Atlantic Ocean. An astonishingly rich variety of mountain and valley, lake and stream, rugged cliff-bordered coast and gentle wave-kissed strand, brings to the Ulster scene a beauty that is never monotonous, but this cannot: be unexpected in an area of such geological diversity. If you will draw a line on your map, from Magilligan Point to Portadown, and continue that line to Belfast, you will enclose that typical north-eastern terrain which takes the form of a great basaltic Gateau of upland moors. These basalts are the youngest of our Irish rocks, erupted about sixty million years ago but geologically speaking the products of yesterday, and so great was the mass of molten material then cast up, that the centre of the area was robbed of support and subsided into the vast basin of Loch Neagh, and into the fertile valley which drains it. The southern line of this basaltic area, projected south-westwards to the Connacht boundary, marks the northern fringe of a great area of immeasurably older rocks, the Ordovician and Silurian slates, and all of this region is hummocky, but highly fertile and well cultivated. The granite splendour of the Mourne Mountains is a later intrusion, of about the same age as the basaltic outpouring, into this immense area of ancient slates. A further line, drawn westwards from Loch Neagh to Donegal Bay, defines another area of granite; of the metamorphic rocks of Donegal and the north-west which are the oldest in Ireland; and of the limestones and other strata, of the Carboniferous period, which we met so often in Leinster, and which here continue into southwestern Ulster. All these rocks give rise to scenery which we have now become accustomed to associating with them, and from such great diversity comes that unending variety of landscape which is the very charm and essence of the Ulster scene.

The Irish word *Ulaidh* means *Ulstermen*, and the present form Ulster emerged long ago when the Norse termination *ster*, meaning the territory of, was tacked on to the old Irish name. And so Ulster means *the Territory of the Ulstermen*, and even to-day you will hear the old three-syllable pronunciation on the lips of people whose good Ulster dialect has not been destroyed by the impact of that monstrosity known as *Standard English*, whatever that may be. For language is a living thing, a growing thing, and it can only become standardised by death. But there is small fear of this in Ulster, where the dialect is unusually hale and hearty, and, for some tastes, aggressively so. Indeed, if you are a stranger to our shores, the first thing to attract your attention will be this virile Northern speech. Not Irish as you know it from stage and screen; rather Scottish perhaps, but not Scots either. In fact, just good plain Ulster, and, like everything else in this part of Ireland, highly individual and self-assertive. For Ulster is above all the stronghold of the hard-bitten, individualistic man.

There are, of course, historical reasons for this individualism, to which I shall make reference later, and as for the dialect, it is in reality a linguistic museum, a storehouse of the English that was spoken in Shakespeare's day, of the Lallans that was current in the Court of Mary Queen of Scots, and of the old native tongue of Ireland. You'll hear an Ulsterman say: *He's a civil wee fella*, and that would have sounded good English to Shakespeare; you'll hear: *God bless the childer*, and you'll find that old plural in the Prayer Book of Edward the Sixth; and any Scotsman of Mary's day would commonly have used dozens of words, such as *scunner* and *fornenst*, which are still current in the North of Ireland. As for the green strand in this piece of good homespun, I have already given you one example in the three-syllable pronunciation of the word Ulster, and it is a curious and significant fact that, whilst the Irish language has almost disappeared from eight of the nine counties of Ulster, folk-memory is astonishingly long, and most of our place-names are still pronounced by the country people with a close approximation to their sound in the native tongue. And many purely Irish words have their secure place in the everyday English of this part of Ireland.

Ireland is supposed to be the home of perfervid politics, and Ulster has always been pictured as having an especially inflammable brand of her own. But in this book I shall say no more of politics than is historically essential, for I never yet had knowledge of any political system that brought more gold to the sunset, heavier salmon to the rivers, or sweeter songs to the lips of the people. Similarly, of religion I shall say only what is necessary to make my book intelligible, and nothing at all in any kind of partisan spirit. No man alive has wandered the length and breadth of Ireland more than I have, and I have never failed to mingle in the friendliest possible manner with the people of our beloved country, north, south, east and west, irrespective of creed or faith, nor to take my full share in every movement of national cultural advancement to which whatever skills and talents I possess have called me. I have known Ireland intimately, and as a whole, in times of peace and in times of war and black hatred, but I have never found religion to be considered other than a man's private concern—unless foolishly he would have it otherwise.

It is true that Ulster stands apart from the rest of Ireland, but this separation was dictated by great natural forces millions of years before the passions of men were even foreshadowed by some faint stirring in a speck of protoplasm floating in a primeval sea. Ireland is an island lying in the Atlantic, a detached fragment of a drowned continent, and a glance at any map will reveal the fact that in its northerly parts it shares the older Caledonian foldings of the mountains of Scotland and Scandinavia, running in great ridges north-east and south-west; whilst in its southerly regions it is part of the younger foldings of the mountain systems of France and Spain and Wales, which run in a distinct east and west direction. These foldings have profoundly affected the character of the country from remote geological times, in scenery, in flora and fauna, and later in the cultural streams of man himself as he adventured forth to populate this last outpost of Europe. The first men to set foot on Irish soil landed on the coast of Antrim nearly seven thousand years ago, in what we call the Mesolithic or Middle Stone Age, and whilst science has established beyond doubt that the first Irishman was thus an Ulsterman, all history goes to show that Ulster has ever since developed a breed of men different from the men of the other parts of our country.

Being no politician at all, but a confirmed wanderer and extreme individualist who is irked by frontiers and borders of any kind, I have looked upon the present political boundary between Northern Ireland and Eire as a confounded nuisance ever since it was set up. But in spite of this personal opinion, as an historian I know that there is good precedent for such a line of demarcation almost as far back as history can go. In the early years of the Christian era, when Ireland was divided into four petty kingdoms whose kings paid tribute to a High King who ruled a fifth or central kingdom from the Palace of Tara, frequent disputes arose about the equity of this system; which was not surprising, for it was a most cumbersome piece of national organisation and in essence a highly defective bit of governmental machinery. The four southern kingdoms were Gaelic in speech and character, but it is not at all certain that Ulster was anything of the kind; indeed it seems likely that Ulster was peopled by a more ancient race than their Gaelic-speaking fellow-countrymen, who were indeed comparative newcomers to Ireland. These Ulstermen were known as *Cruthnaigh*, and it is feasible that they were in part descended from the aboriginal pre-Celtic Irish people, and in part from Pictish-speaking settlers. It is fairly certain anyway that these Ulstermen considered themselves different from the

Southern Irish even of that yesteryear, upon whom they probably looked as a tribe of foreign, Gaelic-speaking interlopers. And whether we take history for our guide, or philology, or even folklore and native tradition, we are led to the irresistible contusion that the Celtic-speaking invaders of Ireland came to this entry no earlier than the year 400 B.C., and that the Gaels, or Q Celts, were the very last of these invaders and did not reach our shores before the year 50 B.C.

In the nature of things it might be expected that the Ulstermen would be even more vehement than their fellows of the three other petty kingdoms, in their frequent objections to the payment of the Tara tribute. And so history confirms, and is itself confirmed by archaeology. For these Men of Ulster built a border which makes its modern counterpart look puny indeed. This indent boundary ran from near Sligo to Loch Allen, and was formed thereafter by the River Shannon as far as Athlone; by a massive earthen wall and trench from Athlone eastwards to Streamstown, north-eastwards to Loch Owel, northwards to Loch Derravarragh, and eastwards again to Teltown; and by the River Boyne from Teltown to the east coast. There were no half-measures about this line of demarcation, and significantly it enclosed almost the whole of that region of the Caledonian foldings to which I have referred. By the year A.D. 300 this border had been pushed northwards by successive waves of Southern invasion, and the retracted line can still be traced to-day from Bundoran, in South Donegal, to Lochs Melvin, MacNean and Allen, and eastwards from there to Slieve Gullion in the County Armagh. At that time the capital of Ulster was Emania, near the present City of Armagh, and Fergus was king of Ulster, and himself refusing to pay the Tara tribute. So that the High King commanded his nephews, the Three Collas, to attack Fergus and to make Ulster their own; and they did little less in the year A.D. 332. They pierced the great boundary near Loch Muckno, in the present County Monaghan, killed Fergus and many of his chiefs, and reduced Emania to ashes. And they drove the Men of Ulster into what is now Antrim and Down and part of Derry, where these stubborn warriors threw up yet another fortified boundary, stretching from the Newry River, near Meigh, to Goraghwood and Poyntzpass, and thence to a point in the Scarva demesne where the Bann Marshes in those days formed an impassable barrier. I have myself traced these old boundaries for many miles, and I shall be showing you a section of them when we visit Scarva later on; a section known to the country people to-day as the *Black Pig's Dyke*, or otherwise as *the Dane's Cast*, probably because the Danes never had anything to do with it!

Climate has also played its part in this differentiation of the Men of Ulster from their Southern fellow-countrymen through the ages, and as Dr. Macalister, late Professor of Celtic Archaeology in the National University of Ireland, Dublin, has pointed out in his splendid book: *Ancient Ireland—He who finds a dwelling in the north-eastern quarter has for birthright an energy, quickened by the winds blowing over the northern snows of Scotland, which the rest of the Irish folk must purchase at a great price, and must fight an ever-losing battle to maintain. It was the north-eastern quarter that created the Black Pig's Dyke. It was the north-eastern quarter which gave the greatest trouble to England. And it was the north-eastern quarter which was first divided into shires, so that the rigours of local government might the more easily be applied to its turbulent inhabitants.* And the good Professor might have added that it was the north-eastern quarter that produced those small dark men, probably Pictish-speaking **Cruitne,** who gave the Roman legions so much trouble in their frequent raids across the border in Northern Britain. They were always the divil, these Ulstermen, and that's no word of a lie!

Agricultural method is also sharply differentiated in Ulster, and for a symbol of this we may look at that most characteristic of all agricultural implements, the spade. You may be surprised to know that our Irish factories have to produce almost two hundred different kinds of spade to suit territorial preferences, though the main division is into two types, the single-eared and the double-eared. The single-eared variety, known as the loy or fack, has long disappeared from Ulster, but it is common in neighbouring Leitrim and throughout the southern and western regions. It is always fitted with a long handle without an end-grip, and almost invariably the movable foot-rest is fitted for right-handed footwork. In Ulster, on the other hand, the two-eared spade is now universal, though less than a century ago these iron spades were looked upon as useless in Donegal, where most farm labourers lacked boots and where the wooden fack was more suited to the bare foot. Usually the two-eared spade is fitted with a handle with a crutch-ended hand-grip, and most significantly the majority of Ulster farm workers are left-footed diggers. One of the commonest expressions in Ulster to this day is: *Och, sure he's a dacent enough man, but he digs with the wrong fut,* and although this now has a religious implication, it cannot be doubted that its origin is much more ancient than any variation in Christian creed, and that we are here confronted with yet another of the innumerable examples of that strong differentiation of the Men of Ulster from the other peoples of Ireland, a differentiation that is much older than recorded history itself.

I have tried to explain how the geological and historical development of Ulster tended from the outset to make it the compact and separate entity which it is to-day, but for the reader who is interested in pursuing this subject at greater length, I can best recommend a study of my larger book: *In Praise of Ulster,* where I am able to discuss the matter in more leisurely fashion. Here, I must proceed with the briefest kind of sketch, just sufficiently detailed through the centuries to provide the intelligent visitor to Ireland with a background calculated to bring his enjoyment of our country into reasonably sharp focus.

In the wake of two great events which were more intimately connected with Ulster than with any other part of our country, the second coming of Patrick to Ireland and the consequent establishment of Christianity here, zealous and mighty Ulster missionaries, like Saint Columba and Saint Columbanus, left these shores and spread the faith throughout Scotland and England and the continent of Europe. The celebrated school of Bangor, in the County Down, presided over by the good Saint Comgall of the County Antrim, was known throughout the civilised world, and missionaries from this community established schools and monasteries in such far-flung places as Saint Gall in Switzerland, Bobbio in Italy, Peronne in France, and Wurzburg in Germany. Then came the Norsemen, those fierce sea-rovers and plunderers, who founded stockaded towns that were to develop into enduring cities in Southern Ireland, but were prevented alike by the rugged Ulster coastline and the rugged independence of the Ulster people from leaving anything more permanent in the north than a few place-names such as Strangford, Carlingford and Olderfleet. But before this, in the sixth century, Ulster had established strong overseas colonies in western Scotland, and had already laid the foundations of that Scottish kingdom which was to emerge later on: a development of events from Stone Age times when Ulster and western Scotland, isolated by the mountainous backbone of Britain, formed a refuge area where the men of that ancient time survived the retreat of the last great ice sheets.

In the twelfth century, with the coming of the Anglo-Normans at the entreaties of a disgruntled princeling of Leinster, the Men Ulster still went their own stubborn way, and, apart from a small region around Carrickfergus and another in the County Down, this latest foreign invasion made no abiding foothold in this Ulster which was to continue, for more than four-hundred years, as that part of Ireland doggedly and successfully determined to keep the English outside her borders. With the emergence of England as a European power in the sixteenth century, it was to stubborn Ulster that the English statesmen of necessity turned their chief attention, for the presence of an independent Ireland so close to her shores rendered her isolation, now intensified by the reformation of her Church, extremely perilous. A long series of wars at length brought much of Ireland under English control, but until the very end of Elizabeth's reign Ulster remained more or less intact, strongly individualistic as all her history would have led us to expect, and a veritable stronghold of Ireland and the Irish way of life, of the Irish language and the old Irish legal system, and uninfluenced by English pressures and ideas, as she had been uninfluenced by the short-lived Scandinavian settlements and the more potent Anglo-Norman adventurings of the years that were gone. And then, as James of Scotland ascended the throne just vacated by the red-haired harridan of England, a final war was planned for the complete subjection of the Ulster fortress. The great Hugh O Neill, Earl of Tyrone, waged a long campaign, of brilliant strategy and bold execution, against the hated English, and had it not been for that curse of Ireland, the spirit of divided loyalties bred of jealousy and suspicion, it is hard to say what might have happened. But in the end the unity and wealth of England triumphed over the disunity and poverty of Ireland, and Ulster became an English province administered by force from a network of carefully placed fortresses, strong-points and bases. The peace which followed could hardly be called a peace, for though the native chiefs were left in possession of their lands, the laws and customs of England were introduced, and this confusion of old ways with new and strange

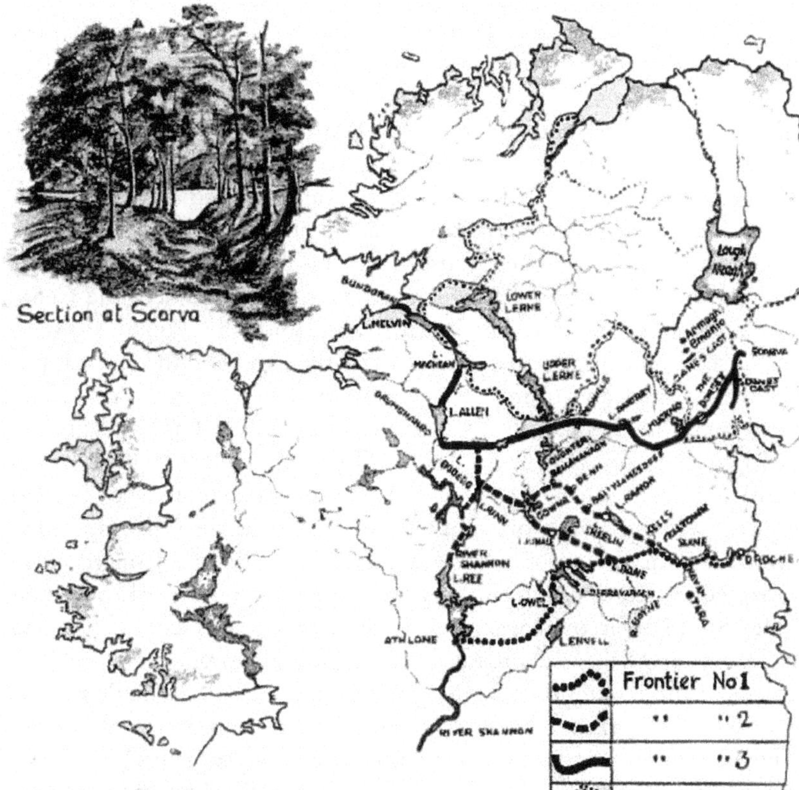

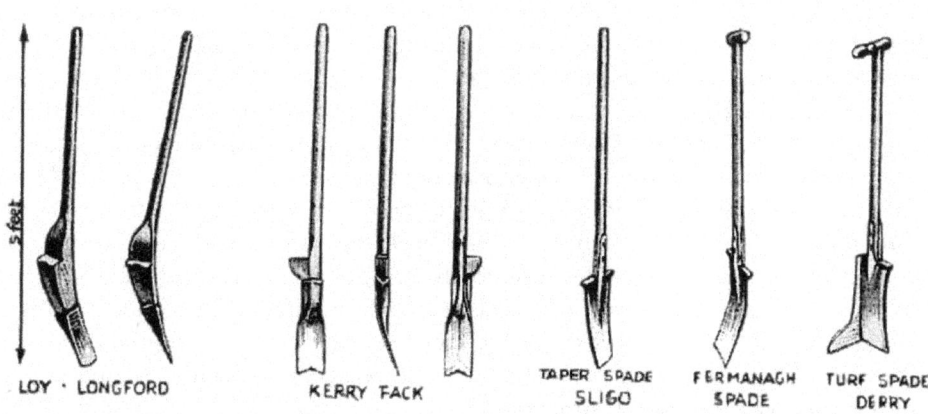

Section at Scarva
Lough Neagh
Bundoran
Lower Lerne
Upper Lerne
L.Melvin
L.Allen
Scarva
Athlone
River Shannon
L.Ree
L.Owel
Frontier No 1
" " 2
" " 3
Present Frontier

The Black Pig's Dyke and Retractions

5 feet
LOY · LONGFORD
KERRY FACK
TAPER SPADE
SLIGO
FERMANAGH
SPADE
TURF SPADE
DERRY

administrations resulted in the utmost confusion. And then, in the September of 1607, O Neill and the best of the Ulster leaders, under fear of broken faith in London, set sail for Europe, from Rathmullan in the County Donegal, and provided historians with a milestone of Irish history which has ever since been known as *The Flight of the Earls*.

Came next, towards the end of 1610, the Plantation of Ulster, at a time when such artificial plantings of alien peoples in subjected lands were very much in favour at the English court. The first of these plantings had only just been made in Virginia, and Ulster was, for obvious reasons, high on the list. Properly considered, the Plantation of Ulster must take its place with those other movements and settlements of peoples which we have just discussed, the Celtic invasion of Ireland, the Scandinavian settlements, and the Anglo-Norman conquest. Like those, it had great virtues and great faults, and like those it sought to dispossess native peoples and to impose upon them a social system and a way of life highly distasteful to them. And if we argue that English kings and queens had no kind of right or business in Ireland, as well we may on the highest moral grounds, we must also be mindful of the fact that the pre-Celtic natives of Ireland must no less have held the same opinions about the invading Celtic-speaking tribes of the fourth century before Christ, thinking of them that they might more justly have remained in Europe and left decent Irish people to work out their own national destiny in their own way. For it is neither good sense nor good history to harp upon one of these distresses and to ignore or forget the other.

The Project of the Plantation was designed to take over Irish lands for the English crown, and to regrant these lands, on certain conditions, to certain people. And the Plantation was to be British this time, and not merely English, probably because of the nationality of the new king of England and the close ties between Ulster and Scotland, and also perhaps on account of the several pockets of Scottish settlers already flourishing in Antrim and Down, a circumstance which made it unnecessary to include those two counties in the geat project. And so the Irish chiefs were deprived of their land by specious and dishonest legal word-spinning, the work of that cunning Jacobean lawyer and considerable poet, John Davies, who preferred this subtle machinery to the usual argument of the strong right arm. Everything was done so legally, and the Irish chiefs were robbed in such a gentlemanly way, that the downright Men of Ulster were left dazed and staggered in their tracks. Three classes of Planters were designated—*Undertakers*, who received two thousand acres and were required to build a castle and bawn for the protection of their new property from the wild Irish, who might be unreasonable enough to attempt to take back that which had been so politely stolen from them; *Servitors*, who received fifteen hundred acres and were required to make adequate but less costly arrangements for defence; and such Irish as swore loyalty to the English Crown and received one thousand acres of their own stolen lands, usually of the poorest quality, as payment for their renegation. This third class was stringently restricted and *Undertakers* and *Servitors* alike were to rid themselves of all tenants and followers not of British race and Protestant religion.

The counties so planted were Donegal, Tyrone, Derry, Armagh, Fermanagh, Monaghan and Cavan, and in these counties diverse systems were applied. I need only refer to the one which differed most markedly from the others, Derry, for here the Companies of the City of London, under duress of their king, purchased the whole county, then known as Coleraine, and planted it according to their own ideas. Derry itself, which they renamed Londonderry though no decent Irishman ever uses anything but the ancient name, they made into a walled city, and to-day, throughout the county, you will find several towns and villages with names to remind you of the London Companies which founded them, such as Draperstown, Salterstown, and many another besides. It was from this planting of alien peoples within her borders that Ulster's dialect arose, a picturesque and racy speech compounded of the native Irish, the lowland Scots or Lallans, and the English of the greatest period of its flowering, the English of Shakespeare. But we have already examined these three strands of the fine strong fabric that is now our everyday tongue.

Earth Foldings

Running true to form, Ulster once more exhibited its individualistic reaction to external influences. In the rest of Ireland the imposed peoples established themselves as a landowning class with servants and retainers, but Ulster quickly digested her interlopers into a community of all social grades, with a backbone of sturdy, independent farmers and merchants, and many of these were already closely allied with the Ulster folk by virtue of the old Scottish connection. Naturally such a community took much deeper root than the landlords of the south and west, many of whom were mostly absent from their demesnes, and were the more easily removed from their vast possessions by the various Land Acts of the last century, and by the violent political movements of this. But these Ulster roots, deep as they were, suffered severe testing in the Rebellion of 1641, doubly terrible because it soon became part of the Cromwellian Civil War of England. Like every great bid for Irish freedom that had gone before it, the 1641 rising was entirely Ulster in conception and execution, and it arose directly from the Ulster Plantation. The country had been wooed into a sense of false security by this settlement, when, suddenly. Sir Phelim O Neill, with the Maguires, took up arms and raised the people with devastating speed. Within a week all Fermanagh, Monaghan, Cavan, Tyrone and Derry were in the hands of the Ulster patriots, as well as much of Down and Armagh, but Donegal remained quiet and Antrim was fiercely resistant. It was a time of wild savagery and barbarous deeds, with no quarter asked or given on either side, and it all ended in a blood-bath prepared by the hated Oliver Cromwell. The Plantation was well-nigh extirpated, but the Men of Ulster were becoming used to such things, and stolidly they set themselves to rebuild their ravaged land. In the midst of this rebuilding, 1690 came upon them like a thunderclap, and, but for the stout work of the Derry men and the Enniskilleners, James the Second, *James of the Fleeing*, would have crossed to Scotland, joined up with the Killiecrankie victory, and gained his devious ends.

Once more Ulster settled down to sort out the inconsistencies of the amazingly artificial social and political structure which had been forced upon her, and in Ulster, alone in Ireland, there grew up a sturdy, individualistic working-class, free from the slavish conditions of labour which were common at the time. Already in the eighteenth century, Ulster farmers had won their Tenant Right, which secured to themselves the value created by their own labour, and made certain that it was not confiscated, as it was in the rest of Ireland, by greedy, rack-renting, evicting landlords and their even more venomous and avaricious agents. And so the Men of Ulster achieved what had never been known, or dreamt of, in Ireland, a decent standard of what was due to labour. And in Ulster, born of the dogged Ulster character, there emerged an immense new power in Irish history, a middle class of substantial farming and trading people, whilst in the rest of Ireland there was nothing of the kind to bridge the awful gap between the eviction-haunted, rack-rented peasants and the parasitical horde of gaming, absentee landlords and their greedy inhuman agents. This strongly individualistic strain in the Ulster character always exerted immense influence on the development of the country, as we have seen, and it was now to continue not only unabated but greatly fortified by coming attempts to force religious uniformity on a people so diverse in spiritual heritage.

The first Presbyterian congregation in Ireland was formed in the County Antrim in 1613, and the first properly constituted Presbytery followed in 1642.

By the eighteenth century the followers of this faith formed a powerful body in Ulster, but in 1704 they were called upon to take an oath recognising the Established Church as the one true body of Christian worship. All history should have warned the bishops of the folly of such a demand, and the Men of Ulster reacted as we would expect them to react. Their refusal to play traitors to the sturdy faith that was in them brought great persecution upon them: they were debarred from teaching in schools, the validity of their marriages was denied, and their ministers and religious services were much interfered with. At the same time drought, famine, sheep disease, smallpox, shortage of silver and copper coinage to the hampering of trade, and absurd legislation against the woollen industry, added to their miseries, and they began to cast hopeful eyes towards the new world across the Atlantic. Small parties began to leave Ulster and the bitter persecution that grew more intolerable every year, and by 1718 what had started as a tiny stream of emigration became a roaring river in full flood. In that year five ships from Ireland arrived in Boston Harbour and landed seven-hundred-and-fifty emigrants from the valleys of the Bann and the Foyle, and some of these adventurers straightway settled the town of New Derry in New Hampshire. Two things these people took with them to Boston which had never been seen there before, the Irish potato and the spinning-wheel, and the ladies of Boston were greatly interested in these strange machines which the women of Ulster never seemed to be without. As for the potato, that was only making the return journey, for it had been introduced into Ireland from America more than a century before by Sir Walter Raleigh. They were tough men, these founders of New Derry, many of them veterans of the famous siege, and they were a terror to the Indians along the frontier. From their settlement no less than ten new towns, of solid Ulster background, arose in New Hampshire during the next twenty-five years, as well as two in Vermont and another in Maine, and pioneering families and groups from these communities set out up the Connecticut River and over the Green Mountains. These settlers, and those who were to follow them in ever-increasing numbers, were to play a vital part in the founding of the United States of America, a part far beyond all expectation and vastly out of proportion to their numbers. For instance, in the War of Independence, General John Stark of New Derry, son of an Ulsterman, led his men from Bunker's Hill to the end of the war, and General Reid, of the same town and blood, fought from Bunker's Hill to Saratoga, and was with Washington at Valley Forge. General James Millar, greatly distinguished in the War of 1812 and afterwards Governor of Arkansas, was of New Derry stock, and Major Rogers, who commanded the famous Rangers, came from the same town. Horace Greeley was of kindred Ulster blood, New Derry to the: ackbone, and so was Matthew Thornton, one of the signatories of *the Declaration of Independence.*

The 750 Ulster emigrants of 1718 were followed by about six thousand of their kindred every year until 1750, when even that figure was doubled. New Derry was repeated over and over again, and to-day there are seven Derrys in the United States, eighteen Belfasts, nine Antrims, twelve Milfords, three Pomeroys, and sixteen Tyrones. As well there is a Coleraine, a Newry, a Banbridge, a Stewartstown and many another good Ulster place-name besides, to bear witness to that flood of our people who made the hazardous journey across the ocean, because of their love of freedom and of the Christian faith into which they were born. From small Presbyterian churches in Ulster whole congregations followed their ministers to the new lands in the west, and in one short period before the Revolution almost sixty thousand Ulster people landed in the American colonies. So much so, that when *the Declaration of Independence* was signed, no less than one-sixth of the total population of the seceding colonies was of sound Ulster stock. Not all of these went to places like New Derry and the New England States, for these were people with the blood of pioneers in their veins, and many of them blazed trails to the Far West, and looked with scorn on the idea of settling down as navvies, policemen, publicans and politicians in the secure towns of the East Coast. No wonder Theodore Roosevelt wrote: *It is doubtful if we have fully realised the part played by this stern and virile people. They formed the kernel of that American stock who were the pioneers in the March to the West;* or President MacKinley in 1893: *They were the first to proclaim for freedom in these United States, and even before Lexington their blood had been shed for America;* or the American historian, Bancroft: *The first voice publicly raised in America to dissolve all connection with Great Britain, came, not from the Puritans of New England, not from the Dutch of New York, not from the cavaliers of Virginia, but from the Ulster Presbyterians.* And Washington held his Ulster troops in the highest esteem, and said that if he were defeated everywhere he would make his last stand for liberty with these sons of Ulster in his native Virginia.

In the War of Independence the record of Congress was not good. It would not give Washington enough troops, nor would it properly clothe or equip those he had. And here the sons of Ulster came forward again, this time on the civil side, and subscribed large sums of money to provide Washington with what he so sorely needed. Blair MacClenaghan gave 50,000 dollars, James Mease and his uncle John gave 25,000 dollars apiece, and John Dunlap did the same; these men came from Strabane in the County Tyrone: Murray of Belfast, Donaldson of Dungannon, and Nixon, Barclay and Nesbitt from other parts of Ulster, gave 30,000 each, and this is only the beginning of a long list. This was the acid test, the money test, of faith and gratitude, and the Men of Ulster passed it right nobly.

One of the greatest events in the history of the world, and by far the greatest single event in the history of the United States of America, was the drawing up and signing of *the Declaration of Independence*. That document is in the handwriting of Ulsterman Charles Thompson of Maghera, Perpetual Secretary to the Continental Congress, and it is signed by John Hancock, President of the same Congress, whose parents were born and bred in the County Down. This world-shaking document was printed from Thompson's transcription by another Ulsterman, John Dunlap of Strabane, and it was first read in public by Colonel John Nixon, whose father came from Ulster. Of the other signatories of this great charter of freedom and democracy, Whipple, Paine, MacKean, Nelson, Thornton, Taylor and Rutledge were all sons of Ulster families, and as if this were not enough, of the thirty-three men who have so far been called to the high office of President of the United States of America, no less than fourteen have Ulster blood in their veins; and no man descended from parents from any other part of Ireland has so far achieved this supreme honour. I have often been asked how it came about that no Southern Irishman ever made a comparable contribution to the cause of American liberty, and I have only been able to give one answer—there was no really significant emigration from that part of our country now known as Eire, until the famine of 1846 drove the poor, half-starved peasants of the south and west across the Atlantic, and already, 150 years before that time, the persecuted sons of Ulster had founded towns, fought wars, spent their blood and their money, and blazed the trails in the covered wagons, in the cause of the great democracy of the West. And these Ulstermen were not peasants flying from starvation, but substantial farmers and traders whose moral qualities alone persuaded them to leave a land governed by a class that would do violence to all that was sacred and holy to them. It was not the fault of our brothers of Southern Ireland, splendid men that they were, that they did not help in this great work of human liberty; it just happened that the work was already done a century-and-a-half before they had any chance to set their hands to it.

In strict justice, I must add that a few Southern Irishmen did in fact distinguish themselves in the cause of American liberty, though their smaller contribution is well-nigh eclipsed by the overwhelming scale of the Ulster effort. Commodore Jack Barry, of the County Wexford, already remembered in my Leinster volume, was one of this small company, and the work of people like Sullivan, Moylan and Carroll cannot be forgotten, but these fine men must stand as the Southern exception which proves the Northern rule. As that distinguished American writer, Owen Wister, has declared with a downrightness which cannot be gainsaid: *It is true that we Americans owe a debt to the Irish; but it is to the Orange Irish, for it was they who fought in our Revolution, and not the Green Irish.* For fuller information on this subject I cannot do better than refer you to that excellent booklet, published by the Quota Press, Belfast, and written by my good friend 'W. F. Marshall: *Ulster Sails West.* Mr. Marshall is the expert on this whole question, and the tale he has to tell is as stirring as it is undeniable.

To return to the Irish scene, towards the end of the eighteenth century the Volunteer movement sprang up. It was entirely loyal to England, but, alarmed by the corruption of the Dublin Parliament and by its subservience to England to the detriment of Irish trade and affairs, it demanded legislative independence. The Ulster Volunteers further called for the relaxation of the Penal Laws against *our Roman Catholic fellow-countrymen*, and this at a time when the Dublin Corporation passed a Resolution that the English and Protestant ascendancy in Ireland must be maintained. Belfast was now thoroughly Republican in sentiment, many of the Ulster Presbyterians had fought for American freedom, and the principles of the French Revolution were in high favour. Wolfe Tone, a Protestant, became Secretary to the *Roman Catholic Committee*, a newly formed body greatly condemned by the people of Dublin, and the citizens of Belfast drew the carriages of the Roman Catholic delegates through the streets, as these gentlemen set off for London to seek redress of their grievances of the king of England himself. The Ulster Volunteer movement now became so extreme in Republican sentiment, that the gentry, who had up to now officered and supported it, scented danger and demanded its dissolution. It was indeed officially disbanded in 1793, by Royal Proclamation, but no such proclamation could stop the march of ideas now in full stride. And so the best of the Volunteers became absorbed in the new *Society of United Irishmen,* and bloody revolution again reared its ugly head. On the 7th of June, 1798, the Ulster Rising took place, but it was ill-timed and ill-planned, and its leader, Henry Joy MacCracken, a Protestant merchant of Belfast, was taken and hanged. Events now moved rapidly, and in 1800 the last session of the old Irish Parliament was held in Dublin, whilst in the following year the first Union Jack floated over that very Market House in Belfast where Henry Joy MacCracken had bowed his head to the hangman's rope but three short years before. Reaction had had its way, Castlereagh was triumphant, and the Union with England was complete—on paper anyway.

When the Act of Union was being pushed and bribed through that most corrupt of all public bodies, the old Irish Parliament in Dublin, its most relentless opponents were Ulster Protestants, and its greatest supporters were the Roman Catholic clergy and laity of Southern Ireland. A glance at the position to-day will confirm the age-old belief that Ireland is, par excellence, the land of contradictions. For whilst Ulster remains largely Protestant and Eire overwhelmingly Roman Catholic, the two areas have changed sides politically in the last century-and-a-half. The Ulstermen of 1798 looked towards France and America for their political inspiration, but the Ulstermen of 1801 began to look towards England, and they have looked in that direction ever since. Contrariwise, the men of Dublin and the South were never more than lukewarm in their support of the ideals of *the United Irishmen,* and were ever inclined to toady to the might of England, but after 1801, when Ulster was changing its orientation, the Southerners changed theirs too, and since that time the fight for Irish independence has been waged mainly in the South, and Ulster has become more and more loyal to the Throne of England. Indeed, so intense has its loyalty become that whilst betimes it has been most comforting to England, at other times, when bargaining was afoot, it has been nothing less than embarrassing to compromising statesmen of that great land.

This turning full-circle of the political barometer is something very difficult to understand and much more difficult to write about. The Union, bringing equal citizenship with Great Britain and the Empire, undoubtedly made Belfast into a great commercial city just as it similarly developed many of the smaller towns of Ulster: and the shortage of cotton during the American Wars, coupled with the vastly expanding Atlantic trade, hoisted Belfast into the position of the world's greatest centre of the linen and shipbuilding industries. Economic considerations are perhaps the most powerful factors in any school of political thought, and it is obvious that Ulster had now every economic reason not only to cleave to the British connection but to nurture and strengthen it beyond all danger of argument or dissolution. And from the religious standpoint circumstances had also wrought great changes. Most of the disabilities of the Presbyterians had been removed, and whilst they still remained loyal to their ideals of freedom of worship and civil liberties for their Roman Catholic fellow-countrymen equally with themselves, events were afoot which gave them pause. Roman Catholics from Southern Ireland were coming north in large numbers, to take the place of those Presbyterians who had gone to America, and the landlords were even prone to evict many of those who remained, in favour of these Southern migrants; for it became clear that the Southerners were content to pay higher rents, and to accept a lower standard of life, in their efforts to share in the sudden prosperity of the North. The upshot of all this was the formation of Protestant societies known as *Peep-o'-day Boys*, designed to protect Protestant interests from this new menace, and the like formation of Roman Catholic *defenders* for similar but opposing reasons. And here, indeed, the seeds of religious intolerance were sown, in a land so far pleasantly free from this ugliest of all human ills.

In the year 1795 two events took place in Ulster so utterly symbolical of the cleavage of two schools of thought, that we must not pass them by. In this year, just before Wolfe Tone left for America and France in search of naval and military aid for the freedom of Ireland, five men stood on MacArt's Fort, at the summit of the Cave Hill, and looked down on the growing town of Belfast which lay almost at their feet. These five men were Henry Joy MacCracken, Thomas Russell, Neilson, Spiers, and Wolfe Tone himself, and in that lovely spot they took solemn oath, one with the other and with their God, never to rest until Ireland was free. That they kept their oath, even unto death, is a matter of history. And in the same year, on September the 20th, in the house of one Atkinson, about six miles from Armagh City, a conference was taking place of some Protestant *Peep-o'-Day Boys*. They were reasonable, solid men, and they were discussing means whereby the senseless feud between their members and the Roman Catholic *Defenders* might be terminated and laid to rest. A faction fight of no mean dimensions was stopped by a flag of truce borne by some of these estimable men, and it was there and then agreed that never again would any man in Ulster be molested on account of the faith he held. It is clear that both parties honourably intended to keep this truce, but it is also the unhappy fact that a body of Defenders, knowing nothing of this agreement, fell upon a party of Peep-o'-Day Boys that very evening, with the result that fighting started again in a more savage spirit than ever. The upshot was the *Battle of the Diamond*, which started at dawn on the 21st of September in that fateful year of 1795. A few days afterwards, in the house of James Sloan in Loughgall, the Loyal Orange Association was born. Contrary to common belief, this was not a religious organisation at all, but a society of men devoted to the cause of loyalty to the British Crown. 1795—*MacArt's Fort—the Loyal Orange Association.* Here surely was the parting of the ways, and whilst Henry Joy MacCracken and most of his

Protestant companions went proudly to the gallows, the rest of Protestant Ulster, almost to a man, rallied to the ideals of the victors of *the Battle of the Diamond*.

The typical Ulsterman of to-day is fiercely and aggressively Irish, but he is Irish in a very special way. Indeed, he considers himself quite a separate kind of Irishman, which, as all his historical background would lead us to expect, he is in very sooth. His speech is rougher and more vital than that of his Southern brother; he has less grace but a deal more sincerity; and instead of the familiar Irish wit he is endowed with an immense command of devastating satirical humour. Protestant and Roman Catholic alike, the Ulsterman is a type well-defined and not to be mistaken for any other variety of the human race, but in the Protestant the Ulster peculiarities have become more completely crystallised, the Ulster traits are in sharper focus, the contrasting lights and shades are more violently set one against the other. And so when we speak of an Ulsterman we usually think of a Protestant, and most of the inconsistencies that perplex a stranger in Ulster arise from this vulgar error. Fiercely and vitally Irish, your Ulster Protestant will yet look with deep suspicion on any Irish movement or tendency; he will, for instance, at once detect the hand of Rome in Irish dancing, Irish music, or the Irish language. On Saint Patrick's Day, if he wears shamrock in his buttonhole, he will wear it with a difference; he will wear it with a defiant air. But if you are in doubt about his nationality, say something disparaging about this emblem of Ireland, and you will quickly learn that if an Ulsterman is a special kind of Irishman, he is nevertheless an Irishman—and a very downright and decided and forcible Irishman at that.

We may pass over the Home Rule movements and the varied political history of the years between the Act of Union and the Government of Ireland Act of 1920, which was responsible for the present division of our country into two separate units. However regrettable this division may be to many of us, and especially to those who view it from the emotional rather than the political plane, it was perchance in the nature of things inevitable, and most certainly it was not of Ulster's seeking. The majority of the Ulster people strongly desired to preserve the British connection, and whilst Southern Ireland was mainly set on complete separation, it is difficult to see how anything but Partition could have solved the problem, if indeed it is solved. At that time a *Council of Ireland* was planned to provide a link between North and South, but whilst Northern Ireland immediately elected its full proportion of members, the Southern Government declined to act on the Council and the body never functioned. That was a pity, for it might have been fruitful in happy relationship or lively constructive discussion.

We have seen how passionately devoted to the British connection are the people of Ulster. When Britain is at war, Northern Ireland automatically becomes a belligerent at her side. The people of Ulster would not have it otherwise. Eire, on the other hand, maintains the constitutional right to dissociate herself from any warlike undertakings of the British Commonwealth of Nations, and in the recent Hitler War she exercised this right, declared herself neutral, closed her ports to the Allies, and permitted the German, Italian and Japanese diplomatic establishments to continue to operate within her borders, as indeed, logically, she could do no other. And it is to the eternal credit of Great Britain that she never made any attempt to coerce Eire from her neutrality, highly disadvantageous and perilous to her operations as that neutrality was. And in 1942, with the arrival of United States troops in Belfast, Eire publicly protested against this decisive contribution of the American people to the liberties of the world, though what happened in Belfast was the business of nobody but the properly constituted Government of Northern Ireland.

The Ulster bridgehead, then established, became the stepping-stone between the great democracy of the West and the tyranny-ridden land that was Europe under the Nazis, and everywhere in Ulster the Americans were received with enthusiasm and pride. For many of these boys it was indeed but a deferred homecoming, for the ancestors of thousands of them were born and bred in these six Counties. Half-a-million fighting Americans came to Ulster—soldiers, sailors, airmen and marines, and with them came guns, tanks, aircraft and equipment in bewildering variety and staggering abundance. It was history in reverse, for if America in the eighteenth century was one-sixth Ulster in population, Ulster was now almost one-third American, and loving every minute of it. At one inspiring time more than one-hundred-and-fifty United States warships and freighters were assembled in Belfast Loch—the largest concourse of American shipping ever seen in any port of the United Kingdom. No wonder General Eisenhower said to the people of Ulster, when he came to receive the Freedom of the City of Belfast:

> *Without Northern Ireland I do not see how the American forces could have concentrated to begin the invasion of Europe. The facilities of the City of Belfast, its people and influence, made possible the very beginning of that concentration, and if Ulster had not been a definite co-operative part of the British Empire, and had not been available for our use, I do not see how the building-up could have been carried out in England.*

I am no politician. I am an extreme individualist, and for that reason I am glad that Eire was able, without interference, to follow the path of nationhood that seemed right and proper to her. For that is the very stuff of true democracy. But I am also glad that the Allies triumphed over the malignancy that was Hitler, and that Ulster was able to play no mean part in that elemental struggle between light and darkness. And it was in every way seemly and historically fitting, that Ulster's effort should have been so closely interwoven with the mighty works of those United States of America, in the founding of which the Men of Ulster, in that momentous eighteenth century, took a share so disproportionately great to the small population from which they were drawn. Their high moral courage, and their unswerving faith in the liberty of man, made them worthy of both splendid occasions.

Typical Ulster Gateposts.

Visitors to Ulster nearly always ask about our curiously massive circular gateposts, built of stone, kept spick with whitewash, and normally capped with a rounded point or a cone; though in some districts the tops are left flat for the fairies to dance on! These gate-posts are more than usually conspicuous because they are so absurdly out of proportion to the light iron gates which they serve, and though many theories have been advanced to explain these erections, none of them is satisfactory, and more especially those based on a supposed ancient tradition. For gates are recent in Irish social history, and without gates there could be no need for gate-posts. Writers about Ireland, up to the eighteenth century, often remark on the absence of gates in Irish countryside, forgetting that with the old rundale system of land tenure, gates would have been of small avail. In the more remote parts of Ireland a slung some thorn bushes piled in a gap, or part of an old iron bedstead, proclaim the native scorn of gates as a whole, and all we can safely say about our typical Ulster gate-posts is that they are not of ancient breed or use, and that for some reason they rank higher in the agricultural mind than the gate which swings between them.

The City of Belfast ~ Béal Feirste

BELFAST, like Dublin, must be one of the most beautifully situated cities in the world. Lying as it does between the basaltic hills of Antrim and the slaty hills of Down, and at the head of a splendid sea-loch, twelve miles long by about four miles broad, it enjoys so much natural beauty that even the heavy hand of the insensitive nineteenth-century builder has been unable to do little more than throw into contrast the shoddiness of his own poor work.

The old valley of the Lagan River marked a boundary between the basalt and the slates, but the river actually eroded itself out of the softer Red Triassic Sandstones, which accounts for the bright red colour of the typical Belfast clays. At the end of the Ice Age the ancient river had thawed out long before the sea-loch had cleared itself of the packed ice, and behind this great barrier a lake formed. Into this lake fine sands were washed down, to form the present Malone and Knock deposits, and many changes took place in the level of the land. On both sides of the river the valley walls fell back to form a vast cup, and in this cup to-day the city lies, or rather stands. For the older central Belfast is a *City on Stilts*, built on long piles which had to be driven thirty or forty feet through the silted blue clays, or sleech, to the firm foundation of the sandstones and hard clays below. This sandstone is too soft for building purposes, and the other local rocks are unsuitable in different ways, but the Belfast clays make splendid bricks, and this circumstance has made the city a place of brick-built houses. But if the sandstone was unsuitable for building, it provided wells of pure water unsurpassed anywhere in Europe, and from this water are made the ginger ales and other beverages, original inventions of a Belfast chemist, which carried the fame of the city around the world in small bottles. And the local distilleries were not slow to send on the heels of those small bottles a little something to take the bare look off their excellent but unexciting contents.

Early man was attracted to the site of Belfast by the flint in the chalk under the basalt hill-coverings, for flint was the gold of those days and from it man made his weapons and his tools. Abundant wildfowl and sea food were additional lures, but this early settlement was made about three miles up the Lagan Valley, for the site of the present city was then a place of dense forest and impassable swamp. You should walk up the Lagan along a pleasant path from Stranmillis to Shaw's Bridge, and there ask your way to the nearby *Giant's Ring,* a ceremonial burial-place entirely unconnected with giants and probably associated with that early settlement.

From this point in the Lagan Valley, four spokes of sandy deposits radiate, and along these the early settlers made their lines of communication, and moved from the hill-top plateaus, on which they lived, to other places connected with their various avocations. At the ends of some of these trails we still find flint implements in terrain where no flint occurs in nature, proof of the use of these ancient ways by the peoples who were settled on the flint-bearing hills. With the coming and advancement of the Bronze Age the climate became drier, and the chief crossing of the Lagan moved down to the present site of Belfast; and we may take it that the modern line of the Newtownards Road, the Queen's Bridge and the Shankill Road follows almost precisely that old, prehistoric trail. A downward curve in climatic conditions coincided with the onset of the Iron Age, and early man then deserted the elevated plateaus and settled on the lower hill-slopes, where the ring-forts which he built abound to this day, and where his underground dwellings or storehouses, known as *souterrains,* and the caves which he occupied and often enlarged, in the Cave Hill and other places, further testify to this movement from the exposed places of the basaltic heights. In those days the shore line lay far inland from its present position, and you may still trace the old sea margin in the cliff-like steep little bluffs that are prominent at Sydenham, Skegoneil and just above the York Road.

The Giant's Ring.

Towns were never part of the Irish economy, and Belfast as we know it to-day was an English creation; as indeed was the much more ancient Dublin after the Danes had been cast out of their old settlement there. Antrim and Down had been disciplined into counties by the year 1200, and a castle had been built in Belfast by de Courcy in 1177, though the later fortress of Carrickfergus was incomparably stronger and more important. From the name of the present Castle Place we know where this Belfast Castle, and its successors, stood, but we should remember that, until about 1600, the whole Lagan Valley area was predominantly Irish, and that the powerful O Neills of Clannaboy ruled with no uncertain hand from their stronghold in the Castlereagh Hills, just outside the town. Theirs was

The Cave Hill and MacArt's Fort, with Belfast below.

the old Irish pastoral economy of townland communities on the hill-slopes, and of the seasonal movement of families and livestock to new pastures during the summer months, a practice known as *booleying* which we shall discuss hereafter. But in 1604 Sir Arthur Chichester, a Devonshire knight of great parts and no little brutality, was granted fifty-two townlands which were filched from Con O Neill on the usual shady pretexts, and within seven years he had converted the damaged Castle of Belfast into *a daintie statelie palace, the glory and beautie of the towne*. A charter was granted by the English king in 1613, a rampart and ditch were built round the town in 1642, and a market-house was erected, in 1665, between the castle and the church which stood at the foot of High Street, near the old ford across the Lagan, on the spot now occupied by Saint George's Church. High Street was then the main thoroughfare, and it followed the line of the Farset River, as it does to this day, but this tributary of the Lagan then flowed openly down the centre of the street, with a roadway on either side. In 1770 this river was culverted and now runs under the consequently widened street. The name of Belfast is a corruption of the original Irish form *Béal Feirste—the Mouth of the Farset*—which is derived from the confluence of this stream with the Lagan. We have a pleasant pattern of feudal life in this part of Belfast to-day, for in Mill Street stood the manor mill, driven by the Farset where it spilled over the ancient sea-cliff at the edge of the slobland; in Castle Place we had the manorial castle; and farther down, at Church Lane, we had the church: church, castle and mill, three symbols of the economy of feudal times. And beyond the rampart were the Old Park and Squire's Hill, place-names still in use, reminding-us of the deer-park and hunting-grounds which every self-respecting feudal lord maintained for his pleasure.

But Belfast, like other places, grew out of its feudal thraldom, and in 1762 an Exchange was built to accommodate the rapidly increasing mercantile interests of the town. The focus of this trading life shifted in the direction of the Exchange, now occupied by the Belfast Bank at Bridge Street, and new thoroughfares, like Waring Street, were built in that region and were favoured by the merchant classes, whilst Castle Place and Donegall Place, until as late as 1840, stood aloof as the section where the country gentry kept their town houses. Another new street was Ann Street, mainly devoted to the traders in provisions, and this thoroughfare has retained much of its specialised character even to this day.

Belfast is a typical example of a mainly nineteenth-century town that has developed far too rapidly. Its rise was phenomenal and left no time for planning or any of the graces of gradual growth. In 1781 the population was about fifteen-thousand; in fifty years it had grown to 53,000; in another fifty years it had again quadrupled itself and stood at 207,671; and in another fifty years it had almost incredibly doubled even that figure, so that to-day it counts a population of 438,000 and ranks as the tenth largest city of the United Kingdom of Great Britain and Northern Ireland. Many people also are concentrated just beyond the city boundary, so that Belfast is really even bigger than its official population

Clifton House, Belfast. Typical Ulster late Georgian with spire instdead of dome usual in comtemprary English building.

would suggest, and we are led to the neat conclusion that about half the people of the Six Counties of Northern Ireland, which muster roughly a million-and-a-quarter in all, are resident in and around Belfast, whilst the other half are distributed over the rest of the area. This remaining area is largely rural, the biggest concentration after Belfast being in Derry City, which boasts a population of 48,000, whilst most of that handful of the remaining larger towns, such as Lurgan, Lisburn, Newry, Ballymena and Portadown, only run to about ten thousand each. As we might expect from these figures, farming is the largest single industry in Ulster and accounts for about one-third of the total trade, the remaining two-thirds being spread over various industries, with linen and shipbuilding well at the head of the list.

We have seen how Belfast grew, with such incontinent speed, from a very small town to a great industrial city, and it cannot surprise us that the people who were concerned with this monstrous growth were not only too busy to bother about town-planning, but were unlikely ever to have heard of such a harebrained notion. These men were mostly strong pioneers, men of hard muscle and harsh faith, men from farmhouse and weaver's cottage, and they came to build a great industrial town on an unpromising but well-situated piece of water-logged marshland. Artistic seemliness was nothing to them—even the churches in which most of them were wont to worship took pride in a tradition of uncomely severity—and their mission was to raise not a lovely city but a great working town. They were hard men, these makers of Belfast, and they had need of their hardness, for their city had to be fashioned laboriously in the midst of a marsh, with every building in danger of collapse if the soft sleechy ground were not properly prepared and piled. Nevertheless, most likely envisaged and encouraged by the rarer spirits in this hard-headed community, some planning of the town was in fact projected and in part carried out. Donegall Square, with the White Linen Hall at its centre, was finely conceived in 1784, and good wide streets of late Georgian houses, similar to those of Dublin, were built; but only scattered remnants of these have survived the fierce industrial-cum-utilitarian plague of later days and may still be traced in Donegall Square South, May Street, Chichester Street, Howard Street and Wellington Place. A further scheme was started, in 1810, for the creation of College Square, with the Royal Belfast Academical Institution, always lovingly referred to as *Inst.*, as its central point of balance and interest; but this scheme was never completed. College Square was never a square other than in name, and the whole gracious plan was blown to smithereens by the much later erection of the tasteless Municipal College of Technology. A more disgusting piece of Philistinism than this raising of an incongruous building, ugly in itself, to the half-destruction of the lovely prospect of a gracious late-Georgian building which is one of the very few architectural jewels of Belfast, it would be impossible to conceive, and I cannot find words sufficiently strong to condemn, as they should be condemned, those city fathers who not only permitted this outrage but planned and commended it. But to return to the early days of the nineteenth century, the half-hearted campaign

The Queen's University, Belfast.

of town-planning then undertaken finally petered out in the creation of Queen's
University, University Square, Royal Terrace, the Deaf and Dumb Institute, and the incompleted Crescent, but enough of it remains to fill us with chagrin and sadness at the thought of what a gracious city Belfast might have been, situated as it is in a position which for beauty and variety must compare most favourably with anything else of the kind in the world.

Something of that beauty and variety must now be mentioned. The very centre of the city of Belfast itself is little more than two miles from the 1000-foot contour of the encircling hills, and to the north and west these noble basaltic escarpments are an ever-present feature of the landscape of even our busiest city streets. *I will lift up mine eyes unto the hills, from whence cometh my help,* sang the psalmist of old, and had he lived in Belfast he would never have been far removed from succour. The Cave Hill itself, a vast playground for the city dwellers, is easily reached by trolley-bus, and whilst the lower slopes are now laid out as a most attractive park, with amusements, tea-houses, and the usual amenities of the kind, the higher peaks remain much as they were when man first came to Ireland. From MacArt's Fort, where Wolfe Tone and his four companions took oath in 1795, the view is grand indeed, and any city might be proud of such a noble vantage-point so very convenient to its centre. So on to a Bellevue bus with you, and then walk to this high place along gradually ascending paths easily negotiated. At your feet you will see the city, and to your left the fine expanse of Belfast Loch; opposite are the Castlereagh and Holywood Hills, and beyond those Strangford Loch with Scrabo Tower at its head; behind your back, over the rolling hills of Antrim, you may glimpse Loch Neagh, the largest lake in all Ireland and England, and to the right of that a hint of Larne Loch. In that direction too is the prominent hump of Slemish, a mountain most sacred to Ireland ever since Patrick herded swine there in the days before he became our patron saint. But what you can't see from MacArt's Fort is more easily listed than what you can see, and I recommend all visitors to Belfast to enjoy this easily gained panorama. It will be at once a delight, and a guide to your further excursions.

Another point of vantage is the dome of the City Hall, and from there you will see many places in the city which are worth a visit, and the view will also serve you as a kind of map for your wider wanderings. From there also you will get a more detached impression of that MacArt's Fort which we have just visited, and from its profile you will understand why it is familiarly known to Belfast people as *Napoleon's Nose*. Architecturally the City Hall is nothing to write home about, and certainly it marks a decline in taste when compared with pictures of the gracefully harmonious White Linen Hall, surrounded by its well-designed wrought-iron railings, which it replaced. That old building served cultural as well as commercial ends, very much in the manner of the lovely Cloth Halls of some parts of Europe, and its passing was symbolical of that disregard for things of the spirit which we have already noted in the rapid development of Belfast from merchant's town to metropolis. In front of the City Hall to-day stands a simple round stone pillar, bearing upon its surface the insignia of the United States Army, Air Force and Navy, together with an inscription proclaiming that on the 26th of January 1942, the first American troops, for the waging of war on Hitler's Germany, landed in Belfast. A simple round, stone pillar, but more eloquent and momentous than all the wedding-cake wurzel-flummery of the great building in front of which it has such an honoured place.

Come with me now to the Art Gallery and Museum up at Stranmillis—*(tSrutháin Mhilis)*—*Sweet Stream*. This modern building is splendidly laid out, and the collections are in the hands of men of taste and intelligence. For your purpose the most significant thing there is the collection of pictures of Old Belfast, known as the MacGowan Bequest, painted for the most part by one of our best Ulster artists, Frank MacKelvey, R.H.A. Look at the shop front of one Gihon in Castle Street (it is No. 4 in the catalogue) and see the Georgian grace that was part of Belfast in the eighteenth century. Look at Nos. 22, 23 and 25, and see how remnants of this lovely town persisted until late in the nineteenth century: what could be more comely than that house of John F. Ferguson, with its fine garden, right in the middle of the city, or what more pleasing than the Royal Hotel, with its harmonious proportions and graceful trees, that only closed its doors in 1897? Look at No. 83 and see what *Inst*, looked like before the monstrous Technical Institute raised its ugly head. But we've dealt with that before. And in place of all this grace and beauty we have been given chromium vulgarity, contrived ugliness, and what is called utilitarian building. As if utility and beauty were mutually destructive and incapable of partnership, and as if beauty did not carry within itself the very highest form of utility.

Before you leave the Museum take a look at the collection of Irish antiquities and give yourself a further background to what I hope to show you, and talk to you about, in the pages that follow. And examine also the set of pictures, again the work of Frank MacKelvey, of those Presidents of the United States of America in whose veins ran the blood of Ulster's most stalwart sons and daughters.

Let us go next to the bottom of High Street, walking beside the now covered Farset River which flows unseen at our side, and regard for a moment the Albert Memorial, a lofty clock-tower lovingly known to the people of Belfast as *the Albert*. It's a good timekeeper, and that's about all I can say in its favour, and what Queen Victoria's devoted consort, Albert the Good, ever did for Belfast that its hard-headed citizens should raise a monument to him, God alone knows, and, as they say in Ulster, *He won't tell*. I look upon this fussy, unlovely monument as a symbol of Belfast's architectural unawareness, just as I look upon Nelson's Pillar in Dublin as an index of the taste and genius that created that splendid Georgian city. Not that the same fell disease, that took its toll of Belfast a century ago, isn't creeping over Dublin to-day. For the gods of neon and chromium are on the warpath there at this moment, and the half-gods of utility are of their barbarous company.

Walking the streets of Belfast you may feel with me that although this place has been a city for more than fifty years, it still wears the air of an overgrown country town. For the most part the people are not more than a generation removed from the land, and their general conversation is besprinkled with phrases which proclaim this close kinship with the countryside: as when one man says that another *brought his lint to a bad market* (*lint* is the Ulster word for *flax*) or that some woman is *as thrawin as an old sow* (*thrawin* is Ulster for obstinate): or assures his companion that *he didn't come into Belfast on a load of hay*, or that *there's little use bolting the stable door with a boiled carrot*. And within the city boundary many of the old townland names survive, such as Shankill—*(Seanchill)*—*the old church*; or Ballymacarret—(*Baile Mhic Airt*)[1]—*MacArt's townland*, where you have another instance of that preservation of the Irish trisyllabic pronunciation of the anglicised *Mac Art*; or Gilnahirk (*Giolla na hAdairce*)—t*he horn-blowing boy* or *gillie*; names which remind us of the ancient social pattern of Ireland, which is still divided into no less than 62,205 townlands of an average acreage of 325 though some reach a thousand acres in extent and one anyway covers only a single acre. The Irish word for townland, or town, is *Bhaile* which is usually anglicised as *Bally*, and this circumstance will explain why so many Irish place-names start with the prefix *Bally*. The townland was the smallest unit of the old division of land, and these townlands are further grouped into baronies, which really represent the ancient petty principalities or chieftainries. Not so long ago many of these baronies had quite distinctive customs and dress, and even to-day regional peculiarities of dress are remembered in the dark blue and damson of Waterford and Cork, the grey of Kerry, and the blue of Galway.

Belfast has an unenviable reputation for religious bigotry, but this reputation is largely undeserved, for sectarian strife has only been in evidence on widely separated occasions, when, for one reason or another, passions were aflame. Indeed, until the year 1850 the segregation of Protestants and Roman Catholics was not at all pronounced, and it should be remembered that the first Roman Catholic Church in Belfast, Saint Mary's in Chapel Lane, was built in 1783 largely with Protestant support, and that the Protestant Volunteers paraded in strength, and marched, with *their Roman Catholic fellow-countrymen*, to attend the first Mass to be celebrated there. And that towards the building of Saint Patrick's Roman Catholic Church, in Donegall Street, in 1811, no less than £1711, out of a total of £2811 publicly subscribed, was paid by the Protestant community.

A town that is conscious of sectarian guilt and bitterness does not make jokes about itself on the subject, but Belfast and Portadown have woven for themselves a garment of railing self-condemnation that is not even excelled by the equally undeserved cloak of stinginess which Aberdeen, in parallel

---

[1] Also perhaps, Baile Mhic Gearóid, (Clachan ed.)

University and Malone Roads, Belfast.

circumstances, has drawn about its own broad shoulders. I will tell you the classic Belfast story in this genre; a story which I have recorded for the Decca Company on a record, obtainable at most gramophone shops: It is about a dying child, and two Belfast mill-girls are supposed to be discussing the small domestic tragedy:

Wee Wullie's dead, says one.

Away ta hell, says the other, *What did he die of?*

He died of a Tuesday, so he did. Dear oh, but ye wud have tuk dear pity on the wee fella, so an' ye wud. He was lyin' yonder in the hospital, cowped up agin a wee pilla' an' as pale an' as wake as death; an' Mary, like, she knowed he wuz goin' ta die, but just ta put him in good form, so ta spake, till meet his Maker, sez she ta him, sez she: Is there anythin' I can do for ya, wee son? An' sez he, the wee loyal mind workin' on the Twelfth day to come [for this all happened on the eleventh a July, the day before the Twelfth day itself, as true as God's in heaven), sez he in a wee wake tremmly voice, sez he: Would ya bring me my wee Orange Drum an' my wee sash.

Och, God love him, the wee craytur, interjects the other girl.

Aye, indeed, an' so you might say, says the interrupted one; *But wait till I tell ya. Sure didn't Mary, just to notion the poor wee fella, bring in the wee drum an' set it fornenst him, an' didn't she hap the ould sash roun' about him, aye, an' set a drum stick in ether hand. An' d'ye know what he done?*

Naw, says the other girl. *What?*

He jist hut the drum one wake wee dunt, an' sez he, Tae hell wi' the Pope, sez he; an' with that sacred prayer on his lips he fell back dead on the pilla' an flew straight to the Gates o' Glory. Wasn't that a gloryus death?

Apart from the story, which shows how Belfast can make fun of itself, this is a very good example of the Belfast city speech as distinct from the Ulster country dialects, and the speed with which these mill-girls can speak is something to marvel at. This whole story would be told with scarcely a pause for breath, and the staccato words would come out with the rattle and rapidity of a machine-gun. Belfast is full of stories of this kind, as is the whole of Ulster, and people who can joke and sing about their supposed weaknesses are not bitter.

The reference to *the Twelfth day to come,* in the story about the wee drum, refers to the celebration of the Battle of the Boyne every twelfth of July, perhaps the most typical institution of modern Ulster. Visitors to Belfast at that time of the year should not fail to witness this great expression of faith in the ideals of the Orange Order. They will see a seemingly endless procession of earnest, serious-faced men, marching four-abreast, every man in his best suit and every man with his Orange Sash slung proudly across his chest. At intervals, marking the point where each lodge begins, a gaily-coloured banner will be held aloft between two poles, and on these banners will be seen painted scenes from Orange and Biblical history. And as well as seeing, they will hear—of a surety, they will hear. For at frequent intervals there are bands of every description— brass bands, pipe bands, flute bands and the real old Lambeggers. The noise is

Donegall Place and City Hall, Belfast.

terrific, and infectious as the measles. For each band is oblivious of every other band, and since the distance between each is never great, the combined sound of perchance a dozen unrelated tunes can be imagined. But indeed it cannot be imagined. It must be heard. And of all the bands, the Lambeggers alone are of the real vintage. Nothing in the world is quite like the Lambeg Band. As an instrument for the production of rhythmic noise it is unique. A battalion of pneumatic drills would be like an infants' choir beside it. The combination is one of four or six gigantic drums, terrifying engines of percussive might, and one or perhaps two flutes which emit a weird sound like a wailing wind riding the thunder. The drums are beaten with schoolmasters' canes, and no drummer is worth his salt who does not produce two livid semicircles of his own heart's-blood at each side of his instrument; for thus, with the laceration of his knuckles, does he best beat out his defiance of all those worldly powers that conspire against the Throne of England.

A visitor—it might have been you from America, or you from England—lost in wonder at the whole proceedings, once enquired of a local onlooker about the meaning of the procession.

What does it celebrate? he asked.

The Twelfth, snapped the man, displeased at being disturbed from his devotions.

The twelfth of what? asked the visitor, unaware of the fact that there is only the twelfth of one thing in Belfast.

The Twelfth a July, shouted the exasperated Northerner.

Oh, I know the date quite well, persisted the visitor, now somewhat nettled himself. *But this procession: does it celebrate some local event?*

Local event! roared the outraged man, *Local event! Ah for God's sake away home an' read yer Bible!*

Perhaps this is the time to take you out Dundonald-way, by bus, to see the Parliament Buildings of the Government of Northern Ireland at Stormont. Built not so very long ago, at a cost of a million pounds which the British Government, in generous mood, paid, this Buckingham Palace-like edifice of Portland stone, set on a plinth of granite from our own Mourne Mountains, occupies a magnificent position. The approach is imposing, up a broad processional avenue which rises gradually from the main road for a distance of about three-quarters of a mile. The view from the terrace is wide and varied, and the modern decoration of the Central Hall and Commons and Senate chambers is well worth inspection. It is often stated by critics of the Northern Government that their administration is a heavy liability on the British Exchequer, but the contrary is the case. Northern Ireland is not one of the wealthiest parts of the United Kingdom, but it makes an annual contribution to the Imperial Government in London which is usually in the neighbourhood of several million pounds. During the Hitler War this Imperial contribution rose steeply, and in 1945 reached the substantial figure of £35,000,000. In the interests of truth and common justice it is well that this fact should be emphasised.

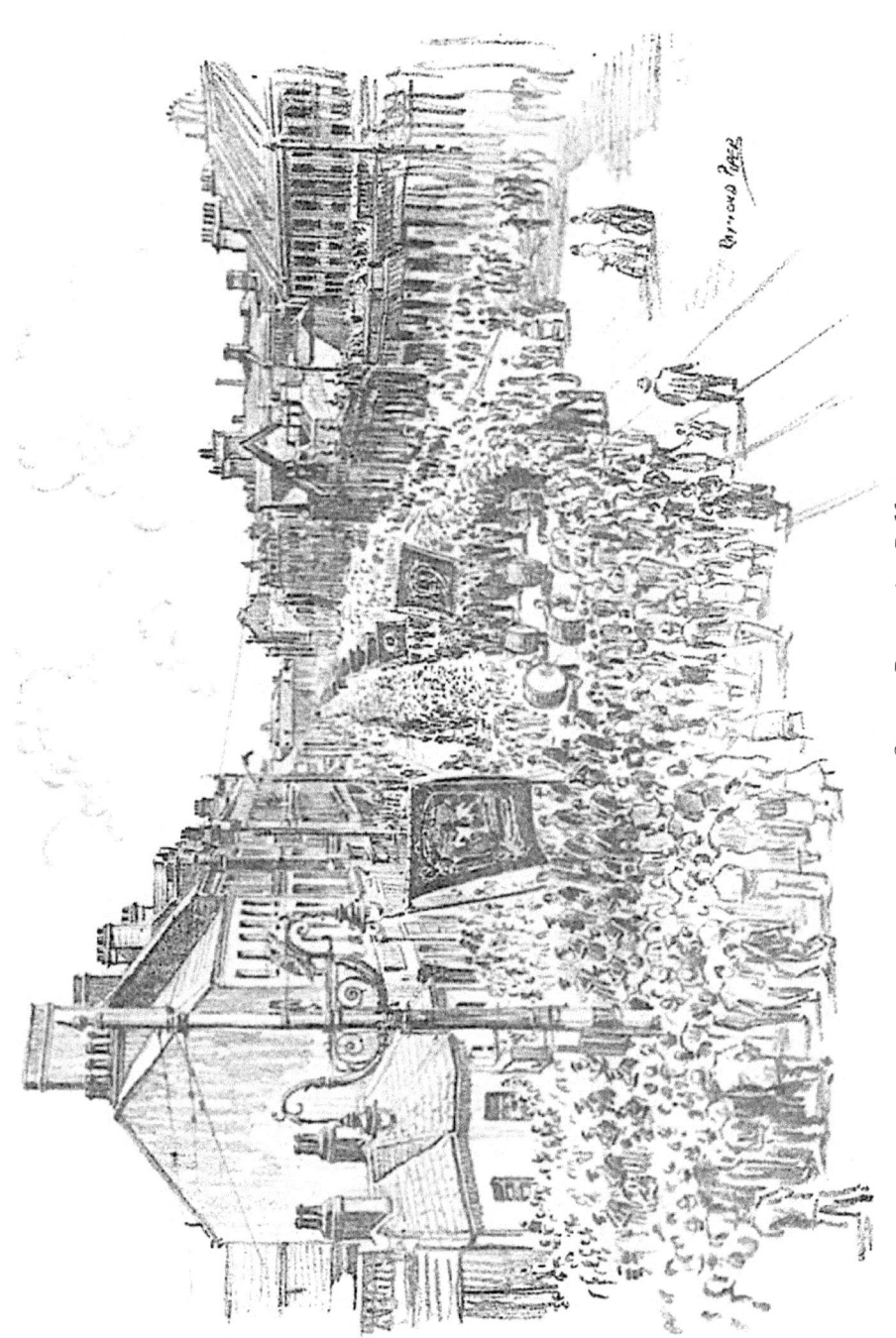

Orange Procession Belfast.

When you are at Stormont you might as well walk over to the near-by village of Dundonald, with the fine mote, built by Richard de Dundonenald in the twelfth century, beside it. In that region also you can see a splendid dolmen, known as Kempe Stones: and as to what motes abd domans are, I have already in Leinster volume, said all that is necessary.

I have now taken you up the Newtownards Road to Stormont and Dundonald, up the Antrim Road to Bellevue and the Cave Hill, and along the Malone Road to Stranmillis and Shaw's Bridge, but go where you will outwards from the centre of Belfast, you'll have the countryside at your elbow in a very short space of time. The Falls will lead you to pleasant mountain slopes and grand views of the Lagan Valley, and the Shankill will take you by steeply rising ground to Wolfhill and Squire's Hill and Divis, which is our highest Belfast mountain and worth the easy climbing; or if you turn sharply right near the top of this road you'll reach the Horseshoe, and be in the way of following a grand road right round the back of the Cave Hill. There you might be a hundred miles from any city, so remote and mountainy it is, but a pleasant walk will land you at Glengormley and the bus for Belfast.

And now, with a glance round a few of the things that should interest you in the city, we may say good-bye to Belfast and start our journey into the County Antrim. But first let us enjoy a transformation scene. From that very hub of Belfast, Castle Junction, come but a few steps up Bank Street and you'll walk into the eighteenth century. At the end of the street is Saint Mary's, Belfast's first Roman Catholic Church, to which I have already referred, and beside you is a public-house that is to-day largely what it was a hundred-and-fifty years ago. Come in for a bottle of stout, and don't mind at all the cobwebs, and the perpetual twilight, that are about you. Sit there on an old barrel, or an upturned bottle case, and say what is your pleasure. And, with first the mouthful down, think back to the days when this was the meeting-place of as merry a gang of poets and playwrights, journalists and pamphleteers, singers and painters, as ever made any house gay with the talk and banter, and the play and thrust of argument, that is blood of their life. Outside again the illusion will hold for a space, for there are the tiny houses of a bygone age, kitchen fires showing cosily through small windows, and the street so narrow that two carts can scarcely pass each other.

Wilson's Court, Belfast.

To the right along Chapel Lane now, across Berry Street, and into Smith-

Parliament Building, Stormont, Belfast.

Saint Mary's Church, at the end of Bank Street, Belfast

field Market. Here the spirit of leisureliness is still with us, even as it was when we supped our sup in Bank Street, for the traders of Smithfield have discovered the secret of repose. Sure there's no hurry anyway, and if this man doesn't want the hacksaw or the or the lock or the coloured lithograph of *King William crossing the Boyne*, isn't there another man will be in soon and his money as good as this fellow's? Ochanee oh, sure the morrow's a new day! And what's the use of wasting your dealing-talk on an old lady anyone with half an eye could see is in no notion of buying? Sure you might as well try to sell the secondhanded book he is reading to yon rickle of a quare fellow, and him without the price of his supper in his pocket, God help him. But why do you let him read on if he'll never buy? Och, God between us and harm, sure you wouldn't have me come between a poor scholar and his larnin'?

And now to the Entrys between High Street and Ann Street, almost as potent as Bank Street in their power of breaking down the years that divide us from the past. Who is that sturdy, assertive-looking man walking towards us down Wilson's Court? Who else but Samuel Neilson, founder of the *Northern Star Newspaper*, price twopence. He is on his way to John Rabb, his printer and publisher, with fresh fiery words for the press. Maybe the words are his own, full of French revolutionary thought, of such new ideas as Liberty, Equality and Fraternity for all men, or maybe they are the words of *Billy Bluff* calling down satire upon the head of Robert Stewart, Lord Castlereagh, *who cut his own and cut his country's throat*. For *Billy Bluff* is Neilson's friend and supporter, and as the Reverend James Porter, Presbyterian Minister of Greyabbey in the County Down, he will soon be hanged, by order of that same Lord Castlereagh, in front of his Meeting House and Manse—and in the sight of his wife. And as for noble

Neilson himself, wasn't he hounded in and out of prison, and the type which printed his vital pages battered to pieces by the Monaghan Militia. 'Twas in a house on the Hudson River he breathed his last, the broad Atlantic between him and the place of his dreams and labours. He kept well the oath he took on MacArt's Fort with Tone and his comrades. Crown Entry now, where *the Society of United Irishmen* was born, nourished and cared for by its fond parents, Neilson, MacCracken and Tone. And it was in Crown Entry, too, that James Sheridan Knowles kept his pathetically comic school, and fell amongst a clatter of original but impossible pedagogic experiments. Poor James, with too much of the Sheridan genius in you to give you any chance of success as an ould dominie, it was small wonder you took to the playwriting and brought *Caius Gracchus* to the old Theatre Royal with resounding success. Soon the proud London folk will give you great ovation at Covent Garden, and the great Hazlitt will hail you as *the first tragic writer of our time*. Across High Street similar evocative Entrys ran through to Waring Street, full of memories of Swift's *Varina, dear Varina Waring*, but Hitler's bombs obliterated these when Ulster stood beside Britain in her dark hour of need. Most precious of these lost footways was Sugarhouse Entry, where Peggy Barclay kept her tavern, and where Henry Joy MacCracken and his friends of *the Society of United Irishmen* held their Muddlers' Club meetings.

Along the line of the ruined Sugarhouse Entry now to the Belfast Bank at the foot of Donegall Street, though, in the days we are thinking about, it was the Exchange. To-night some of the old harpers of Ireland are giving a concert, and you may

Crown Entry, Belfast.

notice that the silver buttons on the faded tunic of one of them bear the ancient crest of the O Neills of Tyrone. And who is that blue-eyed, engrossed-looking young man over there but Edward Bunting, book on his knees and pencil in his fingers, busy taking down the melodies as they fall softly from the enchanted strings. But for this young man much of the old music of Ireland would have been lost for ever, and Tom Moore would never have come by most of those Irish melodies which so unjustly go by his name. And so to another great Meeting of Harpers of a later day, when an older Edward Bunting saw some of his dreams come true, and when Belfast stepped into an imperishable page of musical history.

We must say good-bye now to Belfast, to this great city, which, being so rich in history and in Irishry, is yet so often reputed, by its detractors, to have neither the one nor the other. Its fame and renown will outlive the memory of these poor calumniators, just as its proud history gives the lie to all their judgment and appraisal.

Carrickfergus Castle.

The County of Antrim — Conntoae Aontroma

E start this section with the Town of Antrim, and although this is the County town it is not a very important place to-day, for Belfast is only eighteen miles away and has become the virtual capital of both the counties of Antrim and Down. The name in Irish is *Aontroim,* which means *One Ridge,* though there are other derivations. The town is on the Sixmilewater, a pleasant stream anciently known as the Owenavue, the *River of the Rushes,* and that it is an ancient settlement is testified by the record of a monastery founded here in A.D. 495. Nothing is left of this foundation but the splendid Round Tower, one of the best-preserved in Ireland, which stands on the outskirts of the town. You should see this, and refer to my Leinster volume for a description of these peculiarly Irish buildings. It was in the streets of Antrim that Henry Joy MacCracken led his United Irishmen in battle during the 1798 Rising.

The Parish Church of Antrim is interesting, and, after Saint Nicholas in Carrickfergus, it is the oldest church still in use in the diocese of Connor. It dates from 1596, and although it has been much altered and repaired it is still an authentic Elizabethan structure. Observe the good Tudor stained-glass, and especially the tiny window in the old transept, a perfect little gem brought from Europe in the eighteenth century by the Massereene family. Near the church is Pogue's Entry, preserved as a memorial to the Rev. Dr. Alexander Irvine, who lived there as a boy and was born in an adjoining entry, and who wrote the celebrated *My Lady of the Chimney Corner,* which you should certainly read. In the Town of Antrim, too, the gentle teachings of the Society of Friends were heard from the lips of our first Quaker, the great William Edmundson, who not long before had held his first Irish meeting in Lurgan.

At the end of the town is the demesne of the Massereene family, and though their castle was destroyed in 1922 by accidental fire, you should visit the grounds for the beauty of their two-mile frontage on Loch Neagh. This is the largest lake in Great Britain and Ireland, with an area of 153 square miles, and it is also the oldest in geological time. Loch Neagh is pre-Glacial in origin, and only about forty feet above sea-level, and it was formed by the collapse of the great basaltic plateau of Antrim after the evacuation of vast quantities of molten rock. This is the scientific explanation, but if you want the legendary version of the submerged town, you'll get it from any of the older people round the lake shore, who'll surely quote Tom Moore's:

> On Loch Neagh's banks where the fisherman strays
> When the clear cold eve's declining,
> He sees the Round Towers of other days
> In the waves beneath him shining.

Loch Neagh washes the shores of the five Counties of Antrim, Derry, Tyrone, Armagh and Down, and brings a livelihood to a goodly population in this area. Eels are shipped to England in large quantities, for the Irish won't eat these creatures, and the pollan, a pleasant-eating, fresh-water herring, is also taken in great numbers. Ten rivers feed the great lake but only one drains it, the Lower Bann, which is consequently liable to much flooding. Curiously, whilst the Bann flows almost due north out of the lake, the River Main, only five miles away and almost parallel with it, flows due south into it.

There is a main road from Antrim to Lisburn, by way of Crumlin, (*Croimghlinn*), *the Crooked Glen*—and Glenavy, (*Lann Abhaigh*) *the Church of the Dwarf*—but by following smaller roads which hug the lake-shore you'll get better views of the great sheet of water. Not that Loch Neagh is very beautiful, for it lacks the mountains which bring such charm and grandeur to most of our Irish lakes, and it has few islands to break the monotony of its wide expanse. The largest of these is Ram's Island, and you'll get a good view of that from a point beyond Crumlin, but you should visit the spot if you can get a boatman to take you over, for it is a lush little island and a bird sanctuary to boot, full of melodious warblings in season. It was the seat of an ancient monastery, but all that is left of this foundation is the stump of the ruined Round Tower.

> 'Tis pretty to be in Ballinderry,
> 'Tis pretty to be in Aghalee,
> But prettier far in little Ram's Island
> Sitting in under the ivied tree—
> Ochanee—Ochanee.

Go along the shore as far as Haggan's Point, where the County Down creeps in, and return by Portmore Loch, where Jeremy Taylor, the famous author of *Holy Living*, built an arbour in 1658 on Sallagh Island, where he did much of his writing. The ruins of the old church where he preached are beside the lake, and the later church which he built is near-by and should on no account be left out of your itinerary. This is known as the Ballinderry *Middle Church*, was built about 1665, and, after being relegated to the position of a mere mortuary chapel, was allowed to fall into decay. Luckily the late lamented Francis Joseph Bigger, and some friends, set about its restoration in 1896 and it now endures as one of our bright gems of Jacobean simplicity and grace.

Lisburn is a compact, tidy, prosperous town with a considerable history. Its ancient name is Lisnagarvey—Lios na ngarbac, (Lios na gCearrbhach) the Fort of the Gamesters—and it is built on the site of that old stronghold. But as a town

Pogue's entry in Antrim Town.

it owes its origin to Sir Fulke Conway, a Welshman, to whom the lands were granted in 1609, and a small fragment of his castle still stands in the Castle Gardens, now a public park. Jeremy Taylor, then Bishop of Down and Connor, died here in 1667, though he is buried in Dromore, and there is a monument to him in the dignified cathedral, which you should visit. There, also, is a memorial to one of Lisburn's greatest sons, Nicholson of Delhi, hero of the Indian Mutiny. From the Conways, through the Seymours, Lords of Hertford, the Lisburn properties passed to Sir Richard Wallace, M.P. for Lisburn in the English Parliament, and this good man gave his great collection of pictures to the British nation. So Lisburn is the real donor of the great Wallace Collection in London, for it was the Lisburn rents that paid for that splendid assemblage of masterpieces. The town also produced a great Irish patriot, General Henry Monroe, who commanded the Irish forces at Ballynahinch in 1798, and was hanged for his patriotism in the Market Square, almost in front of his own home.

The Home of the Arthur family, Dreen, Cullybackey, County Antrim.

Lisburn was the cradle of the Ulster linen industry. The Irish woollen trade had been ruined by design of the English Government for its own selfish ends, and in 1698 King William encouraged the manufacture of linen to take its place. Linen had been made in Ireland for many generations, but it was a coarse product for local use and of no value as an export. So from Picardy the King brought Louis Crommelin, and this fine craftsman settled in Lisburn, and organised a community of French artisans to operate a thousand spinning-wheels and looms which had been imported from Holland. Thus a self-contained French colony grew up in the County Antrim, and to this day you'll come across names like Saurin and Delacherois, and you'll see roads planted with sentinel trees in the typical French manner. Lisburn has many other claims to fame, the most curious being the fathering of W. H. Betty, *the Infant Roscius,* to see whose acting, in London, Pitt adjourned the House of Commons.

North of Belfast is Ballymena—*(An Baile Meadhonach), the Middle Town*—which, like Aberdeen, delights in inventing stories about, its own supposed stinginess. *The Ballymena Anthem* is notorious, with its recurring refrain: *What is there in this for me ?* As is the local saying: *Always stand the first round of drinks; the company never gets smaller!* But I have never found any lack of hospitality in this thriving business-town, which owes its prosperity to the linen trade which was introduced there in 1730. The place is of little interest to the tourist, but it is an excellent centre from which to make some interesting excursions. In near-by Cullybackey—*(Coill na Baice), the Woodland of the Cripple or Beggar*—on a farm now owned by Joseph Wright Simpson, is the house where the father of Chester Alan Arthur, twenty-first President of the United States of America, was born. It is little altered since the day when the President's father took his last look at it, and only half-a-mile away lives Mrs. Kenny, whose grandmother was a sister of the President's mother. The countryside here is typical of mid-Antrim and its small prosperous farms, and not far away is the Bann, carrying the waters of Loch Neagh down to the sea. You should run over there to Portglenone for an eyeful of this lovely valley. This little place is often miscalled *Port-glen-ONE* by strangers, but the correct pronunciation is *Port-glen-OWN*, in Irish (*Port Chluain Eoghain*)—*the Landing-place of John's glen,* and from the earliest times it was a much-disputed ford over the river. A great find of ancient weapons, relics of many battles fought over a long period of hundreds of years, was made here, and you may see many of these in the Belfast Museum.

In this spot we may usefully reflect on Ulster farming in general. The holdings are mostly small family affairs, and there are 90,000 of these in Ulster of over one acre each, about three-quarters of these being between fifteen and a hundred acres in extent. The farming is usually mixed, and most of the crops are fed to the livestock, so that the greater part of the farmer's income is derived from the sale of this livestock and its products. Crops are mainly potatoes and oats, known in Ulster as corn, very rarely wheat and barley, and about a third of the farmers grow flax. If you are in the flax-growing districts in August, you'll never forget the smell—and I mean *smell*—of the flax as it decomposes in the retting-holes or ditches. Fruit is largely confined to the County Armagh and the Ards peninsula devotes itself to vegetable growing on a fairly large scale.

About four miles east of Ballymena is Broughshane, *(Bruach Sheáin), Shane's house or farm*—and probably this Shane was one of the O Neills who were paramount in this region. From Broughshane came the ancestors of the man who won Texas from the Mexicans and led it into the Union—Sam Houston. A Houston memorial stands in near-by Racavan graveyard, almost in the shadow of Slemish—*(Sliabh Mis), the Mountain of Mis*—and a relative Houston still lives in the town. Five miles farther on is Skerry Old Church, built where Miliuc had his stronghold or rath. This Miliuc was the master for whom Patrick, not yet a Saint, herded swine on Slemish, and just outside the old church is pointed out a footmark in the rock, which people will tell you was caused by the Angel Victor as he ascended to heaven after his last visit to Patrick. Slemish, the Holy Mountain of Ireland, a mass of crystalline basalt towering over the plateau and filling an old volcanic vent, is only 1437 feet high and very easy to climb. You should certainly make the ascent, for the isolated position of this storied mountain will reward you with a superb panorama. Looking south you will see one of the most picturesque views in Ulster, but if you would prefer to view this the lazy way, and in reverse, just motor from Belfast to Ballyclare and then ask your way to *the Collin*: from the crest of that road the dip down the wide colourful valley towards Slemish will fairly take your breath away.

The Home of President MacKinley's forebears at Conagher, County Antrim.

Ballymoney—*(Baile Monaidh), the Town of the Shrubbery*[1]—has little to detain you, but a few miles along the road to Dervock—*(Dearbhóg* or *Dairbheog), the Little Oak-grove*—in the townland of Conagher, stands the ancestral home of William MacKinley, twenty-fifth President of the United States of America, who guided his country into that association with the Philippines and Guam which was to prove so vital in the Japanese/Hitler War. What some people may consider to be a form of progress has turned the old farmhouse over to the cows and hens, and

---

[1] Also interpreted as "homestead on the peatland'. (Clachan ed.).

only the outer walls and roof remain as they were when the MacKinleys lived there; the furnishings and interior fittings were all sent to America, even to the floors, ceilings, door, windows and the bricks of the fireplace, and with the money earned from this sale the new owner built himself a more modern house beside the old one. In near-by Armoy—(*Oirthear Maí*), *the Eastern Plain*—is the thirty-five-foot stump of a ruined Round Tower, all that remains of a Celtic monastery founded here by Saint Patrick's disciple, the good Olcan.

A by-road will lead you to Bushmills on the coast, and here, in 1609, was granted a licence to make whiskey. Ever since that time *Old Bushmills Whiskey*, celebrated and esteemed the world over, has been made, and you'll be welcome at the distillery if you care to call to inspect the plant and the production methods. But if Bushmills is celebrated for its whiskey, it is even more famous for its neighbour, *The Giant's Causeway*, so much one of nature's queerest pranks that it is rated one of *the Seven Wonders of the World*. It is really a stupendous example of the outpouring of molten rock and the cooling of that rock in a peculiar way. About seventy million years ago Ulster emerged once more from the sea, and, after the deposition of soil on its chalky plains, it must have resembled Holland in the flat uniformity of its landscape. This Cretaceous terrain persisted for several million years, producing its own peculiar flora and fauna of which we still find numerous fossilised remains, until great cracks appeared in the land surface, many miles long and hundreds of yards wide, out of which poured vast floods of molten rock to cover the whole of Antrim, much of Derry, and a great area to the north now submerged beneath the sea. There seem to have been at least five of these flows, which cooled in beds varying from four to forty feet in thickness, and then another flow, different in character from the others, covered the countryside to a depth of a hundred feet and more. This molten mass cooled into a rock of finer texture than the earlier basalts, and in cooling it took that curious columnar form which you will see at the *Causeway* to-day. Watch a basin of starch cooling and splitting into hexagonal cracks, and you'll get a homely illustration of what I'm trying to explain. *The Giant's Causeway* is composed of a series of these many-sided columns of basalt, at present about thirty feet high and divided into blocks by cracking horizontally at intervals of about a foot: most of these columns are six-sided, many have five and seven sides, a few have eight, like the sets at *the Keystone* and *the Wishing Chair*, and there are rare instances of columns with three and nine sides. But the local guides have a far better story to tell than all this dry geological stuff, and you can get it at first hand. *Geology, me fut,* they'll say. *Sure doesn't all the world know Finn MacCool, the Irish giant, built the Causeway with his own two hands, an' him itchin' to get at the Scottish giant that was boastin' about how he could knock the melt out of any Irishman in the world: and isn't the other end of the same Causeway over in Staffa, in Scotland itself, to prove it?* Believe what you like, but don't miss the grand stories these guides will tell you, for that's more than half the fun. They'll tell you, I'm sure, that there are exactly 35,996 columns in the *Causeway*, and if you want to play ball, as you should, you'll ask them how they know. *Ah sure, there was precisely*

36,000 of them in it when I was a boy, but a rich American gentleman bought four of them since; and I wouldn't need to be much of a scholar to know what's left now.

The coast here is superb in the grandeur of its sea-torn rocks and stacks, and you could spend many days of wonder and enjoyment in this magical region. There are two excellent hotels right at the *Causeway*.

Portrush—*(Port Rois), the Port of the Point*—is a favourite seaside resort of bathing strands, amusements and boardinghouses, and it is most beautifully situated on a promontory which is washed on three sides by the Atlantic Ocean, a circumstance which makes it a most bracing place for a holiday. It boasts three magnificent golf courses, the longest being of championship status and taking its place in a list of the world's finest and best.

We are now on the borders of the County Derry, and working our way back to Belfast by the coastal road we shall retrace our journey as far as Bushmills. Along this road runs an electric tram, first operated in 1883, and whilst this was the first electric tramway in Great Britain and Ireland,[1] another similar County Antrim record was set up in Larne, the first town to have its streets lit by electricity. The tramway skirts the coast and soon gains a fine elevation above the Atlantic: here the chalk cliffs have been eroded into fantastic shapes by the ocean, and the dazzling white of this rock shows up in striking contrast with the blackness of the massive overlying basalts.

Soon, on our seaward side, we come to one of the glories of the Antrim coast, the ruined Castle of Dunluce—, *(Dún Libhse), the Fort of Enclosures*—built in 1300 on the lines of Conway Castle, in Wales, which it greatly resembles. An Anglo-Norman castle for many years under the de Mandevilles, and then under the MacQuillans who were the same people with an adopted Irish name—*more Irish than the Irish themselves*—it was taken by the Scottish MacDonnells about 1560 and reconstructed by them. The Earl of Antrim, who lives in near-by Glenarm Castle and is the representative MacDonnell to-day, handed the ruin to the Northern Ireland Government not long ago, and you may now visit this noble relic and hear all about its stormy history from the guide who is there to show you around.

Ballintoy —*(Baile an Tuaigh), the Town of the North*—is an old-world village through which your road runs, but you should not miss the rock scenery to which the winding way to Ballintoy Harbour will lead you. Out to sea is Sheep Island, and at your elbow is the glory of Whitepark Bay, famous site for finds of Bronze and Iron Age pottery; for this is a spot where we may say Early Man went to the seaside. Beyond the far end of the bay is the shattered Dunseverick Castle— *(Dún Sobhairce), the Fort of Sobhairce*—strikingly placed on a rock standing out from the shore. Centuries before the present structure was built, this was the home Conal

---

[1] As this book goes to press, the closing-down of this historic tramway is being discussed, (Original footnote).

The Town of Antrim

The Antrim Coast Road, near Glenarm.

Cearnach, great hero of the Red Branch legends. Farther along the road is Carrick-a-rede—*(Carraig a' Ráid), the Rock in the Road*[1]—and you should certainly make your way down to the of celebrated rope bridge, which is flung sixty feet across a terrific chasm to a great seastack of an island that does battle with the mighty Atlantic. You will find the walk across this swinging, swaying footway quite an experience, and the view of the ocean-torn coast from the far side is truly superb.

Near-by Ballycastle, finely situated at the foot of Knocklayd mountain—*(Cnoc Leithid), the Hill of Breadth*—is a grand place for a quiet holiday, and there is good accommodation in the hotels there. The bold cliffs of Rathlin Island present a solid barrier to your seaward prospect, and to your right is the majesty of Fair Head. Ballycastle was the town of the redoubtable Sorley Boy MacDonnell, and it was his castle that gave the place its name. The cliffs towards Fair Head contain coal strata, rare in Ireland, for most of our coal-bearing rocks were swept away in remote geological ages, and the Carboniferous outcrop here is as unexpected as the sudden area of Old Red Sandstone beside near-by Cushendall. In the eighteenth century one Hugh Boyd worked this coal in a big way, mining as much as 15,000 tons a year, and it is estimated that there are still about twenty million tons in this coalfield: but it is difficult and expensive to mine. On the right bank of the Margey River is the ruined Bonamargey Franciscan Friary, said to have been founded by the MacQuillans in 1475 and restored by Sorley Boy in the sixteenth century, and about a mile to the north-west is a fragment of Dunanainey Castle—*(Dun an eidnig), the Fort of the Ivy*[2]—built in 1550 and one of the first MacDonnell strongholds in the County Antrim. Two miles west of this again is the ruined Kenbaan Castle—*(Caisleán Ceinn Bán), White Head*—set on a lofty perch of chalk, and one of the most picturesque things of its kind in Ulster: it was built in 1547 by Colla MacDonnell.

Ballycastle is associated with two of the most celebrated stories of early Irish romantic literature—*The Sorrowful Story of the Children of Lir* and *The Fate of the Sons of Usna*. You will find these in nearly all the collections of such stories in our public libraries, and you can easily visit *The Rocks of Usna* on the coast near Ballycastle.

Fair Head is the *Robogdium Promontorium* of the ancient Greek geographer Ptolemy, and to stand on this mural precipice of great basaltic columns, each of which is almost thirty feet wide, is an experience not be to missed. There are three small lakes on this promontory, and in one of these, Loch-na-Crannog, is an artificial island, or *crannog*, a type of lake-dwelling introduced by Iron Age people identified with the La Tene civilisation. A steep and broken path, *the Grey*

---

[1] Also interpreted as 'rock of the casting', (Clachan ed.).
[2] Also interpreted as *Dun-an-aenaighe*, 'the fort of the fair or the games', (Clachan ed.).

Man's Path or *Fir Leit*, leads to the beach through a mighty chasm which is bridged at one point by a gigantic fallen column.

Rathlin Island, Rhikina to Ptolemy, *Reachlainn* to the Irish, and Rachery to the present inhabitants, is a place you must visit if you have half a chance. You may best go there from Ballycastle, but the weather will be your dictator, for the Sound between the island and the mainland, known as *Sloc na mara—the Hollow of the Sea*—is as capricious a piece of water as there is anywhere round Ireland. From Fair Head you'll get a grand view of Rachery and its white chalk cliffs capped with black basalt, a combination which has caused it to be likened to a drowned magpie. On that island is the cave where Robert the Bruce watched the patient spider, and many another bit of history and fun forbye, but I must refer you to my *In Praise of Ulster* for a full description. Go to Rachery in May or June for a wonderland of multitudinous seabirds and the great cliffs which they inhabit, and go there at any time for a piece of heart-warming Irish life and laughter, and all the magic of that old Irish way of life which is slipping away from us all too quickly in most parts of the country.

Farther along the coast, and close beside each other, are Cushendun—*(Cois Abhann Duinne), the Foot of the Dun River*—and Cushendall—*(Cois Abhann Dalla), the Foot of the Dall River*—from which you may best explore *the Glens of Antrim*. There are hotels in both these places, and magnificent scenery wherever you go. From Fair Head the coast-keeping road of steep gradients will lead you, far more rewardingly than the main road from Ballycastle, to Cushendun, by way of Torr Head, Murloch Bay and a majesty of rock scenery you'll not soon forget; and if you travel the farther bit of old road from Cushendun to Cushendall, visiting on the way the ancient church of Layd, with an unusual *Priest's Kitchen* at its west end, and the delectable little fairy mountain just to the left of your road, you'll have covered a few miles of that off-the-beaten-track country which, to me, is always the best of Ireland. From Cushendall itself rises the superb road up Glenballyemon, which must be seen to be believed. But indeed each of *the Nine Glens of Antrim* has a champion for its loveliness, and it's not for me to take sides. There's Glenarm—*the Glen of the Weapon*; Glencloy—*the Glen of the Sword*; Glenariff—*the Rough Glen*; Glenballyemon—*the Glen of Edward's Town*; Glenaan—*the Little Glen*; Glencorb—*the Glen of the Slaughtered*; Glen dun—*the Glen of the Fort*; Glenshesk—*the Sedgy Glen*; and Glentaise—*the Glen of Taise Taoibhgheal*, who was daughter to a king of Rathlin. The Nine Glens cut right into the rocky fringe of Antrim, and their narrow floors are composed of fine farming land weathered down from the crumbling basalt: and the men who inhabit these lovely valleys, the glensmen, are a race apart, closely of kin in speech and tradition with their cousins of Scotland, and yet Irish as they make them—and proud of it. A grand breed of people these, and you should not fail to make as close acquaintance with them as their friendly reserve will allow.

The celebrated *Coast Road* runs from Cushendall to Larne, a highway that for sheer boldness of conception has few equals anywhere in the world. It was designed by Sir Charles Lanyon, in 1834, as a work of famine-relief, and had the great engineer worked with a poet and a painter at his elbows he could scarcely have brought more pleasure to the eye and the imagination. Lord Northcliffe said that this was the second finest coast road in the world, excelled only by the *Grand Corniche,* but I hold that it is even more beautiful than that far-famed continental way, because there are no tramlines or railway here to mar the majestic beauty of the sea, no stiff rows of exotic palms to detract from the soft flowing lines of the lovely native flora, and nothing to disturb the spell of wonder that is Ireland and the Irish way of life. Onward goes the grand highway with the glory of the Atlantic Ocean beside it, and the smaller beauty of the North Channel in due time, and always with the towering magnificence of the chalk and basalt cliffs, and the hinterland of quiet braes and hillsides, to bring variety and splendour to the unforgettable scene. Here was the El Dorado of Stone Age Man, for these chalk cliffs are packed with flint, and flint was the gold of that era. You'll notice everywhere the horizontal bands of flint nodules in the white rock.

Round Garron Point we go, and here a great landslip, caused by a geological fault in remote ages, provided a natural plateau on which a Marchioness of Londonderry built a castle during the nineteenth century. This castle is now a religious house, and you should leave the main road to visit this remarkable spot: you will stand on the plateau there, the top of the downthrow, and see far above your head the edge of the mountain of which this plateau was once a part, and you may reflect that no earth movement of the kind, on such a colossal scale, is known anywhere in Europe. And you should certainly climb to Dunmaul, *the Bare Fort,* which is in the castle grounds, for an elevated view that commands a wide beauty.

We pass next through Carnloch, home of the late lamented Ulster playwright, George Shiels, and Glenarm, and come within sight of the bold mass of Ballygally Head, which displays a columnar basaltic structure known as *the Cornsacks*. Here is Ballygally Castle, now a fine hotel, and never really a castle at all, but a lofty fortified manor-house, of typical Scottish coastal type, built by the Shaw family of Scotland in 1625. Over the doorway of the well-preserved tower is the motto: *Goddis providens is my inheritans,* and the initials JS and IB, with the related arms; JS standing for John Shaw, and IB for Isabella Brisbane, his wife. Not far away, on an isolated rock on the seashore, is Carncastle, sometimes called O Halloran's Castle because an outlaw of that name made his stronghold there in the sixteenth century. Also in this region is *The Half-Way House,* a newly opened hotel of excellent repute.

Behind Ballygally Head is a region you should most certainly explore, for there lie the Sallagh Braes, a magnificent amphitheatre of basaltic cliffs, with a two-mile-long safe path along the ridge that will make you think you are walking along the roof-ridge of some Gargantuan cathedral. And what you'll see from there will delight and surprise you—Ailsa Craig out to sea near the Scottish coast, and that coast itself as clear as can be on a decent day, for we are only twenty-five miles from the Mull of Galloway here, and when you were on Torr Head you were actually within twelve miles of Kintyre; *the Maidens,* a pair of small islands with a lighthouse apiece, though only one is in use, looking like a couple of battleships; Trostan—*(Troctan), a Pilgrim's Staff*—away towards Cushendall, and dozens of other mountains on every hand. You'll not find a mountain-top view like this, so easily come by, on the whole Seven Ridges of Ireland, and that's no word of a lie at all.

Larne is our next stopping-place—*(Latharna), the River Mouth of Laharna*—named by the rieving Norsemen *Ulfreck's flete*, or Olderfleet in its corrupted form. This is a very ancient place, and the raised beach near the railway contains flint implements which were made and used by the first human beings ever to tread this Ireland of ours. The near-by ruined castle of Olderfleet was built by the English soon after the Bruce invasion of 1315, which actually made its landing here; but long before that the Norsemen came.

The road to Belfast passes through the picturesque village of Glynn, or *the Glen* as the local people call it, and this is surely one of the neatest and cleanest wee places in Ireland, with a great deal of unspoiled thatch still covering most of its whitewashed cottages. You should have a look round this place of twisting lanes, and follow the small stream up the pretty glen. And you should go on to Gleno—*(Gleann Ó), the Glen of the Yews*—for a look at another neat village and a charming waterfall. It was in Glynn that I made the first full-length feature sound-film ever to be made in Ireland—*The Luck of the Irish*.

Ballycarry—*(Baile Caraidh), the Town of the Weir*—comes next on our list, sitting on steep ground to the right of our road, and this small place was the cradle of the Presbyterian Church in Ireland. Here the Reverend Edward Brice established the first Presbyterian Congregation in 1613, and James Orr, the United Irishman who took part in the 1798 Rising, has sung of the event:—

> There thy revered forefathers heard,
> The first Dissenters dared to tarry,
> On Erin's plain, where men felt pain
> For conscience sake, in Ballycarry.

Orr fled to America and was later pardoned and returned to his home, but a namesake, William Orr, went to the gallows, and gave rise to the slogan known to every good Irishman: *Remember Orr!*

Across the main road, and over a long causeway, is Island-magee, island only in name and peninsula in fact. There is much charm there, a removed kind of life, and a coast-line of great grandeur which includes a bold line of cliffs known as *the Gobbins*. I recommend you to visit that beauty spot, if you have the leisure.

Back on the main Belfast road, we soon reach the hamlet of Boneybefore, small in size but big in history. It lies beside the seashore within sight of Carrickfergus, and there the parents of Andrew Jackson—*Old Hickory*—Seventh President of the United States of America, were born, and there they lived for many years before they sailed west. The Jackson home was pulled down about a hundred years ago to make way for the railroad, and over the site of the birth-

Boneybefore, County Antrim, where President Andrew Jackson's parents lived. Carrickfergus Castle is in the background.

place of *Old Hickory's* parents many thousands of G.I.s passed, most of them without knowing it, on their way from Larne to Belfast during the Hitler War. But one of the windows of the Jackson home was preserved from destruction, and it may now be seen built into the Magill home in the village. Assuredly this small place should be a shrine for all visiting Americans who care for the memory of one of their very greatest Presidents.

Carrickfergus now—*(Carraig Fhearghasa), the Rock of Fergus*—and we come to the end of our Antrim wanderings. This was an important place long before the Anglo-Normans built their castle here sometime between 1180 and 1205, and its history goes back into remote ages. The great castle was probably the first real castle to be built in Ireland, for most of our so-called castles are only fortified houses, and, until a few years ago, this fortress had the distinction of being the only stronghold of its kind to be continuously occupied from the time of its erection; for until its recent establishment as a museum it was never without its military garrison. Nowadays you may be shown around by a courteous and not-unimaginative guide, and it is for you to form your own opinion about some of the taller stories he will tell you. The massive square keep, or donjon, is an impressive example of military architecture; the single entrance is round-headed and at the usual one-storey height above the ground, but the forebuilding which originally stood defensively in front of it has been removed; the great Western Gateway, double-towered, is an addition of the thirteenth century, has been altered in succeeding years, and is notable for a still-working portcullis and a machicolated arch which supports a crenellated allure or parapet. Machicolation was an architectural device for extending the parapet over a doorway or window, so that through the provided space the defenders could administer doses of molten lead, and other kindly contributions, to the heads of the attackers beneath. There was originally a ditch or moat round this castle, but this, together with the drawbridge, has disappeared.

Carrickfergus was the chief centre of the Anglo-Norman power in Ulster, but the Bruce invasion gave that power its death-blow, and not until *Plantation* times did the town recover any of its former importance. By 1669, with 815 hearths and 3500 inhabitants, Carrickfergus was again the largest town in all Ulster, and Belfast, with only 150 hearths, was a village in comparison. The soldiers of James the Second held the castle for a space against Schomberg, the great General of William of Orange, but they surrendered it in 1689, and on the 14th of June in the following year King William himself landed at Carrickfergus, on a spot now marked by a tablet.

Apart from the castle, the defences of this old town are not much in evidence. There are some traces of the town walls, and the North or Spital Gate is still almost perfect. And street names, such as *Irish Quarter* and *Scotch Quarter*, remind us of the days when the English garrison-town was within the walls, and the mere Irish and Scottish inhabitants were only tolerated outside the town proper.

The Parish Church of Saint Nicholas is especially interesting because it is one of the only two Anglo-Norman churches still in use in Ulster, the other being the Cathedral of Downpatrick. Saint Nicholas has suffered much at the hands of the restorers, God save the mark! but much thick plaster, with which these gentlemen obscured nearly all the ancient features, has now been removed, and we begin to see the architecture as it was. The date of this church is about 1185, but much of the vandalism of the *restoration* carried out by the Chichester family from 1620 onwards can never be undone. The ferocious Devonian, creator of Belfast as a great town and founder of the Donegall family, cut the nave in half, plastered the walls, cut new windows, and did dreadful violence to the north transept to provide a chapel for himself and his precious family. Into this chapel was intruded the Chichester memorial, a singular thing of marble and alabaster, and unique in Ulster. It contains the figures of Chichester himself, who died in 1625, and of his wife, his infant son, and his brother, Sir John.

Perhaps the most sensational thing in the long history of Carrickfergus is the fact that on the 24th of April, 1778, just opposite the town, the very first naval action took place in which the American flag was flown in British waters. On that day the *Ranger* appeared in Belfast Loch, commanded by the redoubtable Paul Jones, and opened fire on Carrickfergus Castle. The *Drake,* an English sloop of twenty guns, drew close and ran up the English flag. The *Ranger* promptly ran up the American stars, and, with a raking broadside, put the *Drake* out of action. The English ship called for quarter, and the magnificent seamanship and bold attack of Paul Jones won the day for America. Alarm swept the country, and Ireland demanded that since England was demonstrably unable to defend her against foreign aggression, she must be permitted to raise a defence force of her own: and this led directly to the formation of the Irish Volunteers, to which I have already made reference, two months after Paul Jones had departed on his further excursions[1].

And so Carrickfergus and Belfast Loch share the distinction of having staged America's first naval victory.

---

[1] 'Occasions' in original, which seems unlikely, (Clachan ed.).

Fireplace of Dobbin's Castle, Dobbin's Castle Hotel, Carrickfergus.

The County of Down — Conndae an Dúin

N account of the manner in which much of its surface is broken into a series of little rounded hills, the County of Down has been likened to a basket of eggs, but who could look on the little rounded hills of Down and not love them. This a large county, and it will impress you at once with its fertility, and with the obvious prosperity of its many farms. We are no longer in a region of basalt and chalk, as we were in the County of Antrim, for here the rocks are mainly of the immeasurably older Silurian period, and the light friable County Down soil, easy to work and fruitful in yield, has been produced by the weathering down of these slaty rocks. Down is remarkable in having a coast-line of almost two hundred miles, although in itself the County is less than fifty miles long, a circumstance which is due to the considerable sea lochs of Strangford, Belfast and Carlingford, the first-named being wholly within the County. Generally speaking, Down has not the historical interest of Antrim, but it can claim two events of outstanding importance—the second coming of Saint Patrick, which took place in the year 432 in Strangford Loch; and the first setting-up of the Anglo-Norman power in Ulster, which was achieved by de Courcy when he captured Downpatrick and established himself there. Much of the coast of the County Down is low, with dangerous reefs projecting far out into the sea, and that part of the coast which lies along the Ards peninsula is the most easterly land in Ireland.

Downpatrick is still the County Town, and although it is now a small quiet place it is of great antiquity. In early times it was known as *Rath Celtair* named (in modern Irish: *Cealtachair* —*The Fort of Celtar*, who was one of the Knights of the Red Branch. This chieftain is described in *The Book of the Dun Cow* as *an angry terrific hideous man with a long nose, huge ears, apple eyes, and coarse dark-grey hair*, and on the earthen mound on which this charming warrior built his stronghold now stands the Cathedral of Down, built by de Courcy late in the twelfth century. The fine building which you see to-day is but a fragment of the splendid edifice erected by the Anglo-Norman knight, for in 1316 it was largely destroyed by Edward Bruce and lay in ruins till 1790, when reconstruction began. By that time the fabric of de Courcy's great church had been used as a quarry by the townspeople and the near-by farmers, every removable bit of cut-stone had been pillaged and used elsewhere, and even the Round Tower had been ruthlessly pulled down to provide material for the building of anything from a cow-house to a town hall. In 1662 the cathedral was in such a state of dilapidation that the Parish Church of Lisburn was then created the Cathedral Church of Down and Connor, and all that is left of de Courcy's noble building to-day is the chancel; the nave, transepts and cloisters have all disappeared, and the original Anglo-Norman building must have been almost three times as long as the present structure. The ten pointed arches, which divide the present nave from the side aisles, are very fine, the columns handsome and massive, and the capitals curiously carved: look, in the northwest corner, for the series of female heads on one of the capitals, the expressions of the faces ranging from broad laughter to the merest smile. There is a strong tradition that de Courcy built this cathedral on the site of a Celtic monastery founded by Saint Patrick himself, and there is also a legend that the knight, in a fine piece of political window-dressing of which we know him to have been fully capable, gathered the bones of Saints Brigid, Patrick and Columcille and buried them here in his great cathedral:

> In burgo Duno tumulo, tumulanter in uno,
> Brigida, Patricius atque Columba pius.
>
> In Down three Saints one grave do fill,
> Brigid, Patrick and Columcille.

Though how de Courcy located these hallowed remains, and was permitted to remove them, is not recorded. Indeed it is not at all certain that even Saint Patrick rests here, for Saul and Armagh have at least equal claims to that distinction, and in any case you may ignore the massive granite boulder which stands outside the cathedral, and which is pointed out as marking the grave of the Saint; for this stone, despite its pseudo-antique and quite spurious inscription, was only placed where it is about fifty years ago.

It is fairly well established that Patrick and his sisters were in Wales when a raiding party, under Niall of the Nine Hostages, captured them, with many others, and sold them into slavery on their return to Ireland. Patrick was bought by Miliuc of Skerry Hill, which we have already visited in our Antrim pages, and employed by him as a swine-herd, and it was during his long years of loneliness and hardship on the slopes of Slemish that he developed his vitally religious quality of mind. In the twenty-third year of his life, and the seventh of his captivity, Patrick was commanded, in a vision, to make good his escape to Europe and there prepare himself for the conversion of Pagan Ireland to Christianity; and so to his uncle, Saint Martin of Tours, he fled, and then to Auxerre, and in the year 432 he returned to Ireland and landed near the present town of Wicklow. But he was not welcomed, and anyway his mind was set on the conversion of his former harsh master, Miliuc, and it was Ulster that called him most strongly. And so he sailed north into the Slaney, a Strangford stream known to-day as *the Fiddler's Burn* and greatly shrunken in size, and there he was uncommonly well received by Dichu, an Ulster chieftain of that region. Dichu became Patrick's first Irish convert, and for the accommodation of the first Irish Christians here he gave Patrick a barn or granary, known in Irish as a Saḋal, from which the place is still known as Saul, the sound of the Irish word.

Going down the hill from the cathedral, you will pass, on your left hand, the old gaol, in front of which Thomas Russell, *the man from God knows where* of Florence Wilson's grand ballad of that name, was hanged for his noble part in the

1798 and Emmet rebellions, and opposite this place of memories you will see a lovely group of Georgian buildings, the Bluecoat Schools and Almshouses. These were erected in that flowering time of Irish building, 1733, by Edward Southwell, whose mother, the Lady Elizabeth Cromwell, was the only daughter and heiress of Vere Essex, fourth and last Earl of Ardglass. The schools and houses still flourish, the fabric is perfectly preserved, but the picturesque uniforms of the scholars have gone with so many other good things, and the gracious prospect of the Georgian architect has been wantonly destroyed by the raised roadway to the cathedral which was subsequently constructed. This act of barbarity, which makes it impossible for the eye properly to enjoy the best thing of its kind in Downpatrick, is but one more example of that curious lack of public taste in Ireland, to which I have so often drawn attention. Across the garden of the school, and within the grove to the south of the cathedral, John Wesley preached in the open air at a time when the cathedral itself was a roofless ruin.

From the top of Rathceltair, on which the Cathedral of Down stands, you will see another mound, not an ancient Irish rath but the earthen mote-and-bailey raised by de Courcy after he had taken Downpatrick from the Irish. On that mote stood the wooden archery-tower, or bretasche, from which the knight ruled this region until he built his stone castle, the only possible remnants of which are the old church tower and the vaulted chamber under the present Post Office. From the cathedral you will also see, away across the River Quoile, the beautiful remains of Inch Abbey—*(Mainistir na hInse), an island*—built by de Courcy in 1180 for Cistercians from Furness Abbey in Lancashire, and evidently intended as a strong centre of English influence, for no Irish monks were admitted. The ruins are singularly lovely, and on no account should you fail to visit them, for the peace of that place will fall upon you like a balm.

Not far from Downpatrick are the Struel Wells, the name coming from the Irish word for a stream, and these, forming the most remarkable series of Holy Wells in Ireland, are associated with Saint Patrick, though it is likely that they were of earlier Pagan origin and were only dedicated to the new faith after its introduction. These wells, celebrated for the cure of diseases of the eye, the skin and the stomach, are covered with stone buildings of primitive type, and hither, on Midsummer's Day and on the Friday before Lammas, come many ailing pilgrims from the surrounding countryside, though their numbers are not so vast nowadays as they were up to fifty years ago.

Farther afield, in Saul, you'll find a modern church and Round Tower, built to commemorate Saint Patrick's first foundation, but you'll find little or nothing of the monastery established there in the twelfth century by the holy Malachi, though parts of an old gable and two much-restored tiny stone buildings with high-pitched roofs may date from that time: these little structures may have been hermitages or confessionals, for each could only accommodate a single person in a sitting or kneeling position. Near-by is Slieve Patrick, surmounted by a gigantic statue of the National Saint, and you should climb this small hill for a fine prospect of the County Down in all the endearing charm of its basket-of-eggs landscape. If you are so minded you will notice the crag-and-tail shape of these little hills which rise all around you, with their clear indication of the direction taken by the great ice sheets which carved out the face of this countryside so long ago and gave it its characteristic appearance.

About a million years ago a gradual and long-established drop in temperature covered Northern Europe with a great sheet of ice, and, as this coldness increased, that ice crept farther south until it covered Scotland and Ulster; arctic conditions brought arctic animals to our country, and for thousands

Saul Memorial Church, County Down.

of years vast ice-fields see-sawed backwards and forwards, so that we can now trace several distinct oscillations of a great *Ice Age*, with milder periods between each of them. From Scotland came one of these sheets, and from Donegal came another, to meet in the valley of the River Bann, and there to jockey for position and supremacy in the gigantic business of overwhelming our countryside. Not more than twenty thousand years ago Ulster was as desolate and almost as snow-bound as the North Pole, and then a gradual improvement in climatic conditions set in, the ice melted and receded, and about eight thousand years ago the country was once again clear of its devastating mantle of cold. These little rounded hills of Down, at which we are now looking, are the work of that master-sculptor which held our country so long in thrall, and otherwhere great ridges of gravel, known as eskers, tell us of swift rivers that ran for a space beneath this enveloping ice, and long straggling moraines of boulders remind us of the glaciers which filled our valleys in those yesteryears, and, melting under the ever-waxing warmth, dropped these rocks and stones from their disintegrating embraces. As you wander round the country with me, you may find it profitable to reflect on some of these vast elemental forces which created that beauty of mountain and valley and plain which now brings such pleasure to your roving eye.

A couple of miles from Saul is Raholp—*(Rath Cholpa), the Fort of the Heifer*—and here stands the ruin of one of the very earliest of our Irish churches. Saint Patrick is said to have received his last Communion there, at the hands of his beloved disciple, Saint Tassach, and this building is so old that it pre-dates the use of lime-mortar in Ireland and is bound together with yellow clay.

From the region of Saul it is a pleasant jaunt to the small port of Strangford—*the Strang Fiord: violent inlet* of the Norsemen. In this place-name, and a few others of similar derivation, we find about the only trace of these fierce sea-robbers still remaining in our country, and Strangford was an ideal place for the headquarters of a piratical community, as a glance at a map will quickly reveal. This sheltered arm of the sea was created by a dip in the land which took this region down below sea-level, and made of the little rounded hills of Down, those drumlins of glacial drift, a grand company of small islands. In Strangford itself is the square tower of Strangford Castle, and just opposite is Portaferry, standing almost at the southern tip of the Ards peninsula, and you may visit that small place by ferry if you so desire. This whole region is rich in defensive castles, and you will be struck by the difference between these and the castles of the County Antrim, for here the architecture is full of English influence as against the predominantly Highland-Scottish character of the Antrim strongholds. Near Strangford is Audley's Castle; in Lord Bangor's demesne is Ward's Castle, now a part of the farm buildings; and a short distance away, in Myra, is the almost perfect Walshe's Castle. Farther south, towards Ardglass, is the Castle of Kilclief, meaning, in Irish, *the Church of the Hurdle*, and these five strongholds formed a combination of considerable defensive strength, which tells us of the importance attached by the English settlers to this great arm of the sea which ran like a spearhead into the territory over which they held uneasy sway.

We have already noted that after the Bruce invasion, in 1316, the Anglo-Norman or English influence in Ulster became almost extinct, and was indeed wellnigh confined in Ireland to a small area, in and around Dublin, which was known as the English Pale. But at Ardglass—(*Ard Ghlais), the Green Height*—there was a vigorous English revival when a trading company first founded a colony there, and, sometime later, a Corporate town, the seal of which can still be seen in London on a document of the year 1500. In Ardglass to-day you will find the remains of the fortified mansions of these traders of long ago, although they have been much destroyed and disturbed by incorporation with later structures. The Castle of Simon Jordan, a merchant of the late sixteenth century, was built more than a hundred years before that good man took possession of it, and it remains the best preserved thing of its kind in Ardglass to-day; it is in the care of the Government, is open to the public, and you should not fail to visit it. Nor should you neglect to take a walk along the spreading pleasant downs, nor fail to visit the little harbour which is famous for its herring fleet. There is a very sporting golf course in Ardglass too, and sea bathing *to make your toes open and close.*

Two miles south of Ardglass is the fishing village of Killough, and beyond this the northern boundary of the great sweep of Dundrum Bay is marked by Saint John's Point with its fine lighthouse. On your way here you passed Coney Island, from which place Ulster emigrants took the name and put it on the great amusement park outside New York City. On Saint John's Point is the ruin of a very early Celtic church, with that typical Irish doorway which narrows as it rises, the better to bear the weight of the great single stone which forms its lintel. This type of trabeated doorway is associated with the very earliest stone churches to be built in Ireland. From this spot the panorama is truly magnificent, for the grand semicircle of Dundrum Bay, with its splendid strands of Rathmullan and Tyrella, and its great sand dunes, is backed by the serried peaks of the storied Mountains of Mourne, and Lambay Island stands out a little to seaward away down near Dublin.

A winding road to the west leads us to Dundrum—(*Dún Droma*), the *Fort of the Ridge*—with its splendid castle, with circular donjon, fortified gateway and drum towers, standing on an older earthen mote-and-bailey high above the town. This fortress is commonly attributed to de Courcy, but it is certain that it was erected later, probably in the reign of that Henry the Third who built Windsor in England, for the two towers are similar. In 1539 the Lord Deputy Grey described it *as one of the strongyst holtes that ever I sawe in Irelande,* and even to-day the fifty-foot-high donjon gives an impression of great and massive strength. Lower down the hill is the ruined Jacobean mansion, built by the Blundell family about 1660, presumably of material from the castle after its destruction by Cromwellian artillery in 1652.

On the road to Newcastle, just over the hedge at your right hand in the townland of Slidderyford, is a very fine dolmen worthy of your notice, and in Newcastle itself you will perforce admire the superb situation of this popular watering-place, right at the foot of the highest peak of the Mountains of Mourne, the mighty Slieve Donard itself, and with the wide waters of Dundrum Bay dancing before it. The golf links here are world famous, the bathing is excellent, and the district is rich in lakes and streams which are well supplied with trout, sea trout and salmon, but I am sure it is the mountains that will make the most compelling tug at your heart. You should start by winning the highest peak first, Slieve Donard—(*Sliabh Dónairt), the Mountain of Donard*—with the massive hermit cell of Saint Donard on its summit, away up 2796 feet in the sky, for although this is the highest mountain in Ulster it is both safe and easy to climb. And the view from the top will take your breath away with its expanse and beauty, so that it would be easier to list what you can't see from up there than to describe the manifold delights that you'll find spread all around you. Most useful of all will be the wide embracing general view which will guide you in planning your further excursions among these grand peaks, but wherever you go you'll have beauty and majesty beside you and around you. Whatever you plan, don't miss the ascent of Slieve Bingian—*(Sliabh Binneáin), the Mountain of the Sharp Peak*—by way of the lovely little Blue Loch; of Slieve Commedagh—*(Sliabh Coimhéideach), the Mountain of Watching*—for the fairy-tale feeling of its great lonely pillars of granite; or of Slieve Bearnagh—*(Sliabh Bearna), the Gapped Mountain*—for the joyful uplifting traverse of the Hare's Gap: nor should you neglect the eastern sides of the Eagle and Pigeon Rock Mountains, the delights of Cove and Lamagan, and the magical descent from Slieve Muck, the Pig Mountain, to the singing shores of Loch Shannagh—*(Loch Seannach), the Lake of the Foxes*. Many a fine moraine you'll see in the valleys up there, where the retreating ice dropped its burden of boulders in the long ago, and in the drusy[1] cavities of the Diamond Rocks, near the Hare's Gap, you'll find splendid crystals of topaz, emerald, beryl and smoky quartz. And maybe in the quiet hush of the evening, and you resting yourself after a hard day's climbing, you'll hear the soft music of our Irish Pan, *Boirche of the Benns*, and it stealing out of one of the lonely valleys; for the kindly people of these uplands say they often see the shadowy shape of Boirche the Piper, as it winds in and out of the mountainy mists, when the hour of dayligone[2] is upon the age-old Kingdom of Mourne.

The Mountains of Mourne are composed of granite of about the same age as the Antrim basalts, and so, geologically speaking, they are amongst our youngest hills. This youthfulness accounts for their sharp steep outlines, for the hand of time has not yet worked its full period of mellowing on their often jagged contours. A zone of the older Silurian slates, through which this granite thrust itself, lies between the Moumes and the much older granite of Slieve Croob, Slieve Gullion and the mountains of Louth, and this juxtaposition of two granite upthrusts of widely separated ages is often puzzling enough. The older granites go back to the time of those Caledonian foldings which fashioned, once and for all, the present face of the northern parts of Ireland.

And now from Newcastle we take the coast road to Kilkeel—*(Cill Chaoil), the Narrow Church*—past Maggie's Leap, the Bloody Bridge and the ruined little eleventh-century church of Ballaghanery, the *Pass of the Shepherd*. The sea is far below us, and on the other hand the Mountains of Mourne bear us company in ever-changing shapes; and away up there is the Silent Valley, where the waters of the Kilkeel River have been impounded to keep the taps of the citizens of Belfast

---

[1] A rock fracture with coating of fine crystals on its surface, (Clachan ed.).
[2] Scots and Ulster Scots word which means *twilight* or *dusk*, (Clachan ed.).

running as they should. Past Annalong, too, the *Ford of the Ships*, with its picturesque small harbour, and into Kilkeel itself, where you will find a good hotel, excellent bathing, and several things of interest like that fine dolmen known as the Crawtree Stone; the pleasant Parish Church built within a rath on a fifth-century foundation of Saint Colman; and some interesting and fantastically shaped sections of boulder clay down by the shore. Near-by is Greencastle, for centuries the capital of the Kingdom of Mourne and later an important stronghold of the Anglo-Norman power in Ulster. The ruined castle there is most impressive, built about 1260 and similar in design to the splendid Castle of Carlingford, which we visited in our Leinster wanderings. You can see it there, away over the waters of the loch, grim and massive on its rocky boss. At Rostrevor Quay is one of the best hotels in Ulster, and I think you would find it difficult to choose a lovelier spot in which to spend a few days of quiet relaxation. The colour symphony of Carlingford Loch, which faces the hotel, backed by the varied splendour of the rugged Carlingford Mountains, must be seen to be believed. The loch itself is a true fiord, deep at the top and shallow at the mouth, and it owes this peculiar conformation to the great glaciers which carved it out during the Ice Age. The climate here is unusually mild, and many exotic shrubs and trees flourish in this region which you will only find elsewhere in Ireland in Kerry and West Cork. Take the path through the pretty woods at the back of the hotel and climb to the Cloughmore—*Big Stone*—for a sweeping view of such rare beauty that you will remember it all the days of your life. This Big Stone is an erratic boulder left in its present extraordinary position by a melting sheet of ice long ago.

The village of Rostrevor is a mile farther on towards Warrenpoint, and up the steep road to Hilltown you will find an old graveyard in which stand the ruined church of Saint Bronach and two ancient Stone Crosses. The old bronze bell of this foundation may be seen in the near-by Roman Catholic church, where it is kept for preservation. Also in the graveyard are the remains of Paddy Murphy, a local youth who grew to the height of almost nine feet and was exhibited throughout Europe as *The Irish Giant*. He died of smallpox in Marseilles, at the age of twenty-eight, and was brought home to be buried here. In the Church of Ireland, a little down the road, you will find an interesting memorial to General Robert Ross, who was killed in Baltimore during the American Wars. Ross captured Washington in 1814, and also achieved a great victory at Bladensburg against vastly superior odds; and ever since that time the family name has been *Ross of Bladensburg*. You will see an obelisk to this great Ulster soldier as we move on now to our next place of call.

Warrenpoint calls for little more than the observation that its situation is one of extreme loveliness. What you saw from Rostrevor Quay you will see again, but with the added delight of the Rostrevor and Mourne Mountains to fill up the left margin of your prospect. There is good golf here, and good bathing, and if you spend a few pence on the ferry to Omeath you will enjoy all the thrills of foreign travel in a matter of minutes, for Omeath is in Eire and you'll have to

The Mountains of Mourne from Slidderyford dolman, County Down.

pass through four Customs examinations on the double journey! Ireland is wonderful!

On the way to Newry we pass the picturesque ruin of Narrow Water Castle, built by a Magennis early in the seventeenth century, and across the road from this is the entrance to the Hall demesne, in which the fine residence has now been converted into a splendid hotel with all the amenities. You should spend a week-end here, for the surrounding countryside is one of many delights, or at least you should stop for a meal and a walk round the charming grounds. Over the Newry River you will enjoy the sweet sight of the richly-wooded steep slopes of Fathom Mountain—(*Feadan), a streamlet*—which is the only part of the County Armagh that touches sea water. Along the side of Fathom runs one of the most adventurous little roads in Ireland, and I cannot too strongly recommend you to traverse that delectable highway when you are in Newry. Ask for the Flagstaff Road, for that is the popular name, and enjoy an elevated view of astonishing loveliness which you might normally gain only from an aeroplane. This region properly belongs to my Armagh pages, but it is most conveniently reached from Newry, which is in the County Down. If you are motoring take care not inadvertently to cross the Border into Eire, for this is an *Unapproved Road* not provided with Customs facilities, but when you are at the Flagstaff, turn to the right and travel half-a-mile to see the splendid Horned Cairn of Clontygora—*the Meadow of the Goats*.

This cairn is a fine specimen of its class, which takes its name from the semicircular, or horned, facade of standing-stones, which bounds what was most likely a sacred, or ritualistic, garth in front of the entrance to the contiguous corbelled and segmented gallery-grave. Originally this grave itself was covered by a parabolic long-cairn of loose stones, but these stones have been removed, by various agencies, from most of our specimens, just as they have disappeared from our dolmens. The people who built these Horned Cairns seem to have reached Ireland by way of Carlingford Loch, from which primary focus they spread out into the interior, but their settlements were, in the main, restricted to the Ulster region, and their culture does not extend beyond the boundaries of our north-eastern homeland. I have already remarked on the ancient division of the Men of Ulster from their fellows in Southern and Western Ireland, and if *the Black Pig's Dyke* was dug, to mark that dichotomy, before the beginning of the Christian era, well over two thousand years before that time these Megalithic people, who built the Horned Cairns, set themselves almost the same limits as those marked not only by the Black Pig's Dyke, but by the present political border as well. In further emphasis of this long-standing difference between the Men of Ulster and their Irish fellows of the south and west, we may call in the evidence of pottery. The sherds associated with the Horned Cairns of Ulster bear ornament of the strictest severity, whilst the pottery taken from the graves of Loch Crew and Carrowkeel, which lie just beyond the ancient boundary, are decorated in the most rich and lavish manner. So great indeed is the contrast, that it is tempting to think of an Ulster of more than four thousand years ago already charged with that spirit of Puritanism in religion, art and culture which is to this day such a strong characteristic of the typical Ulster man and woman.

Newry is an ancient place, and, like Armagh, it owes its modern origin to a religious house founded there by Saint Patrick. *The Annals of the Four Masters* tell us that the Monastery of Newry was burned down in 1162, as well as the yew tree which Saint Patrick himself had planted there, and this reminds us of the Irish name of the town—*(Lubhair Cinn Tragh), the Yew Tree at the Head of the Strand*; this was shortened to *An Iúraigh*, which sounds in English something like *on ewer*, and the final corruption to the present form of Newry was but a step. The old town was burned by the Duke of Berwick, in 1689, when he was fleeing before Schomberg, and since Dean Swift came here only a few years after this desolation, we may the better understand his celebrated but ungracious couplet:

> High Church, low steeple,
> Dirty town, proud people.

But if the Church of Newry was high, so too are the hearts of the Newry people, even though they have suffered great disadvantages in trade from being so close to the Border; for Newry was the commercial centre and market town of a great agricultural tract of country which is now cut off from them because it is in Eire . The town is a curious mixture of busy, modern streets and derelict old warehouses, and from its position, and the composition of its population, it is sharply divided in its allegiance to Northern Ireland and Eire. John Mitchel, author of the *Jail Journal* and brilliant leader of the Young Ireland Party of 1848, lies in the old burial-ground here, for though he was transported for treason-felony he was permitted to return home to die, in Dromolane, in the year 1875. He was the son of the minister of the First Newry Presbyterian Church. I have two favourite prospects of Newry, one from the hills around Goraghwood when the old town is in its sleeping, and when, in certain lights, it breathes a curious beauty from its mountain-fringed hollow; and the other from a bridge across the canal in the town itself, when the gathering twilight plays tricks with the old barges and warehouses and washes everything into a magical dreamlike monotone.

Instead of going to Banbridge by the main Belfast road, take a circuitous course through Hilltown and Rathfriland and you won't regret the extra mileage. About two miles out you'll see the *Crown Mount*, a fine but overgrown twelfth-century mote-and-bailey that looks, because of its bushy top, for all the world like a royal crown, and soon after that you'll be in Hilltown, a cheerful mountainy village near the source of the River Bann, and close neighbour to the Mountains of Mourne on their westerly side. There are fine roads running from this small place, right through the heart of those storied peaks, to Kilkeel and Newcastle and elsewhere, and I cannot commend them too highly for the great vistas of rugged beauty and grandeur that their leisurely exploration will yield.

If you go along the Bryansford road from Hilltown, and walk up the first lane on your left through Megaw's farm, you'll be beside the *Goward Horned Cairn*.

This has a façade of eleven stones, and the grave is three-chambered, but its chief interest lies in the fact that when it was excavated, in 1932, it yielded the first pottery, definitely recognised as Neolithic, to be found in any Irish megalith, some fine polished shouldered bowls. This must have been an important place of early settlement, for in the field immediately above are several upright and recumbent stones, evidently the remains of a ruined chambered grave, and just to the left of this site are more stones which look like the remnants of a segmented gallery grave. Especially interesting is the local pronunciation of this place-name, phonetically GOO-ARD, with the accent on the first syllable. This coincides with the Irish name—*Gut ard, the High or Raised Voice*—and is but another example of the persistence of Irish forms on the lips of people who have no Irish at them. You'll never hear the English form *Goward* in this district at all. Farther along this same Bryansford road, at the next turn to the left past Morgan's shop, is a winding road which would eventually lead you back to Hilltown. A mile along this road is a little lane to the right, and along that lane, past a cottage, is the so-called *Pat Kearney's Stone*, standing in the field to the left. This is a splendid dolmen with a massive capstone, and it may at one time have had a façade, for there are slight traces of such a structure at the sides of the slender front slab. Apart from the interest in these monuments, the countryside round here is especially attractive and most typical of the County Down. You may either retrace your way to Hilltown, or continue along the winding road as I have already observed.

Rathfriland—*(Ráth Fraoileann), O Freelan's Fort*—is perched on a high hill three miles due north of Hilltown, a typical Ulster market town, and about the same distance north again is Ballyroney—*(Baile Uí Ruanadha), O Rooney's Town*—with a perfect specimen of a twelfth-century mote-and-bailey and a stone castle which was built about half-a-century later. Captain Mayne Reid, the celebrated *Boys' novelist*, who fought for the United States in the Mexican War of 1848, was born here in 1818, the son of the local Presbyterian minister. And, since we have touched the world of letters, about four miles west of Ballyroney, in the townland of Ballynaskeagh, is the home of the father of the Bronte sisters, who changed his good Irish name of Brunty in a fit of anti-Irish snobbery, though he could not quell the Irish spirit that shines through much of the work of his daughters, despite their careful English upbringing in that gloomy parsonage on the Yorkshire moors.

Banbridge is a stout market town with an English name which means just what it says, for the Bann flows through here. Locally it is known as *The Town of the Cut*, from the fact that its main street, instead of climbing a hill as it does in Rathfriland, goes through a deep cutting which was excavated as a work of famine relief. Captain Crozier was born here, that Crozier who was with Franklin at the discovery of the North-West Passage, and who took command of the expedition when Franklin died, only to die himself, a little later, at the post of duty. He is fondly commemorated by a statue in the town.

Lochbrickland—*(Loch Brícleann), the Lake of Bricriu*—lies a few miles back towards Newry, but it is worth a visit. This was the home of *Bricriu of the Bitter*

Tongue, a poet who gave a famous feast to Conor MacNessa, and his court, about which you may read in any of the popular collections of traditional Irish stories. The lake is pretty and quite good for coarse fishing, and the crannog set in its midst was probably one of the homes of our unpleasant bard.

Old Cottage of Flemish weavers Waringstown.

Scarva—*(Scarbhach), the Bough Place*—is not far away, and there a great pile of stones, known as Carn Cochy, commemorates a battle fought in the year 332 between the Three Collas and Fergus Fogha. I have already recounted how the Three Collas pierced the Black Pig's Dyke and destroyed Emania, and here, within the Scarva demesne, you may see the finest section of the great earthwork still intact; it is yet wide and deep and you may walk along it due south for a mile, until it disappears into the natural barrier of Loch Shark and reappears at the other side of that pleasant small lake. This was a heavily fortified district in early days, and in the neighbourhood you will find some of the best earthen ring-forts in the country, and obviously associated with the defence of the great dyke; Lisnagade, *the Fort of the Hundred*, is especially notable, with its multiple rings and ditches. But to-day Scarva is chiefly famous for the Sham Fight which takes place there every 13th of July, when the Hosts of William of Orange and James of the Fleeing face each other and fight their battles all over again. It is great fun, and if you are in Ireland at that time of the year you should not miss this colourful pageant, about which you can read in Miss Alexander's well-known book.

Dromore—*(An Droim Mor), the Big Ridge*—through which the Lagan flows on its way from Slieve Croob to Belfast, is famous for its cathedral, built by Jeremy Taylor in 1661 and restored by that other great churchman, Bishop Percy, who lies asleep there. Percy was a member of Doctor Johnson's circle, with Goldsmith, Joshua Reynolds and Boswell, and was the author of the of the world-famous Reliques of Ancient English Poetry. At the cathedral wall stands the reconstituted ninth-century Market Cross of Dromore, which was cast down by the Cromwellians and lay in pieces for two hundred years, during which time one of the fragments was used as a seat for the town stocks. The old stone castle of Dromore stands near-by, so much dilapidated that it is hardly recognisable, and dominating the town is a superb Anglo-Norman mote-and-bailey which is one of the best specimens of its kind in Ireland. A close examination of this splendid example of Norman military engineering, in the gamut of fortifications of the advance-guard type, will bring home to you all I had to say on the subject in the Longford section of my Leinster book.

Warringstown House, from the yard.

A detour of six miles to the west, towards Portadown, would take us to Waringstown, a picturesque village with at least one of the old cottages of the Flemish weavers, introduced by Samuel Waring early in the eighteenth century, still extant. The thatched roofs, high brick chimneys, and tall pointed doorways of these little houses made Waringstown a real gem of a village until about thirty years ago, but one by one they were demolished in favour of more utilitarian dwellings, more's the pity. A Waring still presides over the destinies of this peaceful place, and the residence of the family, Waringstown House, built in 1667, is one of our best examples of Jacobean architecture. Its walls were built of mud, and its front façade, with two *pepper-pot* defensive towers, is good Renaissance; but the side elevation, viewed from a noble lawn, brings the delightful contrast of *William and Mary* architecture, with curving gables, high chimneys and dormers. Across the lawn is a lovely fern-leaved beech, elsewhere is a splendid weeping beech, and a graceful young tulip tree takes its place with the magnificent timber of the wide parklands, whilst a venerable clipped yew hedge is beside the house, where it was planted nearly three hundred years ago. Within the house is a fine Jacobean staircase, carried out, like the floors and panelling, in good Irish oak, and lovely old Jacobean curtains add to the delights of this grand old home.

Beside the house is Waringstown Church, built by William Waring, in his own demesne, for the use of his family, servants and tenants. It is dedicated to the Holy Trinity and dates from 1681, when it was erected by James Robb, Chief Mason of the King's Works in Ireland. It was originally rectangular, and all the woodwork was of carved Irish oak, but a south aisle, north transept and chancel were later added, and though some pine was employed in this work, the harmony of the structure has not seriously been disturbed. The lovely timbered roof, the quaint gallery and the carved pulpit which was once a double-decker, will remind you of that church of Jeremy Taylor's which we visited in our Antrim pages, and, since William Waring and Jeremy Taylor were close friends, it is not unlikely that Waring modelled his church on that earlier structure at Ballinderry, which was finished in 1665. These two churches are the best examples of Jacobean ecclesiastical architecture in Ulster, and I would ask you to notice especially the manner in which the transept at Waringstown has been achieved without the use of an arch. The oak hammer-beams have been carried over, in the manner of flying buttresses, to massive yet graceful timber pillars.

We go through Ballynahinch now, *the Town of the Island*, and from this place you should seek out the Spa, with its medicinal wells, its excellent hotel and its pleasant golf course; Lochinisland with its three interesting churches of early date; and above all the tall and splendid dolmen of Legananny—*(Liagán Áine), the Hollow of the Marsh*[1]—which stands on the side of one of the hills of the Slieve Croob range—*(Sliabh Crúibe), the Mountain of the Hoof*—and is perhaps the most strikingly beautiful monument of its class in Ireland. The view from this point is superb and shows the County Down at its loveliest best. In Ballynahinch, in 1798, General Monroe, who had defeated the English forces but three days before at Saintfield, was in turn vanquished and was sent to the gallows in Lisburn. At Killyleagh—*(Coillid Liat), the Grey Wood*[2]—on an old mote-and-bailey, stands a splendid castle which is, in part, of thirteenth-century construction, but which was renovated, with German architectural influences, in 1850. It must hold the record for continuous occupation of any castle-residence in Ireland, and it makes a striking picture in this quiet village. In this place, in 1666, was born Sir Hans Sloane, President of The Royal Society in succession to Sir Isaac Newton, and virtual founder of the British Museum, and his modest birthplace is now marked by a tablet bearing the simple inscription: *1637: GS: MW*. His memory is more pretentiously perpetuated in London by such places as Sloane Square, Sloane Street, and Hans Place.

Comber derives its name from the Irish word *An Comar, a confluence,* which obviously refers to the confluence of the Comber River with Strangford Loch at this place. The local people call the place *Cummer*, which is the sound of the Irish

---

[1] Also interpreted as *Áine's standing stone,* (Clachan ed.)
[2] Also interpreted as *Cill Ó Laoch, church of the descendants of Laoch,* (Clachan ed.)

name, and this is but another example of the persistence of Irish sounds amongst people who have not spoken their native language for generations. Near-by, on Mahee Island—*(Inis Mochaoi), Saint Mochoe's Island* — are the remains of the Celtic Monastery of Nendrum—*(Noindrum). the Nine Ridges*—established there by Saint Mochoe, a disciple of Saint Patrick, in the fifth century. Saint Mochoe was a son of Bronad, and she was a daughter of that fierce old Pagan, Miliuc, whom Patrick served as a slave on Slemish in the County Antrim. This site on Mahee Island had been forgotten for centuries, and the very name lost, when, in 1844, it was discovered that what was long reputed to be a limekiln was really the stump of a Round Tower. Even so, nothing was done about it for many years until the Belfast Natural History Society made a thorough excavation in 1922-24, with the interesting result which you may examine to-day. The remains are surrounded by three concentric defensive cashels, for even religious houses had to be fortified in those wild times, not only against the rieving Norsemen but against the Christian Irish themselves, and, let it not be forgotten, against rival Christian monasteries on occasion; and you may now see what is left of the eighth-century school, the tenth-century Round Tower, the twelfth-century church, the foundry, the workshops, and all those other offices which went to make up the economy of a completely self-contained and self-supporting community. Many other things you may see as well, which I have not the space to list, and you may care to know that no other Celtic monastery remains in anything like so complete and perfect a state as this. Most of our ancient religious houses are cluttered with ugly tombs, and burial rights forbid excavation, but Nendrum was destroyed at such an early date, and lay forgotten for so long, that the archaeologists were able to work there without hindrance. You will probably find the old sundial especially interesting, for this is not marked with the hours but with the five periods of prayer: *Prime or Matins; Terce; Sext; None; and Duodecima or Vespers.*

Newtownards, the New Town of the Ards of Sir Hugh Montgomery, owes its rise to the commercial acumen of that wily Scot who got the better of poor Con O Neill at the beginning of the seventeenth century. The old Mercat or Town Cross still stands, and close at hand are the remains of the Dominican Priory, founded in 1244 by the Savage family, and subsequently used as a dwelling by the Montgomerys and their friends; it was they who built the tower and gateway which look so fine in their decay to-day. The cylindrical pillars and slightly pointed arches of the nave of the old Priory Church are noteworthy. Outside the town the ancient Abbey of Movilla, built on the site of a Celtic monastery founded by Saint Finnian in 450, will repay a visit because of the series of grave-slabs preserved there, one with an inscription in the Irish language which was rarely used for such purposes—*Or do Dertrend, a prayer for Dertriu.* Some of the old dated street-name signs in Newtownards are worth inspection, as well as the fine eighteenth-century Market House, with its sun fanlight and its distinctively Scottish appearance. On the neighbouring hill of Scrabo—*(Scrabac), the Sward of the Cows*—is a tall memorial tower erected to the memory of the third Marquess

Waringstown Church, County Down.

of Londonderry in 1858, and you should ascend that tower for the sake of a tremendous panorama of Strangford Loch and the surrounding countryside; and then you should descend it for the sake of a real Ulster meal of tea and goat's milk, soda bread, fadge, potato bread and everything that goes with it, for this is one of the few places where you can be sure of our authentic Ulster fare, and it will do you more good than all the nostrums in the British Pharmacopoeia. The tower stands on the site of a Bronze Age cairn and within an ancient circular defensive enclosure, and some hut circles, on the charming little golf course that surrounds the hill, tell us that this was an old booleying place, where farmers of an earlier age moved their live-stock to upland pastures in the summer season, and lived on the spot till the time for harvest took them back to their lowland farms. Geologically, Scrabo is interesting because the basaltic cap of the hill has preserved the Triassic sandstones that elsewhere in this region have been swept away.

Down the eastern side of Strangford Loch we go now, past the lovely demesne of Mountstewart where you should seek permission to view the fine Italian gardens, and on to Grey Abbey. Here are the impressive ruins of a Cistercian Abbey founded in 1193 by Affreca, daughter of Godred, king of the Isle of Man, and wife of John de Courcy, as an act of thanksgiving for salvation from shipwreck. The remains follow the usual Cistercian plan, and a guide on the spot will indicate the many points of interest in this especially fine example of conservative Irish Gothic. In the adjacent graveyard sleeps the Reverend James Porter, who was hanged in front of his own manse, which you may also see, for his courageous part in the 1798 rising.

You may go on now to Portaferry, which we have already considered, and make the full circle back to Donaghadee, by way of Portavogie and Ballyhalbert, where Miss Pedelty weaves lovely fabrics on her hand-looms, along the coast of the Ards Peninsula which fronts the Irish Sea; or you may cut through to Ballywalter, on that same coast, and save yourself more than twenty miles of travelling at the expense of much good scenery. Donaghadee is a pleasant little port, dominated by a mote-and-balley erected by one William de Coupland, a de Courcy knight, who also gave his name to the Copeland Islands which lie just out to sea. On the top of this mote is a modern decorative tower, built to house the explosives used in building the fine harbour, and from this neat haven the mail-boat used to sail to Portparick, in Scotland, before the Larne-and-Stranraer service was established as a more convenient and less weather-bound route.

Bangor—*(Beannchar), the Pointed Horns or Rocks*—is a go-ahead seaside resort that is often called *Belfast-by-the-Sea*. It has the third largest population of any town in Ulster, being exceeded in this respect only by Belfast and Derry, and most of its inhabitants are business people of Belfast, though it has an enormous influx of visitors in the summer months. It is a pleasant place, charmingly situated, with a fine strand at Ballyholme and a bold coastline of jutting masses of Silurian rocks and slates, but its most enduring his great monastic fame lies in the past, for

Priory Church, Newtownards, County Down.

Saint Comgall founded schools here in the year 559.

Saint Bernard speaks of this most celebrated foundation as *a noble institution, the parent of many thousands of monks, the head of many monasteries ... so fruitful in saints that one of its sons, Luanus by name, is alone reputed to be the founder of one hundred monasteries.* Indeed, for eight hundred years and more the schools of Bangor were famous all over Europe, and missionaries from this place went forth into many lands, and founded, amongst other celebrated houses, the monasteries of Saint Gall in Switzerland, of Peronne in France, of Wurzburg in Germany, and of Bobbio in Italy, the founder of the last-named establishment being none other than that illustrious son of Bangor, the great Columbanus himself. The priceless *Bangor Antiphonary*, the *Antiphonarium Benchorense*, written between the years 680 and 691, is all that is left of this once-great school with its more than three thousand students, and that sole relic owes its preservation to the fact that it was taken to Italy in the ninth century and has remained one of the most cherished treasures of the great Ambrosian Library of Milan ever since. For the Norsemen plundered Bangor again and again, and when Saint Malachy visited the place in 1121 he found it a desolate ruin. His attempt to revive its ancient glories was only partially successful, and the fragment of a wall in the vicarage garden of the present Abbey Church of Bangor may be all that remains of one of his buildings. In the near-by Clandeboye demesne stands Helen's Tower, raised to the memory of Helen, Lady Dufferin, who wrote *The Irish Emigrant* and many another deathless song, and you should seek permission to visit this memorial. Helen's Bay, another remembrancer of this gracious lady, is a pretty cove down by the sea, and in the neighbouring village of Crawfordsburn is a lovely little glen with a waterfall at its head, and an old and well-graced inn which is the best thing of its kind in Ulster.

Holywood Priory, County Down.

Nearer Belfast is Holywood, spelt with a single *l* and pronounced as though it had two like its famous sister in California. But its ancient name of Sanctus Boscus—*Holy Wood*—shows us that it is the pronunciation that is at fault. Saint Laisren founded a Celtic monastery here in 650, and a Franciscan Friary was established in the fifteenth century, but the ruins of the church of this later establishment are all that is left of Holywood's one-time ecclesiastical importance. Above the town, on a highway still known as Jackson's Road, is Garden Lodge, and from this pretty home the Jackson family emigrated to the United States and gave to that country a son who was to become famous in her service as General Stonewall Jackson.

And now, on the Castlereagh Hills above the busy City of Belfast, we may finish our tour of the County of Down. Here is the site of the old Grey Castle of that branch of the O Neills of which poor Con was head when his wide and pleasant lands were filched from him by the wily strangers. The very name of the place reminds us of this old home of the O Neills—Castlereagh—*(an Caisleán Riabhach), the Grey Castle*. But you will look in vain for the ruins of this place, and that for a most curious reason. For during the nineteenth century, when all that was left of this storied pile was in danger of final extinction by cattle, ivy and the weather, some gentlemen of good will made representations to the landlord for the preservation of the crumbling remains. To his credit, this nobleman suitably instructed his land steward to build a protective wall about the ruin, but that official was thrifty and resourceful, and he had his own ideas about such things. He built the wall, and made it good and strong at that, but he saved himself the trouble, and his noble employer the expense, of carting material to the top of a hill, by pulling down what was left of the old castle and building his wall with the salvage. So that you may now enjoy the spectacle of a well-built protective wall which protects exactly nothing! Yes indeed, this is Ireland!!

I wonder, Con O Neill, does your spirit still haunt the groves of Holywood, or kneel in prayer within the insubstantial precincts of old Saint Laisren's house, where you were wont to go, and you in your great sorrow for the calamity that had come on the Yellow-haired O Neills. Rest in peace, Con O Neill, last Tanist of the Yellow-haired clan, for sure if we can't find your forgotten grave in Ballymaghan, can't we keep a wee place in our hearts for you and your sorrows. It was you I was thinking of when I wrote a little poem many years ago, a poem of which this is the cadence:

> No, there's little known about him round the hills of Castlereagh,
> And the grass has hid his grey old home
> This manys a day:
> But they tell me out in Holywood they sometimes see the man,
> Late afoot and sorrowing
> For the Yellow-haired clan.

The County of Armagh — Contae Árd Macá

IT is impossible to stand in the City of Armagh and not sense in the air all around you ghostly whisperings of the tremendous influence which this ancient and venerable city has had upon the history of Ireland, not only through the long centuries of the Christian era but also for many centuries before that time. Armagh is one of the select company of the towns and cities of Ireland which assail one with an indefinable but subtly personal atmosphere all their own; in this company one thinks of Dublin and Kilkenny and Derry, and very much of Galway, that most Irish of all towns, but one thinks pre-eminently of Armagh; for there is atmosphere in every stone of this place, something springing from the generations of great people and of lowly people, of secular princes and princes of the church, of all who have made their homes here and transmitted to the very bricks and mortar some ineffable quality of their own humanity. And in this gracious mellow place the regrettable but inevitable division of the Irish people into two divergent schools of thought seems to find some kind of agreement, for here the two chief Irish Cathedrals of the two main persuasions of the Christian Faith stand in friendly proximity on neighbouring elevations, and seem to whisper to each other that the worship of God, in whatever form or manner, is as high as heaven over the human follies of argument and discord. For Armagh is the ecclesiastical metropolis of the whole of Ireland to-day, just as it was on that other day when Saint Patrick set up his initial bishopric here and declared it to be the Primacy.

Saint Patrick loved this place, and you cannot wonder at it. It is the very cry of his heart that we hear in *The Book of Armagh: It is Armagh that I love, my dear thorp, my sweet hill*, and I often wonder whether he ever thought, when he chose this Holy City of his, how much it resembled that other Holy City of Rome. For Armagh lay close to the seat of royal power in Ulster, and Saint Patrick sought the co-operation of the Ulster kings and chieftains just as in Rome the Popes sought the power of the emperors as soon as they became Christian; and as well as this, Armagh, like Rome, stands partly on a number of small hills and partly between them, and *the Seven Hills of Armagh* are still pointed out to visitors. Not that the Celtic Church founded by Saint Patrick had much contact with Rome, for it was an Irish Church and a National Church, but it was never a State institution, which explains why there is no instance of the Celtic Church ever having used *the Sword of State* against pagan or heretic. Rather were these elements wooed to the bosom of the Church by a wise and gentle forbearance, and by a far-seeing incorporation, recommended by Saint Patrick himself in the plainest words, of the most cherished pagan beliefs and customs into the general body of

Scotch Street, Armagh.

The Observatory, Armagh.

Christian practice. For the Celtic Church was isolated geographically from the Church of Rome, with a solid pagan barrier in eastern and southern England between it and the Eternal City. Indeed in the matter of rites and doctrine the Patrician Church differed markedly from that of Rome, so much so that when Augustine, who was unaware of the already highly developed Christian communities of West Britain and Ireland, sought to bring them into conformity with Roman doctrine, he was dismayed at the bitterness with which these Christians of the Celtic Church opposed his reforms. And it was not until 1152, at the Synod of Kells, that complete uniformity was reached and the first Roman Catholic archbishops were appointed in Ireland.

The beauty of Armagh is the beauty of an old woman who has aged gracefully. Beauty is there, and dignity, and a deep understanding which comes from more than three-thousand years of intimate connection with the business of humanity. About the year 684, Aldfrid, soon to become king of the Northumbrian Saxons, was a student at the celebrated School of Armagh, and he wrote a little poem:

> I found in Armagh the splendid,
> Neatness, wisdom and prudence blended.
> Fasting as Christ hath recommended.
> And noble councillors untranscended.

And if the date of that poem impresses you with the antiquity and importance of Armagh, I would ask you to reflect that even at that time Armagh was already a very ancient city.

As a county, Armagh resembles in surface its neighbouring County of Down, though the little lakes which bejewel Down are rare here, and the limestone and Loch Neagh clays in the northern terrain bring their diversifying qualities to that countryside. Some of the streets of the City of Armagh are paved with a handsome red marble which is quarried locally in a sudden outcrop of Carboniferous strata, but, sad to relate, these distinctive and beautiful pavement slabs are gradually being replaced with the characterless artificial products of modern commerce.

Armagh, in Irish *Ard Mhacha*, —*the Height of Macha*—is named after a queen, and although Macha was the name of three famous queens, it is generally accepted that the lady who gave her name to this venerable city was that wife of Nevry who came to Ireland 608 years after the Deluge, and who lies buried on the famous hill. This would confirm the belief that Armagh is one of the most ancient settlements in Ireland, a circumstance further confirmed by the fact that the city is placed where two great roads meet on their way to the Ulster basin. It is also likely that the Moyry Pass was part of that great road which stretched from the extreme south of Ireland, through Tara, to Armagh, connecting in Christian times the seat of secular government with the seat of spiritual power. You may trace many of these ancient roads in this region, just as I have traced them, if you have the inclination and keep your eyes open.

The City of Armagh, from the Cathederal Tower.

Emania is the Latinised form of the Irish *Eamuin* a compound word which refers in part to a brooch; and *Eamhain Mhacha*, now known as Navan Fort, is close to Armagh City on the road to Killylea. For nearly seven hundred years this was the palace of the kings of Ulster, and the headquarters of the *Knights of the Red Branch*, Ireland's most notable order of chivalry of which the mighty Cuchulainn was the shining bright jewel. Macha founded this palace in 352 B.C., and herself drew the plan of it with her brooch, which accounts for the place-name. The end of Emania came with the conquest of the *Black Pig's Dyke* by the Three Collas, and to-day you will see there no more than you will see at that other greater Royal Palace of Tara, a few grass-covered mounds and entrenchments. For the Irish builders of ancient times wrought their palaces and dwellings out of timber, and wattle-and-daub, and even the earliest churches and monasteries were made of these perishable materials, so that all we can ever see to-day are the earthen mounds on which these structures stood, and the earthen rings and trenches, or the stone cashels, which surrounded and protected them from man and beast alike.

Saint Patrick arrived in Armagh a hundred years after the destruction of Emania, and Daire, a descendant of the Three Collas, ruled the region from a rath on which the ancient cathedral stands to-day. Saint Patrick wanted that site the moment he saw it, but Daire refused his request and granted him ground where the Bank of Ireland, once the town house of the Dobbin family and still a lovely Georgian mansion, is at present situated in Scotch Street. There Saint Patrick built his first Church of Armagh, a wooden structure of which no vestige remains, and there his sister Lupita was untimely laid to rest. Which brings us to the controversial question of the burial-place of Saint Patrick himself, for the people of Armagh deny the claims of Downpatrick to this great honour. They point out that The Calendar of Cashel states that the relics of Patrick repose at Armagh in the place called *The Monument of Patrick*; that the *Lebor Brec* declares that these relics lie in a stone tomb in Armagh; that the holy Saint Bernard has recorded: *as the great Saint Patrick presided at Armagh in his lifetime, so in his death his remains repose there;* that William of Newbridge, in the twelfth century, said that the Primacy was bestowed on Armagh because the remains of Saint Patrick lay there; and, finally, they say that since Armagh held the Bell, Book and Staff of the Saint for so long, a fact which is not questioned, it is certain that had the Saint been buried in Down these personal relics would have gone with the body; for there is no instance anywhere of a Saint's lying buried apart from his personal relics. And there I leave both you and controversy.

In the course of time, when probably Daire himself had embraced the Christian faith, Patrick was given the site of the royal rath on which he had set his heart, and there he built a church which was known as the *Sabal*; and thereafter he built another church known as the *Toga*; and then between these two wooden buildings arose the *Daimliag mor—the great Stone Church*—and about the year 445, in the strictly modified sense in which the term may be related to the early Celtic

Church, Saint Patrick conferred upon the bishopric a Primacy over all Ireland, a Primacy which has existed through the centuries to the present day. The Great Stone Church persisted in altered forms until the year 1268, when it was entirely rebuilt by the Primate, Maelpatrick O Scannail, for it had suffered periodic damage and devestation at the hands of the Norsemen who had settled in Loch Neagh. But in 1566 this new structure came in for even worse treatment, for in that year Shane O Neill reduced it, and the surrounding city, to ashes, *to prevent the desecration of the holy sanctuary by vile English troops,* as he said, perchance with his tongue in his cheek. So once again the people of Armagh had to set their hands to the rebuilding of their cathedral and their city, this time under the direction of Primate Hampton, and once again an O Neill, Sir Phelim of that ilk, burned everything down with the 1641 rising as the pretext this time. And yet, despite wars and ill-usages and the later heavy hand of the restorers. God save the mark! O Scannail's successor to the Great Stone Church of Saint Patrick still remains as a considerable part of the fabric of the present cathedral. The oldest portion is the crypt, with arches of ninth-century construction, and there you may see an amusing *Sheela-na-gig—(Síle na gcíoch), Julia of the Paps*—a stone figure recovered from a spot on the rath which is not recorded, and you will observe the horse's ears of this grotesque little creature; the legend relating to this figure is a variant of the Greek Midas story. In 1834 the cathedral was completely restored by Primate Lord John George Beresford, who paid for the entire work out of his own pocket, and the architect Cottenham, who restored Saint Albans, was in charge of the operation; which explains why Armagh, like Saint Albans, was shockingly *over*-restored. The external walls were refaced with freestone, the internal walls were covered with plaster, windows and doors were ruthlessly altered to conform with the excessively bad taste of the time, and little remains to tell the casual observer that this is Ireland's oldest cathedral; except the curious inclination of the chancel. This is a feature which you will only find in the very oldest churches in Ireland, in Saint Nicholas at Carrickfergus and in the great cathedral on the Rock of Cashel, and this slant of the chancel from the line of the nave is usually explained as a representation of the inclination of our Saviour's Head on the Cross. But for a detailed description of Armagh Cathedral I must refer you to the Armagh official guide, though before we leave.

I would like you to climb to the top of the tower with me for a look at the Armagh district as a bird must see it. Over there lies Emania, and there is Niall's Mound beside the River Callan, named after that Mall Caille, king of Ulster, who was drowned there, in 846, when he plunged into

Sheela-na-gig, at Armagh Cathederal

the flood in an attempt to rescue one of his soldiers during a battle with the Norsemen. Niall lies in the graveyard just below us, where Colman also sleeps, disciple of Saint Patrick and the first Christian to be buried there. Brian Boru is also of that silent company of the dead, for he was brought to this holy place, in 1014, in deference to his last wish expressed on the victorious field of Clontarf— *My soul to God and my body to Armagh* . The rings of the old rath of Daire will be plainly visible to you from this lofty perch, and within these ramparts once stood the Abbey of Saint Peter and Saint Paul, the Culdee Priory, and the famous library, whilst without the fortifications were the churches of Saint Brigid and Saint Columba, and the thirteenth-century Franciscan Friary of which alone any remnant remains, a picturesque fragment in the grounds of the Primatial palace which you may visit hereafter. And over there is Tuflyard Mound, traditional grave of the Sons of Usna; there Ballybrawley Stone Circle; and, away in the Fews—*(na Feá/Feadha), woods,* for in earler times that region was densely timbered—you'll see Carrickatuke and Blackbank, with one of the ancient roads from Tara to Emania between them. There are the churches of Grange, Lisnadil, Killylea, and Kildarton; and Dungannon Town all on its hill like Rathfriland; and that building on the road to Portadown is the Royal School, moved there in 1774 from its old site in Abbey Street. Near the school is the Observatory, founded by the great Primate Robinson in 1790 and with a distinguished record of work to its credit, and you should certainly visit that pleasant Georgian house with its historic equipment now rubbing shoulders with the latest instruments. Under my good friend Doctor Lindsay, and with a distinguished and recently amplified staff of astronomers, the old observatory has taken its place with the best establishments of the kind in the world to-day. But we could go on like this all day, and before we descend I would only ask you to observe one thing more, the manner in which the City of Armagh has grown round the cathedral like the spokes and rim of a wheel round its hub. And as for those graceful twin spires over there, come with me and we'll examine them at closer range.

These spires, soaring heavenwards for well over two-hundred feet, belong to the splendid Roman Catholic cathedral of Saint Patrick, magnificently situated on an eminence reached by a seven-terraced stairway of white limestone. This cathedral is largely the personal creation of Archbishop Crolly, and its building was commenced in 1840—*Cum Gloria de agus onora na hEireann* —*To the glory of God and the honour of Ireland*—with money subscribed by Irish people living in every part of the world. It was dedicated in 1873, when its design was altered from Perpendicular to Decorated Gothic, and on July the 24th, 1904, it was consecrated at a great ceremony at which the Pope was represented. You may spend a pleasant hour or more in an examination of this sumptuous building, but once again I must refer you to the official guide for a full description of its many treasures and excellences.

I would ask you not to leave Armagh without visiting the County Museum, first of its kind in Ireland and greatly beloved of its originator, T. G. F. Paterson, the present Curator. If Mr. Paterson has the leisure he will tell you more about Armagh in a few minutes than I could transmit to you in many pages, but a mere examination of his carefully arranged collection will afford you a background against which you will be able to consider what I have written, with heightened interest and intelligence. And, People of America, do you know that it was an Armagh man, the Reverend William Tennant, who founded your Log College, which has since grown into Princeton University; and do you know that George Buchanan Armstrong, born in Armagh City, founded your United States Mail Service? Even if you do know these things, it is well that you should ponder them in contemplation of the strong and imperishable bonds which bind our Ulster and your great democracy so closely together.

The Museum stands beside the Mall, a gracious and most-English-looking enclosure of greensward, with a fine cricket pitch in its midst. Through the graceful trees which border this green, the splendid Charlemont Terrace shows up superbly in all the glory of its magnificent Georgian conception, one of the finest things of its kind in Ireland. Its very name will chime in our heads at once, and remind us of those greater glories of Irish Georgian, the superb Charlemont House in Dublin, and the entrancing Casino, also built by Lord Charlemont, at Marino on the outskirts of that same city. Lower down this side of the Mall, near the Courthouse, is the famous Crooked Door. Look at it, and you'll see how it came by the name!

The road to Portadown, by way of Richhill, will take you through that lovely orchard country which makes up much of the northern parts of the County Armagh, and if you are here in blossom-time you'll enjoy as pretty a picture as there is in Ireland. Armagh was planted by Warwickshire folk in the time of James the First of England, and these people brought something to Ireland which we never had before, the pleasant custom of planting an orchard as the necessary adjunct of every dwelling. This custom has lived on, and the gardens of fruit trees, and the thick-set damson hedges, which you'll see everywhere around here, have given this region the name of *The Orchard of Ireland*. A little to the north of the main road is Kilmore—*(an Chill Mhór), the Big Church*—with a modern church built on to a tower of great antiquity, square and massive, and with walls nine feet thick. But what makes this tower especially remarkable is the fact that it is built around, so as to enclose, the almost perfect Round Tower of the ancient monastery founded here on the fifth-century site of Saint Mochto. This is one of the most astonishing architectural freaks in Ireland, and no explanation of it has ever been found or suggested. Richhill is an English name, probably bestowed on this district because of its richness and fertility, and the only thing of interest I can tell you about it is that the gates of Richhill Castle, of superb mid-eighteenth-century wrought-ironwork, were taken away in 1936, and now adorn the entrance to Government House, which is in Hillsborough in the County Down. What Armagh thought of this high-handed piece of piracy is nobody's business. From neighbouring Ahorey, Thomas and Alexander Campbell went out to the United States, in 1807 and founded the Baptist Church of America.

Portadown, on account of its name, is often mistakenly associated with the County Down, but it is an Armagh town pure and simple, and not so very simple at that! It is the Aberdeen of Ireland, in the matter of stories invented by itself to its own discomfort, but I have already dealt with this aspect of its being. The place-name is *Port an Dúnáin—the Landing-place of the Fortress*—the fortress in this case being, in all probability, an earthen dun or rath, long since disappeared, situated beside the River Bann which flows through the town. This crossing of the great waterway must have been of immense importance ever since prehistoric times, but I can only recommend Portadown to-day for its stories, and as the starting-point of a pleasant little boating trip up and down the wide and gentle stream. As for the stories, here are two more.

A ticket-collector at Portadown station espied two nuns in a carriage, and at once his Orange hackle rose. In his rudest and most aggressive manner he demanded their tickets, and the elder of the two, after fumbling awhile, politely explained that she must have mislaid them, but would surely have them ready when the collector returned from his attention to the rest of the train. *Yid better*, said the official, shortly and sharply, as, with a slam of the door, he departed for a space. Upon his return the elder nun confessed that she could not find their tickets but would furnish their names and addresses. *Too safe ye will*, snapped the collector, *and who are yiz anyway?* We're two Sisters of John the Baptist, faltered the somewhat-ruffled religious, and . . . *Well that's a damned lie for a start*, roared the outraged official; and the rest of the story is not recorded.

A certain editor of a country newspaper found, to his horror, a reference in his Orange Sheet to a *Father Rafferty*. *What's this you have here?* he shouted at the reporter who was responsible for this enormity, *Father Rafferty, is it? Father nothing at all! If you must mention the like of that you'll call him the Reverend Mister Rafferty, the same as you would an ordinary decent minister.* And such terror was struck into the hearts of the whole staff that when the late Plunket Greene sang at a concert in the town, the following words appeared as part of a long eulogy: *In response to repeated demands for an encore, Mr. Plunket Greene rendered, in his inimitable style, that well-known Irish ballad, The Reverend Mister O Flynn.*

From near-by Lurgan came AE, celebrated Irish poet, mystic, painter and economist, often claimed as a Dublin man; and Sir Robert Hart, first Inspector-General of the Imperial Customs in China, and a man whose immense integrity won him almost fabulous respect in the Far East, was born in Portadown.

Lurgan—*(Lorgain), a Shin or Long Hill*—is an entirely modern town created by the Plantation. John Brownlow, a Nottinghamshire squire, was the undertaker here and was presented with fifteen hundred acres of good Ulster soil filched from the O Neills. One of this family, the Lord Lurgan of Victorian days, was the owner of the greatest coursing dog the world has ever known, the celebrated *Master MacGra*, famous in song and story, which won the Waterloo Cup no less than three times. But Lurgan is equally noted for the manufacture of linen

Georgian House, The Mall, Armagh.

diaper, a trade introduced here by William Waring in the reign of Queen Anne of England, and still extensively carried on. James Logan, born in Lurgan in 1674, became in turn Secretary to William Penn, Secretary of the State of Pennsylvania, and President of the Council, so that, like most Ulster towns, Lurgan has enduring links with the United States.

From Lurgan it is a pleasant jaunt to the shores of Loch Neagh, to Ardmore Point, Charlestown, and Bann Foot at the mouth of the Upper Bann. You will enjoy a superb view from there, of the wide lake and the grand mountains of Derry and Tyrone on the far side. At hand is Coney Island, where Shane O Neill is reputed to have kept his treasure-house; and maybe the fragment of a circular keep, which you will find there amongst the charming paths and woodlands, is part of that ancient safe-deposit.

In Charlemont village stood the famous fort built by Mountjoy in 1602, but this was destroyed in *the troubles* of 1920, and all that remains is the gateway surmounted by a clock and the Caulfeild arms. The first commander of this fort was Sir Toby Caulfeild, from whom the Lords of Charlemont are descended.

Lochgall, *the Lake of Cal*, is as English-looking as the orchard country in which it lies, but, as if to show that it was very Irish at one time, there is a crannog in the lake. In Lochgall, in Jackson's house, was drawn up the Constitution of the Loyal Orange Society, and not far away is the Diamond, famous for its battle.

Blackwatertown was in earlier times a major station on the ill-fated Ulster Canal, and signs of its decayed commercial greatness are now heavy upon it in the form of derelict warehouses and dwellings. But behind all this looms a page of history as stirring as anything in the Irish annals, for this quiet village, known as Portmore at that time, was *the Gibraltar of Ireland* in the Elizabethan era. Here, in 1575, the Earl of Sussex built a strong fort, of which you may still see the ramparts, in an endeavour to keep the powerful and turbulent O Neills in order, and for that reason this fort was always particularly hateful to the Yellow-haired clan. In 1598 Hugh O Neill, the great Earl of Tyrone, exasperated at the gradual penetration of his lands by the English, made a full-scale attack on this stronghold, and he was so successful that the English were forced to send a relieving army from Armagh . In command of this force was O Neill's greatest enemy, both in public and in private, the doughty Bagenal, whose sister O Neill had carried off in elopement and subsequently discarded. An explosive mixture was amaking, beyond a peradventure. O Neill, with masterly strategy, managed to divide Bagenal's forces into three parts and to attack each part separately with his full weight, and the result was the greatest disaster ever suffered by the English arms in Ireland, the death of Bagenal in battle, and the loss of Ulster to the invaders. Had the Irish been able now to achieve that unity which only once came to them, under Brian Boru, the resultant rising in Munster might have freed Ireland once and for all. But it was not to be, and within weeks the old Irish jealousies and treacheries and divisions were again operating to the advantage of the English. This great Irish victory which I have described took place at the

Derrymore House, County Armagh.

Yellow Ford, on the banks of the River Callan, between Blackwatertown and Armagh.

The southern part of the County Armagh is rugged and mountainous and wildly beautiful, but for some strange reason its rather remote mountainy grandeur is as little known to our own people as it is to visitors to our shores. So come with me to the Slieve Gullion region, which is steeped in ancient history and romantic legend. We'll start from Bessbrook, away over near Newry and the Down border, a model industrial town founded by that good Quaker, John Grubb Richardson, as a centre for the manufacture of linen. It was planned on the lines of a Penn Settlement, and a visiting Cadbury was so impressed by it that he straightway decided to build his celebrated model village of Bourneville. The relationship between the Richardsons and the townspeople is still almost patriarchal, and we may here reflect on the seemly kind of world we might enjoy if all industry were organised on such idealistic yet solidly practical lines. Close to Bessbrook is Derrymore House, low and pleasant and with an entrancing, old thatched roof, which was built in 1780 by Isaac Corry, last Chancellor of the Exchequer to the Irish Parliament, and here, in 1800, Corry and Castlereagh drew up the fateful *Act of Union*. South of Bessbrook is Camloch—(*Cam Loc*), *the Crooked Lake*—lying in a deep and beautiful hollow beside Camloch Mountain; the village is picturesque and tree-lined, and the lake supplies Newry with its water, and countless anglers with good sporting trout, which are mostly taken on the western shore where wading is easy.

From Camloch a small rising road will take you, by the eastern shore of the Crooked Lake, to Meigh—*(an Mhaigh), a Plain*—and from almost anywhere along this highway the scenery will tear the heart out of you with its tender loveliness. Our path now lies due west to Killevy—(*Cill Shléibhe*), *the Church of the Mountain*—and to that storied mountain itself, Slieve Gullion—*(Sliabh gCuillinn), the Mountain of the Holly*—but if you have time to spare I can here recommend a journey of twenty miles north to Tanderagee—*(Tóin re Gaoith), Backside to the Wind*—and back again. This would lead you along the Down border through as varied and interesting a countryside as you will find anywhere, through the delectable Beamish, which means, in Irish, *a Little Gap*, where you'll find a Horned Cairn at Ballymacdermot, and over elevated country which commands sweeping wide views of Dundalk Bay, of the Cooley country over which Cuchulainn held sway, and of the surrounding mountains full of the glory of heather and bracken and fragrant whin, and with those atmospheric blues about their majestic slopes which you'll only see in such perfection in this lovely Ireland of ours. At Tanderagee the modern castle of the Duke of Manchester—how strangely that incongruous name strikes our ears in this most Irish region!—is worth a visit, if only for the charm of its grounds and the sombre beauty of its Dark Walk; and a mile or two away, towards Hamilton's Bawn, is Marlacoo Lake—(*Marla cuaic), the Marl of the Hollow*—with its historic crannog. Sir Henry Sydney tried to capture this for the English in 1566, but without success, and the great Earl of Tyrone occupied it in 1595, and kept there, for their safety, *greate store of munitions, plate and jewels, and his wife and children,* notwithstanding the fact that he had then, at Dungannon, *a fyne handsome stone castell all roofed with leade,* an indication of the tardiness with which the Irish deserted their accustomed homes of timber and wattle for the new-fangled stone dwellings. The ancient cemetery of Relicarn is not far away, in the direction of Scarva, and there sleeps Redmond O Hanlon, Ireland's most famous highwayman, aristocrat turned outlaw and rapparee because of the filching, by James the First of England and his crafty lawyers, of the wide pleasant lands which were his ancient patrimony.

Back through Poyntzpass, one of the three old passes into the County, and owing its name to that English soldier of fortune and *the 1641,* Sir Charles Poyntz, we go on to Goraghwood, and from this road you will see many good sections of *the Black Pig's Dyke,* on the small hills to the right. And from hereabouts you will also get that distant view of Newry Town which I have ever found most endearing and most rewarding.

Back to Meigh, we may now take our way to Killevy to look at a ruin which is the most remarkable thing of its kind in Ulster, for here are the remains of two ancient churches built end to end. The western structure is the earlier, as you may see from its trabeated[1] doorway with inclined jambs, which, as I have already explained, belong only to our most ancient stone buildings but the window here is eleventh-century Hiberno-Romanesque and tells us of a later alteration of the ancient fabric. The eastern church has a pointed window of the fourteenth century, and both these buildings are especially interesting because they show not the slightest trace of English influence. And that these sacred places were under constant threat of attack, in this wild and remote region, is suggested by the unusual *chevaux-de-frise* which stands before the doorway of the older church, a fine array of stumbling stones to take the sting out of any sudden rush by a hidden enemy.

The best approach to the summit of Slieve Gullion, from this side of the mountain, is through the grounds of the modem house known as Killevy Castle, so let us seek permission from the friendly owners and move on our way to that high region of beauty and old romance and legend. We are 1893 feet above sea-level up here on the summit, but from this modest altitude we may enjoy one of the grandest and most extensive panoramas in Ulster. This mountain is intimately associated with Cuchulainn, and with the later Finn MacCool, who, in the popular imagination, was the giant who built *The Giant's Causeway* and many another mighty structure, but who in reality was that *Fionn mac Cumhaill* who founded the Fianna, a kind of National Militia, and who is the central figure of the oft-printed and oft-translated stories of the *Fenian Cycle*. I must refer you to those stories, of which you will find a version in every library in Ireland, and in particular to *The Chase,* which you will find in *Reliques of Ancient Irish Poetry,* for a

---

[1] The use of horizontal beams which are borne up by columns or posts, (Clachan ed.).

proper understanding of the legendary and romantic background of our storied Slieve Gullion, but here on the summit you may now see the magic lake from which poor Finn emerged an old man with grey hair, and you may examine the house of the witch or *calliagh* who wrought this dreadful deed, *the Calliagh Birra's House*; and don't let it break your romantic heart when I tell you that this pile of stones is really an unusual and highly important hill-top cairn, closely resembling the cupola-tombs of Spain and Portugal. There is nothing quite like it anywhere else in Ulster, and it is a pity that it is so dilapidated.

Slieve Gullion is part of a complex of ancient rocks which is the delight of every geologist. It is not within the scope of this book to deal with such a fascinating and complicated subject, but from the summit of the storied mountain you may care to observe that you are virtually at the centre of a far-flung circular rampart of smaller hills. These form the famous *Gullion Ring Dyke*, and if geology is one of your interests you have a text-book countryside at your feet in this lovely region of South Armagh. And you have beauty too, in full measure, and romance and history to bring colour and perspective to the wonder of it all.

A very ancient road runs due south from Killevy through the Moyry Pass to Faughart, where Edward Bruce was defeated and slain in 1318. But sure Faughart is in the County Louth, and that's in Eire, God help us! and over the Border; but we've been there already in our Leinster wanderings, so no matter! Most of the roads round here are old roads, very old roads, but the Moyry Pass must be the oldest of them all, and every line of communication, north and south, must have come through this *Gap of the North*, including the great highway from Tara to Emania itself, for there was no other possible passage except that around the Carlingford coast. Here the Men of Ulster would gather to make war on the Men of Leinster; here the mighty Cuchulainn made his single-handed stand against the hosts of Queen Maev of Connacht, whilst the rest of the Ulstermen lay in their magic sleeping; and here the O Neills kept the English at bay, until, in 1601, my Lord Mountjoy decided to put an end to all such resistance. This able soldier first cleared the ancient pass of the forests and woodlands which the Irish soldiers used so skilfully, and then he built the celebrated Moyry Castle in conformity with his idea that every danger-point of this kind should have the protection of *a littel keepe or tower of stone*. And you may see this *littel keepe* to-day, three storeys high and in ruins, and neatly and compactly placed on a small rocky eminence. In the valley below you'll find the Pillar Stone of Kilnasaggart—*(Cill na Saggart), the Church of the Priest*—which belongs to the period of about A.D. 700 and which is the earliest inscribed Christian monument so far discovered in the whole of Ireland. This is South Armagh at its splendid best, packed with beauty and romance and historic incident, and if you can engage in easy conversation some of the old people in this region, you'll hear many a thing that never gets the length of books. And that's no word of a lie!

Clontygora Horned Cairn, County Armagh.

To Forkhill now—*(Foirceal), the Cold Wood*—by way of Dromintee—*(Druim an Tighe), the Ridge of the House*—and if I can't do anything more for Forkhill than recommend its extremely picturesque surroundings, with Carrickastickin and Carrickbroad Mountains awaiting your exploring feet, and the wild beauty of Glendhu, *the Black Glen*, unrolling itself before you like a magic carpet, I can tell you something quite unexpected about Dromintee. For from this tiny village of a few houses, from which, by the way, runs another excellent approach to the summit of Slieve Gullion, went *the Pahvees*, to encircle the world in the selling of cloth, to Canada, to Australia, to New Zealand and to the United States of America; and the bright check shirts favoured by the men of the old mining camps were the creation of these pedlars who lived in the shadow of Slieve Gullion. Dromintee ragmen were also famous in their day, and if this seems a humble or unpleasant trade it is not unprofitable, and one Dromintee man anyway left his home *to gether regs*, as they say, and finished up as Lord Provost of a great Scottish city.

Crossmaglen—(*Crois Mhic Lionnáin), Maglin's Cross*—is very close to the Border and boasts a huge market square which seems much too big for it. The fairs here were formerly notorious for the undesirable characters who frequented them, and this circumstance is reflected in many an old song and ballad:

> From Carrickmacross to Crossmaglen
> There are more rogues than honest men.

Close to the town is what might be called the Lake District of Armagh, and these small lakes, and the associated River Fane, are all much favoured by anglers. In the midst of one of the lakes, Loch Ross, is the crannog on which the plans for the 1641 Rising were discussed and completed, and near-by is the fine earthen ring-fort of Corlis with a good souterrain about its centre; and since most of these underground chambers have been closed, on account of their danger to straying cattle, you should examine this one, which is open, for a sight of the general lay-out of these ancient and rather puzzling structures.

It is a pleasant run, partly through a gracious agricultural countryside and partly over a mountainous upland of wide vistas and a kind of desolate grandeur, from Crossmaglen through Newtownhamilton to the City of Armagh, and in that ancient place we may end, as we began, this tour of a lovely County that is almost as historically important as it is, beyond all comparison, ecclesiastically famous and revered and greatly beloved.

Slieve Gullion, County Armagh, Hills of the Ring Dyke in the right background.

The Moyry Castle, Gap of the North, County Armagh.

The County of Tyrone ~ Conntae Tír Eogain

YRONE among the Bushes! That's a saying you'll hear all over the world, for the Tyrone men are great travellers, and when they meet that's the phrase will be most often in their mouths. Ireland is full of these regional sayings—*Dear dirty Dublin,* for instance, which has a grand sound to it, and a heartening sound, but still an' all it's a bit playful and that takes the ache out of it; and as for *Were you ever in Larne?*—well, that's just neighbourly and calls for nothing more than a glass of whiskey, or maybe two; *Clonakilty, God help us!* is only humorously despairing and can be taken and offered as occasion demands; whilst *G'long, you ould Lurgan spade!* should only be used with extreme discretion. Yes, Ireland is full of these regional sayings, but of them all *Tyrone among the Bushes* has the real quality of heart about it, a deep nostalgic tug that seems to stem from that great love of their wild countryside which burned so constantly in the hearts of the fierce O Neills. For Tyrone—(*Tír Eoghain*), *the Territory of Owen*—derives its name from that wellnigh mythical Owen O Neill who is reputed to be the founder of that princely race which bears the greatest name in Irish history. From very early times Tyrone and the O Neills meant one and the same thing, and until late in the Middle Ages, Tyrone extended far beyond the borders of the present County, and included large tracts of the modem Counties of Armagh, Derry and Donegal.

The capital of Tyrone to-day is Omagh—*(an Ómaigh), the Perfect or Sacred Plain*—and the Irish sound of the name is preserved on the lips of Tyrone people when they pronounce it, as they commonly do, OH-ME, with the accent entirely on the first syllable. Compared with Armagh or Downpatrick, Omagh has little history, though no town has none, and there is little here to detain you except the crack of the good-hearted townspeople. But then Omagh has only been the County Town since the end of the eighteenth century, for before that time Dungannon—*(Dún Geanainn), the Fort of Gannon*—was the capital of Tyrone; but that ancient town lies far to the south of the County, almost on the Armagh border, and no doubt Omagh, more centrally situated, was found to be in better equilibrium as an administrative centre.

Dungannon was the paramount stronghold of the O Neills, but nothing remains of their stone castle but the name of the place on which it stood, a fine eminence at the head of the town, from which a wide and splendid prospect may be enjoyed, still known as Castle Hill. The four towers which stand there to-day, with traces of connecting curtain-walls, belong to a comparatively recent building, erected there in 1790 by one Hannynton, and even before that date Chichester had built a Plantation castle on the site of the ancient and storied native stronghold. As for the contiguous brick structure known as *O Neill's Chapel*, this is of no antiquity and has no connection with the princely family. And one would not expect to find any traces of the O Neills here, for their age-old refusal to acknowledge the alien government of England involved their town in a long series of assaults and devastations, and no place in Ireland is more intimately and honourably identified with the struggle for national freedom than this town on the hill. Even as late as 1782, Dungannon was the chosen spot for that great *Meeting of Volunteers*, which demanded the proper recognition of the Irish Parliament as the one lawful body for the making and enactment of laws for the government of Ireland; the freedom from arbitrary English legislation which was designed for nothing but the destruction of Irish commerce; and a thorough-going relaxation of *the cruel Penal Laws operating against our Roman Catholic fellow-countrymen*. The Presbyterian Church in Scotch Street is where this epoch-making gathering took place.

A mile or two west of Dungannon is Castlecaulfeild, and here the church, built about 1681 by Lord Charlemont, is architecturally confused but most interesting. In the south wall of the nave is a window brought from the old abbey of Donaghmore, and there are other carved stones, belonging to that old house, incorporated in this church. There is also a dated sundial on the tower, and within is a simple memorial to the heroic Walker, Governor of Derry in 1690. The Reverend Charles Wolfe was rector here in 1817, the year in which he wrote *The Burial of Sir John Moore*, a poem known all over the world but printed for the first time in *The Newry Telegraph*. The ruins of Castlecaulfeild Castle, which was really an Elizabethan-style manor-house, built by Sir Toby Caulfeild in 1612, stand on an adjacent spur of limestone which was the site of an old stronghold of the Donnellys. This Irish family was dispossessed by James the First, at the Plantation, and waged incessant warfare on the Caulfeilds, to whom their stolen lands were presented.

Donaghmore—*(Domhnach Mhór), the Big Church*—is a little to our north, but nothing remains of the Celtic monastery which gave this place its name. At the head of the village stands a tall and beautiful High Cross, obviously belonging to this ancient house, but unfortunately it lacks the two upper rings and part of the top arm. This cross was thrown down in *the 1641*, and was not raised again until 1776, by which time it was much dilapidated, and of the fine pictorial decorations which adorned the shaft we can now only trace a representation of the Crucifixion. The middle section of this shaft is missing, and the cross must originally have been higher than its present fifteen feet. In 1674 the gallant Walker, more

Georgian Doorway, Dungannon, County Tyrone.

famous as soldier than priest, was rector here, and his widow brought his remains back from the Battle of the Boyne for burial in this quiet spot.

Pomeroy is the highest town in the County Tyrone, and the Mountains of Pomeroy are famous in song and story. I'd like you to go there for the grand mountainy feel of the little place, typical of mid-Tyrone and never to be forgotten, and if you happen to be there on the Tuesday before either the 12th of May or the 12th of November, you'll see something quite remarkable. For on those days the Hiring Fair is in full swing, and bargaining in flesh-and-blood is carried on in its most primitive form.

The road from Pomeroy to Cookstown has many inviting little cross-roads, and some of these will lead you to elevations from which you may enjoy views of rare beauty. Cookstown owes its entirely English name to one Allan Cook, who did not receive his lands in the usual manner of the Plantation but leased them from the See of Armagh. For this was a district of termon lands belonging to the Church. The Stewarts of Killymoon subsequently acquired the property, and in 1726 William Stewart decided to carry out a bold scheme of reconstruction which is really one of the earliest examples of town-planning in Ireland. Instead of the accepted narrow roads and lanes, Stewart called for a single wide street, very wide indeed, for it is 130 feet across, and he ordered that it should stretch for an unbroken mile and be furnished with neat and wide side-avenues leading into it. All of which accounts for the quite remarkable appearance of Cookstown to-day, and for its nickname—*The Long Town*. Not far away is the Loughry demesne where Dean Swift used to visit, and where his arbour, in which he wrote many of his vitriolic satires, is still pointed out; but his friends the Lindsays no longer find joy in their seventeenth-century manor-house, for that gracious home has been taken over by the Government and is now a dairy school. Near at hand is Tullaghoge—*(Tulach Óc), the Hill of the Young*—a splendid example of an earthen ring-fort, and here for centuries the O Neills were inaugurated and crowned, and indeed this is the traditional pre-fourteenth century capital of Tyrone.

Eight-and-a-half miles along the road from Cookstown to Gortin, in the townland of Dunamore, is *the Eskera Bar*, owned by mine host MacCracken, and, from that hospitable house, a by-road, running northwards for two-and-a-half miles along the top of a grand esker, leads to Beaghmore—*(Bheitheach Mhór), the Big Birchtree*. Another derivation of this place-name could be *Beact mor, the Big Circle*, but I have no authority for this form, which is only attractive because of what I have now to tell you. At Beaghmore that most active and genial archaeologist, my good friend Andrew MacL. May, has recently discovered a fine complex of Stone Circles, alignments and cairns, which was obviously a most important burial and assembly place of *Beaker people* who came to Ireland towards the middle of the Bronze Age. A deterioration of the Irish climate scattered these settlers from their centre, and smothering mosses soon covered their structures, and the whole area, with deep bog. The removal of this bog, during turf-cutting operations, recently laid bare this ancient tribal concentration of ritualistic monuments, and it is likely that, as more turf is cut away, many features will be revealed to add to the already remarkable interest of these circles, with their associated and orientated avenues. This bog lies at an altitude of about seven hundred feet in typical country of the Tyrone uplands, and on every hand, especially in the series of splendid eskers, are abundant evidences of that great Ice Age which, eight thousand years ago, carved the face of our countryside into new contours. On the way to Beaghmore the valley of the Ballinderry River is most picturesque, and the wide grandeur of the Sperrin Mountains is spread before us in remote but entrancing loveliness. From this place you have a choice of several winding ways back to the main road, and which of these you follow I can best leave to your own fancy.

Coagh—*(Cuach), a Cup-like Hollow*[1]—is right on the Derry border, and its wide market-place bears the absurdly irrelevant name of Hanover Square; a little bit of blarney put on the first George of England when the landlord of that day was seeking a charter to hold a market. On the outskirts of the village is the fine Clochtogle dolmen—*(Cloc Togala), the Lifted Stone*—with a massive quartzite capstone, weighing about twenty tons, perched twelve feet up on four supporters. From Coagh it is a pleasant run to Newport Trench and Quay on the shores of Loch Neagh, where you will see the fishermen packing eels for London and pollan for Manchester, and a little to the south, amongst typical lake-shore scenery, stands the Celtic High Cross of Ardboe—*(Ard Bó), the Height of the Cow*—in this case a magical cow of astonishing yield. This is one of the finest High Crosses in Ireland, and whilst it bears no actual date it can safely be described as of tenth-century workmanship and doubtless belonged to the Celtic monastery founded here in the sixth century. Like most of its fellows it is elaborately decorated and designed as a kind of pictorial Bible, for the purpose of teaching Scripture stories to people who could not read. The top stone was dislodged in 1816, and the arms fell thirty years later, but the entire Cross was restored thereafter by Colonel Stewart of Killymoon. The decorations are now much weathered and difficult to decipher in places, but you'll be able to pick out Adam and Eve under the Tree of Knowledge; the Sacrifice of Isaac; Daniel in the Lions' Den; the Three Children in the Fiery Furnace; and the Day of Judgment, with angelic forms and a pair of scales under the central figure of Christ. Behind the Cross are the dilapidated remains of the Old Church of Ardboe, with the famous Wishing Tree in which you must stick a pin if your wish is to be granted; and about two hundred yards away is a formless fragment which is most likely part of the ancient abbey.

Coalisland lies between this place and Dungannon, and, as its name suggests, it is the centre of the extensive Tyrone Coalfield. This coal rests on the Dungannon limestone, with the higher ground largely covered with Triassic and

---

[1] Also interpreted as *a round hill*, (Clachan Ed.).

Stone Circles at Beaghmore, County Tyrone.

been worked here for many hundreds of years, such working can never be economically sound, as a recent large-scale attempt, with the most modern machinery, abundantly proved. For, owing to geological faults and intrusions, it is wellnigh impossible to sink workable shafts; the shaly nature of the roof-rocks makes propping very costly; and floors are almost impossible to maintain because of the highly absorbent nature of the clays. For all of which I breathe a prayer of thanks, for the last thing I want to see in Ireland is a region comparable in ugliness and misery with the coal-mining districts of England and Wales.

Moy—*(an Maigh), a Plain*—is always referred to by Ulstermen as *The Moy*, and for generations this quiet place was the scene of one of the most famous horse-fairs in Ireland. It will strike you as an unusual-looking village, with its tree-lined square and picturesque aspect, but you will understand why when I tell you that it was planned and built by a Lord Charlemont as a fairly close replica of Marengo in Italy. Moy is on the Blackwater, and just across the bridge is Charlemont, in the County Armagh, which we have already visited.

Benburb—*(Beann Borb), the Proud Peak*—is aptly named, for nothing could look prouder than the splendid crag, above the Blackwater, on which stands the ruined Benburb Castle. This site was occupied by a stronghold of Shane O Neill in the sixteenth century, but the present remains are of a tall fortified mansion, set within a square bawn, built here in 1615 by Sir Richard Wingfield, a Plantation grantee who later became Lord Powerscourt. The charming Parish Church was built by the same landlord in 1618, and the bell, said to have been made for the Capuchins of Limerick in 1688, and some other interesting features and memorial stones, are well worth inspection. But the chief fame of Benburb arises from the smashing victory won there by Owen Roe O Neill, in 1646, over the English Puritan and Scottish troops, as decisive as that other Irish triumph at the Yellow Ford not so far away. For those more peacefully inclined, the fishing here will commend the place, for the Blackwater flows in this region in a series of little falls and pools, and in those pools the fat salmon lie, whilst with the August floods the celebrated dollaghan comes down, a grand trout that may run to anything from five to twelve pounds.

The splendid nineteenth-century mansion of the Bruces, which stands above the ruined Benburb Castle, has been purchased by *The Order of Servants of Mary* and is now known as *The Priory of Our Lady of Benburb*. This is the first foundation of this Order in Ireland, and, since it belongs to the Chicago Province of the Servites, American voices, which rang through the stately house when United States troops were billeted there during the Hitler War, may still be heard in this quiet part of the County Tyrone. But those Transatlantic accents, then concerned with preparation for dire and dreadful war, now fall from the lips of Black-robed servants of the Mother of Peace. It was a son of Irish parents, Chicago-born Father Keane, who was mainly responsible for this Irish foundation of his Order, and it is fitting that he should be the first Prior. He has all the gifts to make of this House a holy and lasting blessing to his people.

Benburb, and the River Blackwater, County Tyrone.

We move through delightful country now, along the banks of the Blackwater, until we reach Caledon, in ancient times Kenard—*(Ceann Ard), the High Head*—and taking its present name from the landlords, the Earls of Caledon, of which family is Field Marshal Lord Alexander, the brilliant British soldier of the Hitler War. Kenard was a great stronghold of the O Neills, and Sir Phelim O Neill had a castle here of which you may see an inscribed stone in the Caledon demesne to-day. You may also see, in the same place, a Celtic High Cross which belonged to the near-by Monastery of Glenarb, as well as a freak or folly, known as *The Bone House*, which is most amusingly described in the celebrated *Orrery Papers*. Just across the County boundary, in Armagh, is Tynan Abbey, abbey only in name and with no monastic pretensions ancient or modern, and in the grounds of this charming residence of the Stronge family, where the United States Field Artillery trained during the Hitler War, are three splendid Early Stone Crosses, whilst a taller cross, probably of eighth-century date, stands in the village.

We travel north-west now, along the Tyrone-Monaghan border which is also the Eire Border, through that famous trio of towns which provide a choice mouthful for any English visitor, Aughnacloy, Augher and Clogher; and the stagger which some of our tourists make at these Irish gutturals is a joy to hear! We are now in the Clogher Valley, lying entirely in Tyrone but stretching from Armagh on the one hand to Fermanagh on the other. There is nothing to detain us in wide-streeted Aughnacloy—*(Achadh na Cloiche), the Field of the Stone*—but at Augher—*(Eochair), a Horse Enclosure[1]*—you may want to see the square Plantation Castle of Spur Royal, still used as a residence, with one of the circular towers of its protective bawn still standing, whilst you will certainly wish to examine Tyrone's most interesting ancient monument, the large circular cairn known as Annia's Cove. This stands on the summit of Knockmany Hill—*Cnoc mBaine, the Hill of the Monks[2]*—and whilst the capstones of the graves and the covering cairn have disappeared, three of the remaining supporters are ornamented with such an assortment of incised concentric circles, wavy lines, zig-zags and cup-markings, that you have seen nothing like them since you went with me to New Grange in the County Meath; though what these markings mean no man can say, except that they may be related to the Cyprean and Cretan inscriptions, and that it is not impossible that they have some connection with those ancient merchants who travelled *the great Eastern Trade Route*. Knockmany Hill, now a Government forestry station, rises so abruptly from the plain that it affords an unrivalled view of *Tyrone among the Bushes*, and indeed I cannot think of anything more inspiring than the varied and far-flung beauties of this old territory of the O Neills which will unroll themselves before your eyes from this commanding eminence. Carleton loved this prospect himself, and this was his country; *Carleton, the greatest*

---

[1] Also interpreted as *an edge or border*, (Clachan ed.).
[2] Also interpreted as *the Hill of Queen Baine*, (Clachan ed.).

novelist of Ireland by right of the most Celtic eyes that ever gazed from under the brows of storyteller, as W. B. Yeats said. You must read his *Traits and Stories of the Irish Peasantry*, published in 1830 when Carleton was thirty-six, for with that book modern Irish literature began. The author was born in Prillisk, not so far away, the youngest son of a humble peasant family of fourteen, and a heap of stones now marks his birthplace. But you will find Carleton's peasants very different from the creatures of Lever and Lover, for they have a dignity which those lack, and they do not revolve round *the Big House* like so many clowns especially created for the amusement of the gentry. Read Carleton, and wander around this lovely region which is the Carleton country, for it is still largely unspoiled and many stories and customs of an Ireland that is dead still linger here.

The ancient cathedral city of Clogher, *(Clochar), a Stony Place*—is close beside us, but it is now a very small village. This See was founded by Saint Patrick, and its first bishop was his beloved disciple, the celebrated missionary Saint MacCartan; whilst later came Saint Aidan, who was soon to leave for England, to convert the coarse Northumbrians to Christianity, and to make his home on bleak Lindisfarne. The chief relics of Clogher are in the National Museum in Dublin, the lovely *Domhnach Airgid*, given by Saint Patrick to Saint MacCartan, with an outer and later box of silver and gold of magnificent fourteenth-century craftsmanship; and *The Cross of Clogher*, one of the most entrancing things of its kind in existence. The present cathedral is not ancient, for it was built between the years 1717 and 1744, but in the churchyard are two fine Early Stone Crosses and a most interesting sundial. This sundial pillar, because of its shape, was mistakenly pointed out as a *statue menhir* for many years, but its real interest lies in the omission from its dial of the prayer-hours of *Matins* and *Vespers* which were not observed in the early Celtic Christian Church; a circumstance which marks this dial as of seventh-century date. No bishop lives in Clogher nowadays, and the Bishops' Palace, built in 1799 by Primate Lord John Beresford, is now a Roman Catholic Convent.

Nine miles north-west of Clogher is Fintona—*(Fionntamhnach), the whitish field*—which glories in a slogan almost as famous as that of the County itself: *Go to hell, are you from Fintona?* To hear one Fintona man assail another with this picturesque greeting is something you can never forget, and when you speak of the town always place the accent entirely on the first syllable. On the outskirts of Fintona is the comely demesne of Ecclesville, the home of my old theatrical friend Raymond Browne-Lecky, who maintains a private theatre in his elegant mansion, and not far away dwells another old artist comrade of mine, Matt Mulcaghey, famous for years on radio as *The Ould Besom Man*, and as the operator of his own private experimental wireless station. The *Eccles Arms* is a neat and comfortable inn just opposite Fintona Railway Station, and although that station is a full-blown establishment of the renowned Great Northern Railway Company, the trains which frequent it are pulled by a force of no more than one horse-power. They are, in sober fact, pulled by a single horse, along a track which runs for over half-a-mile to Fintona Junction, where the main line steam trains pick up the pioneering horse-drawn adventurers. I pray that these indefatigable old vehicles, of most ancient and honourable lineage, first and second class inside and third class on the open top, may never be taken out of service, for they are a link with the past, a lovely memory of old and more gracious days, and something unique of which Fintona should be proud and most truly jealous. That you may see what *the Fintona One-horsepower Railway* looks like, I have asked Raymond Piper to make the accompanying sketch of the gallant old vehicle, God bless it!

Directly south of Clogher, on the borders of Tyrone, Fermanagh and Monaghan, is the mountainy wonderland of Slieve Beagh—*(Sliabh Beatha), the Mountain of Bith*; and Bith was a legendary chieftain who came to Ireland with the Princess Ceasair forty days before the Deluge, and about whom you may read in collections of early Irish legends. His cairn is on a mountain-top not far away. Here is South Tyrone at its best, and I cannot too strongly recommend you to take time to explore it. You should seek out, amongst many other chief delights, the splendid cairn of Carnagat, with its four burial-chambers and double horns; the sombre secluded valley of Altnadavin, in which you will find Saint Patrick's Chair, Holy Well and Cairn; and *The Three Counties Hollow*, where you may sit in Tyrone, with one leg in Fermanagh and the other across the Border in Monaghan, which is in Eire —though what good that will do you I have never been able to discover! Here too you should explore the grand demesnes of Fardross, Aughentain and the Windy Gap. This is all *off-the-beaten-track country*, but it is wild, unspoiled Ireland and more rewarding by far than most of the highly publicised beauty spots of this most beautiful island.

Our road now runs north-west, through Fintona and Omagh, to Newtownstewart, known of old as *Lislas—the Fort of the Grave*—and pleasantly situated, between two hills known as Bessy Bell and Mary Gray, on a fine gravelly bend of the River Strule where it joins the Owenkillew and later becomes the River Mourne. This is great country for the angler, and for the lover of scenery too with its grand background of the Sperrin Mountains. These mountains, composed of schist and quartzite and with broad, bog-covered summits, rise to more than two thousand feet, and present such a formidable barrier that the railway between Belfast and Derry has to traverse more than a hundred miles of track to cover a distance which a crow would count as about seventy miles—if crows are given to such mathematical exercises! Known both as the Munterloneys—*(Muintir Lúinigh), the Family of O Looney*—and the Sperrins—*(Speirín), a Sparrowhawk*[1]—they extend right to the Benbradagh basalts, and provide an entrancing region for anyone who is not averse to walking and is in search of remote beauty and the wider prospects of unspoiled mountainy grandeur.

---

[1] Also interpreted as *little pinnacle*, (Clachan ed.).

The One Horse-power Railway.

The Castle of Newtownstewart, now in ruins, was built in 1618 by Sir Robert Newcomen, in the style of a contemporary English manor-house, was taken by Sir Phelim O Neill in the 1641, and was burned in 1689 by order of James the Second, after he had spent the night in it during his flight from Derry. The fine bridge of six arches, which spans the Mourne, was built in 1727, about which time the castle was repaired and inhabited for a space by the landlord Stewart who gave the town its present name. In the neighbourhood is the pre-Plantation castle of Harry Avery, a curious corruption of the name *Aimbreidh*, one of the O Neills who died in 1392, and near-by is the splendid demesne of Baronscourt, seat of the Duke of Abercorn, wherein are many objects of interest, including an unusually ancient crannog on which stand the ruins of the later Island MacHugh Castle.

The main road to Strabane runs through Douglas Bridge and Sion Mills, a model village born of the linen industry and reminding us, by its origin and neatness, of Bessbrook in the County Armagh; but I will take you to Strabane by a more picturesque route, for it's not on the main roads we find the real Ireland. Another memory of Armagh and Redmond O Hanlon should come to you by the mention of Douglas Bridge, for you surely know Carlin's fine ballad:

> On Douglas Bridge I met a man
> Who lived adjacent to Strabane,
> Before the English hung him high
> For riding with O Hanlon.

> The eyes of him were just as fresh
> As when they burned within the flesh;
> And his boot-legs were wide apart
> From riding with O Hanlon.

I confess I can never pass the place without seeing the shadowy figure of that old rapparee with his wide-apart horsey legs.

From Newtownstewart we'll go to Gortin—*(an Goirtín), the Little Field*—which is so romantically placed beside the Owenkillew River—*(Abhainn Coillead), the River of the Wood*—that it is a favourite spot of picnickers for miles around. Gortin Glen and Gap are extremely picturesque, cut deep as they are into the Sperrin country, and bejewelled with a cluster of charming little lakes which are perfectly set off by the predominant greenish and dark browns of these elevated lands. Not far north of Gortin is Plumbridge, a typical Tyrone village pleasantly placed on the Glenelly River, and a great centre for fishing and shooting. The Glenelly holds good brown trout, and white trout and salmon in its wider reaches, and it can be fished freely as far down as Drumnaspar Bridge; but from that point the angler would need to enquire about rights.

And now, from Plumbridge, you can enjoy two of the finest stretches of the Tyrone countryside, and of all Ireland for that matter, by journeying either east towards Draperstown, which is in the County Derry, or west into the historic Tyrone town of Strabane. And if you take my advice you'll do both! So we'll go east first, through the charming little upland village of Cranagh—*(an Chrannóg), the Tree-clothed Place*[1]—to that spot of quiet beauty, the little hamlet of Sperrin itself, where Miss Carleton keeps a small inn wherein you can get a good Ulster meal—and maybe *a drop of the craytur* too if you are minded that way—as I am! The Glenelly keeps you singing company all the way along this small little road, and the majestic Sperrins rise beside you on your left hand, so that for a piece of unfrequented lovely country you will be hard put to it to beat this place that you are in this blessed minute. From Sperrin a most rewarding little road runs to Park, and you should certainly not leave this region without climbing the 2240 feet of Sawel, king of the Sperrins, from whose summit you may enjoy a glorious panorama of mountains and valleys, boglands and glens, and wild rolling plains with all the magic of Ireland in every acre of them.

From Sperrin we retrace our way, westwards now, to Plumbridge, and from there we go to Strabane. But about four miles short of that town, just where the road reaches the summit of a long ridge, let us stop and look around. It will be worth our while. Behind is the impressive tumble of the Sperrins, green and dark brown and mysterious, whilst before us lies a wide and superb prospect of distant Donegal. That is the tall slender cone of Errigal you see there to the left,

---

[1] Also interpretted *the crannóg*, (Clachan ed.).

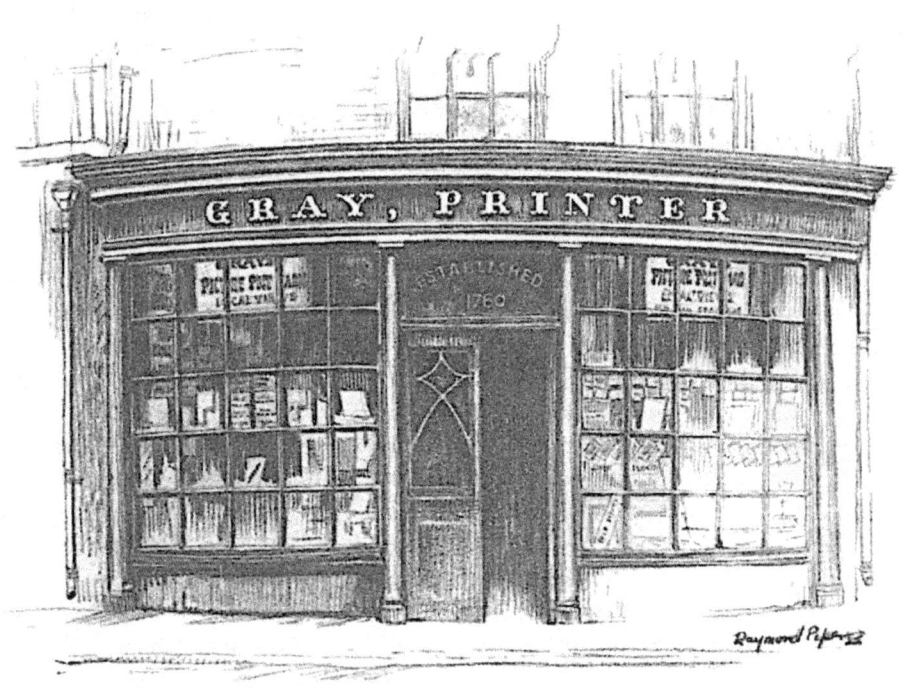

Gray's Shop, Strabane, County Tyrone, with old Printing Press.

and to the right of that is the pig-backed Muckish, another landmark of Donegal, whilst right of that again are the lovely hills of Inishowen, rising one after the other in a gorgeous symphony of atmospheric blues.

Strabane—*(An Srath Bán), the Fair or Whitish River Meadow*—is the largest town in the County Tyrone and is pleasantly situated on the River Mourne. This river flows into the tidal Foyle just below the town, and, with its tributaries the Strule, Owenkillew, Glenelly, Derg and Finn, comprises the best angling water in the County. Strabane, formerly the scene of fierce and frequent battles between the O Neills and the O Donnels, into whose territories it was the chief gateway or pass, is a thriving market town to-day, nor is it backward in industry, for shirts and collars are made there in great quantity and variety. Across a fine bridge of many arches lies the small town of Lifford, so small indeed that it seems to consist mainly of a church, a courthouse, and the offices of the Eire Customs authorities, and yet it is the capital of the large County of Donegal. So that you may walk but a short distance over this bridge and see the Border machinery between the two parts of Ireland working at full throttle. But it is Strabane we are considering and not Lifford at all, and Strabane is especially famous because it gave to the world three people who were to alter, in no mean way, the great course of global history: John Dunlap, the printer of *the American Declaration of Independence*, and James Wilson and Annie Mills, who, after sailing to America, became the grandparents of the greatest idealist the White House has ever known, President Woodrow Wilson. By the strangest coincidence, John Dunlap and James Wilson both went to work in the same place, the old printing-shop of the Gray family, which still does a thriving business in Strabane; and in the workshop of the Gray establishment to-day the actual press on which those two world-shakers served their apprenticeship is still busily turning out showcards and posters and auctioneers' bills.

I cannot end this Tyrone section on a happier note than this further reminder of the vital part which Ulster played in the building of the United States of America, nor with a more significant memory than that of John Dunlap, good son of Tyrone, learning his trade in Gray's of Strabane, and using that skill to print, in the great new land of his adoption, that tremendous document which was to chart a new course for democracy.

Knockmany Cairn, County Tyrone.

The County of Fermanagh — Conndae Fear Manac

FERMANAGH derives its name from the Leinster tribe known as the *Menapii*, or, in Irish *(Fear Manach)*, *the Men of Manach*, who settled around the shores of Loch Erne just before the coming of Christianity to Ireland, but who, like the Norsemen in other parts of the country, left no enduring trace of their residence other than that which survives in the place-name. The County as a whole may aptly be described as one great valley of the River Erne, which has carved its island-studded winding course, and its expansion into two great lakes, by the solution of the Carboniferous Limestone of which the terrain is composed. Loch Erne—*(Loch Éirne), the Lake of the Ernai*—preserves in its name a legend similar to that which seeks to explain the origin of Loch Neagh, in which we are told of the triumph of *Fiachu Labrainne*, Monarch of Ireland, over the Firbolg tribe of Ernai: *after the battle was gained the lake flowed over them and their dwelling place*, and from them the lake is named, though we hear of no submerged town here, and no Tom Moore has sung of Round Towers shining under these sweet waters. But the name which rings like a clarion call down the pages of Fermanagh history is Maguire, and wherever you go in this lovely County you will find yourself confronted with some memory of that great and warlike clan. Fermanagh of the Maguires! Fermanagh of the Lakes and the soft-spoken friendly people! What a well-graced County it is, to be sure.

It was not until 1585 that Fermanagh became a County on the English model, when Ulster was shired, as far as it could be, for its better government by the invader. And always the history of this region has been moulded by the river, and the two great lakes, which virtually split it in half, for no passage of men between Ulster and the West could take place without a crossing of this formidable water-barrier; and as a commentary on the long series of struggles which took place, from times immemorial, along this great divide, we have a splendid collection of weapons, discovered mainly at the more fordable points, ranging from early axes of stone, copper and bronze to the lethal instruments of comparatively modern times. The Erne spreads its wide and mazy course over the countryside in a singular and curious manner, and a most interesting holiday can be spent, with a canoe suitable for spells of portage, tracing this wayward waterway from its source in Loch Gowna, up in the County Cavan, to its mouth at Ballyshannon, seventy-five miles away on the Atlantic coast of Donegal.

The capital of the County Fermanagh is the beautifully-situated island-town of Enniskillen—*(Inis Ceithleann), Ceithle's Island*—and this Ceithle was wife to the dreaded Balor of the Blows, that single-eyed king of the Fomorians who looms so large in early Irish legend. The town, situated like the Swiss Interlaken on an island between two lakes, occupies a spot which must always have been important from the military point of view, for it is fair and square on the only crossing, for many miles in either direction, of the great water-divide of the County. Here the Maguires built their castle, and the bottom storey of its great central keep still endures, but the picturesque double-towered Water Gate, which will claim your chief attention to-day, was added early in the seventeenth century by Sir William Cole, ancestor of the Earls of Enniskillen, who had been granted many acres, along with the old Maguire stronghold, in this region. *The Annals of Ulster* tell a stirring tale of siege and warfare which beset the old castle through the centuries, but the very complicated story of takings and re-takings by O Donnels, O Neills, Maguires, and divers English commanders and adventurers, is too long for me to attempt to recount it here.

The present town of Enniskillen serves a wide agricultural area, and its single long winding undulating street gives it a pleasant appearance, but the chief fame of this place must always arise from the two famous regiments of the British Army, the Inniskilling Dragoons and the Inniskilling Fusiliers, which bear its name in one of the numerous variations of its spelling. From the Battle of the Boyne, when King William singled out *the Ould Skins* with the words: *Gentlemen, you shall be my guards this day,* to that supreme moment at Waterloo when both Wellington and Napoleon, from their opposite viewpoints, paid magnificent tribute to their fighting qualities, these regiments covered themselves with glory, and their later history in the Indian Mutiny, the South African campaign, and the two great World Wars has been no less glorious.

Beside the main street stands the old Parish Church, now the Cathedral of the See of Clogher, rebuilt in 1840 but with the old tower of 1637 still standing and bearing above its door a dated stone carved with an *Agnus Dei*, whilst on the near-by Fort Hill, in the midst of a pleasant little park, is a lofty monumental pillar erected to the memory of General Lowry Cole. You may ascend this pillar, by means of an internal winding stairway, and from the railed platform which surmounts it you can enjoy a wide view of the town and its most attractive surroundings. Near the lake-shore is the celebrated Portora Royal School, founded in 1626 by Charles the First, where Oscar Wilde was but one of the many brilliant scholars who were to become famous in diverse walks of life.

Loch Erne, by which we mean both the Upper and Lower lakes, is for the most part sylvan in character, and you need not look in this region for the mountainy grandeur of Killarney. Instead, you will find a veritable fairyland of blue water and unbelievably green islands, green down to the very water's edge, green with a greenness which is positively startling, and around these shores are dotted the ruined castles of Plantation grantees, whilst on some of the islands are the remains of foundations of the early Celtic Church. And in this turbulent region one can understand the desire of *Men of the Faith* to withdraw themselves from the battlegrounds of the warring clans, who were constantly in strife around the shores of the lakes, and to build for themselves, and for the propagation of their holy ideals, those abbeys and hermitages of which, alas, we can now behold but the shattered remnants.

The rivers of Fermanagh are not especially interesting to the angler and white trout do not frequent any of them. The Erne, from Roscor Bridge to Belleek, holds trout and pike, and though salmon enter the waters of Loch Erne, from the fisherman's point of view they might just as well have stayed in the sea; you may kill an odd one near Roscor, on the troll or with the shrimp, but though you may see them rising in numbers elsewhere, the odds are against your taking any of them. There are small trout round the pebbly shores, but the really big fellows take little notice of the artificial fly, and the best time for catching them is during the Mayfly season, or later on with the daddy-longlegs.

A few miles south of Enniskillen, amidst some of the finest limestone scenery in Ireland, is the mid-Georgian mansion of Florencecourt, seat of the Earls of Enniskillen. The park is especially lovely, with fine sweeping views and some grand timber, and most notable of the trees is the celebrated *Florencecourt Yew*, parent tree of the Irish Yew. Three miles farther on, and approached through a deep and lovely mile-long glen, is the so-called *Marble Arch*, a splendid cavern which is really a most interesting example of an underground stream that has eaten its way through the limestone by the solvent action of its contained carbonic acid. We have already seen this corrosive action at work in the outspreadings of the River Erne. In this present case the stream dives underground on the northern slope of Cuilcagh Mountain—*(Binn Chuilceach), chalky*—which stands 2188 feet high due south of the Marble Arch and dominates the whole landscape here. This, like most Carboniferous Limestone country, is a veritable region of disappearing streams, and you should explore Cuilcagh not only for the purpose of examining some of these queer freaks of nature, but also for the entrancing views which those gracious uplands will afford you. The summit of Cuilcagh is composed of Millstone Grit, followed by Yoredale beds, and several streams flow down these hard rock surfaces in a perfectly normal manner, but, as soon as they strike the soluble limestone farther down the slope, they vanish into the holes which they have dissolved for themselves and thereafter go their ways out of the sight of man and beast. You can easily trace their subterranean courses here and there where the roofs of the caves, through which they flow, have collapsed, with the resulting formation of deep, tree-filled ravines, and at the bottom of some of these ravines you may see the stream emerging from one cave and disappearing into another at the farther end. Martel, the French speleoligost, some years ago explored the Marble Arch stream for a distance of three hundred yards underground, and at one point sounded a rock pool to the depth of 150 feet; and the Yorkshire Ramblers' Club have carried out more recent and most important surveys. Belmore Mountain, rising north of the Marble Arch to a height of 1312 feet, is perforated with numerous caverns due to this same solvent action of water, and this whole territory will yield you much interest and delight if you will but take time to explore it. Forget the clock, forget

Enniskillen, County Fermanagh.

the roads, and just walk and scramble and climb and get a joy out of life of which, perchance, you never even suspected the existence.

Over to the west, along charming, small mountainy roads, we go to Knockninny, named after that Saint Ninny who was of the race of Niall of the Nine Hostages, a pupil of Saint Finnian, a contemporary of Saint Columcille, and Patron and Bishop of Inishmacsaint. From the summit of this hill you will get the finest view of Upper Loch Erne that it is possible to enjoy from any one point, and from this spot the amazing contortions of that singular sheet of water can most easily be followed. Almost due north you will see Belleisle through a maze of islands, and there, in the fifteenth century, Cathal MacManus Maguire compiled *The Annals of Ulster*, in the monastery which then stood in that place. Just across the lake from the northern tip of Inniskeen—*(Inis Caoin), Beautiful Island*—is Lisgoole—(*Lios Gabhail), the Fort of the Fork*—and a Maguire founded an Augustinian house there in 1106 which was burned in 1360 and thereafter lay in ruins for two centuries. Then another Maguire, Cuchonnacht of that clan, built a Franciscan friary beside the old site, and as late as 1739 another Maguire, Sir Bryan, sent from France a beautiful chalice for the use of this house. Sir Bryan had sold his sword to France, in the manner of *the Wild Geese*, and had been honoured and decorated by the French king, so that we may picture this gay soldier of fortune, roystering and fighting and living high, striding through the splendour and extravagance of the French Courts and camps, with his heart all the time away in Lisgoole in his own beloved Fermanagh. But isn't that just the aching splendid tug at the heart that every Irishman knows only too well.

The south-eastern region of Fermanagh is full of interest and beauty, so we'll move on to Lisnaskea, and on the way we'll look at Castle Coole, residence of the Earls of Belmore. This is one of the most lovely demesnes of this lovely County, which as a whole will give you an impression of seemliness and grace, and a feeling that here parklands and demesnes are better kept than in any other part of Ireland. And, in truth, in Fermanagh the county families seem to have retained, to an unusual degree, their traditional pride in their estates, and the County is indeed well-groomed and proud of it. Lisnaskea, *(Lios na Scéithe)—the Fort of the Bush*[1]—takes its name from a famous bush under which, for generations, the Maguires were inaugurated, and here, in 1615, Sir James Balfour built his Plantation castle, very much in Scots baronial style. A former stronghold of Conor Roe Maguire stood here, and around this commanding position much of the 1689 fighting took place, leading up to the Battle of Newtownbutler. The Market Cross of Lisnaskea is not of much interest, only the base and shaft being of any antiquity, but the near-by ruined church of Aughalurcher—*(Achadh Urchaire), the Field of the Foal*[2] — where, in 1484, a Maguire slew a kinsman at the

---

[1] Also interpreted as *ringfort of the shield*, (Clachan ed).
[2] Also interpreted as *field of the shot or cast*, (Clachan ed).

foot of the altar, is worth a visit for the sake of a look at the curious carved stone, representing a bishop holding a book and a crozier, which stands in the graveyard.

At the south-eastern end of Upper Loch Erne is Crom Castle, built in 1611 by Michael Balfour, Lord Burleigh, and now an ivy-smothered ruin. This old fortalice had a stirring history during the Williamite Wars, but its end did not come until 1764 when it was accidentally destroyed by fire. The new Crom Castle was built thereafter, and in the grounds is one of the oldest and most gigantic Yew trees in the country. From here you may journey at your own sweet will to Belcoo—*(Béal Cú), the Ford Mouth of the Mist*[1]—a neat little village with a position peculiarly like that of Enniskillen, for it also lies between two lakes, the Upper and Lower Lochs Macnean—*(Loch Mac nÉan), the Lake of the Bird's Son*. This was obviously an important pass, in early days, and the remains of many ancient fortifications in this MacGovern country will not surprise us. The lower lake lies almost entirely in Fermanagh, but the upper lake is almost equally divided between Fermanagh and the two Eire Counties of Leitrim and Cavan, a circumstance which makes fishing awkward and throws into sharp focus the more annoying aspect of this Border which divides our country. About three miles to the north-west is Boho—*(Botha), Huts or Tents*—where you will find the most accessible of the limestone caverns of Fermanagh, and where you may hire a guide to show you around the great galleries and chambers which are the home of a colony of Daubenton's Bats. In this district too, at the top of Upper Loch Macnean, you will find a good section of the Black Pig's Dyke, here known as the Pig's Race.

A long road which skirts the Leitrim border for the whole of its length, and which runs between pleasant heathery slopes, leads us to Loch Melvin—*(Loch Meilbhe), the Lake of King Meilghe*—a sweet sheet of water nearly eight miles long, lying mostly in Eire, and full of grand fish from the humble brown trout to the lordly gilaroo and sonaghan. Gilaroo, in Irish, means *the red servant-boy or gillie*, and the local people will tell you that it is only in Loch Melvin you will find this grand, sporting, full-flavoured fish. There is a good inn at Garrison, a cheerful, lively place full of anglers in the season, and on the lake are one or two islands you should visit. One of these is a crannog, with the ruins of Rossclogher Castle standing upon it, and in this castle De Cuellar, a captain of the Spanish Armada, found refuge after shipwreck on the Sligo coast, and here he wrote an account of his adventures which is in the Madrid Academy of History. You will be charmed with the scenery all round here, and, instead of going to Belleek by the main road, take my advice and cut round the triangle of adorable little boreens—*(bóithrín), a small road*—that skirt the Fermanagh-Leitrim-Donegal border to the west, by way of Derrynacross and Loughill. You will not be disappointed.

---

[1] Also interpreted as *mouth of the narrow stretch of water*, (Clachan ed).

Belleek is aptly named—*Béal Leice, the Ford Mouth of the Flagstone*—for here the Erne has worn down its rocky bed to pavement-like smoothness. From Belleek to Ballyshannon the river passes through a series of fine rapids, and there was a splendid waterfall at Belleek until the great drainage scheme of last century removed it along with nearly a quarter-of-a-million tons of rock. This is a famous spot for anglers, for the Erne here is stiff with salmon and trout, but perhaps a wider fame comes from the celebrated Belleek pottery, which used to be made from a fine felspar quarried near Castle Caldwell but is now manufactured with imported raw materials. Visitors are welcome at the Pottery, which stands on the site of the pre-Plantation Castle of Belleek.

Castle Caldwell lies off the main road to Pettigo and was built in 1612 by Francis Blennerhassett, but in 1662 one James Caldwell, a wealthy merchant of Enniskillen, bought it and gave it its present name. The Caldwells were a very hospitable family, given to entertainment on a lavish scale, and their splendid six-oared barge, with an orchestra to enliven their excursions with what Handel would have called Water Musicke, was a familiar sight on the lake. Opposite Castle Caldwell railway station you will see a memorial stone to one of Caldwell's fiddlers who fell off the barge in 1770:

> On firm land only exercise your skill.
> There you may play and safely drink your fill.

A strange injunction from Caldwell, who obviously liked his music afloat; unless he was referring obliquely to skill in drinking! Anyway, the Caldwell hospitality must have been only too lavish, for the estate was sold up and Castle Caldwell is now a ruin.

Pettigo—*(Paiteagó), the Place of the Smith's House*—lies partly in Fermanagh but mostly in Donegal, and, to obviate the necessity of crossing the Border to reach it, a bridge has been constructed at each end of Boa Island. This island—*Inis Badhbha, the Island of Badhbh*, who was the War Goddess of the Ulstermen—is four miles long, and half-way across you should run down to Rosgole Point for the sake of the view. You should also seek out Caldragh graveyard on the south shore, where you will find a sixth-century stone carved with two human effigies placed back to back. Pettigo is the centre from which the great pilgrimages to Loch Derg take place, but since that lake is in Donegal we shall deal with this subject in its proper place.

We move on to Kesh—*(Ceis), the Bridge of Wickerwork*—a name which reminds us that bridges made of wicker or hurdles were once common in Ireland. Down an old and narrow road, leading to the lake-shore, is Crevinish Castle—*Craob mis, the Branchy Island*—built by Thomas Blennerhassett in 1617 and occupied by Rory Maguire during *the 1641*. Along this same road we journey to Castle Archdale, with superb views of the lake, and of White Island, to keep us

Figure on Boa Island, County Fermanagh.

company. A Latin inscription over the doorway of the bawn tells us that John Archdale, who was a Plantation grantee from Norfolk, built old Castle Archdale in 1615, and you will notice that this castle is much more like an ordinary house than any of its fellows in Fermanagh, which perhaps explains why it was not defended against Rory Maguire, who pillaged it in 1641. After the wars the Archdales rebuilt their old home and lived in it until they erected the present residence in 1773. In the deer-park you should seek out a remarkable multiple cairn, consisting of a central cairn, with two of its stones carved with intricate devices, surrounded by a circle of twenty-two smaller cairns; and as well you should see the Friars' Walk and the scant remains of a Cistercian house which was a grange of that Abbey of Assaroe immortalised by the poet, William Allingham. But above all, you must go out to White Island to see the little ruined church there, a structure which boasts one of the only two Hiberno-Romanesque doorways in Ulster. The North is not rich in fine ecclesiastical ruins, for we had no great church builders in Ulster to compare with Brian Boru, Turloch O Conor and Cormac of Munster, who, in the eleventh and twelfth centuries were building many churches of a beauty unsurpassed by any of that age in Europe. The chief feature of all these churches is the lovely Hiberno-Romanesque arch, a native Irish development about which I had something to say in my Leinster volume.

Figures on White Island, County Fermanagh.

The history of the little church on White Island is unknown, and, neglected for centuries, its beautiful doorway collapsed in 1900. Luckily a splendidly detailed photograph, taken by the incomparable Robert J. Welch in 1896, supplied all the information necessary for a perfect reconstruction of this adorable portal, and in 1928 this praiseworthy task was carried out by the Belfast Natural History Society. Seven grotesque carvings, of probable seventh-century date and with Gaulish artistic affinities, were found amongst the fallen stones on this site, and for their preservation these were built into the north wall of the church, where you may see them to-day. They are the work of artists alien in spirit from the creators of the Celtic High Crosses and decorated doorways, and their purpose is unknown; but a mortice-hole in the head of each figure suggests that they were made to support something.

Devenish, Loch Erne, County Fermanagh

Out from the lakeside road, between this place and Enniskillen, is the Island of Devenish—*(Daimhinis), the Island of the Oxen*—which holds within its small bounds a whole collection of early Christian remains. The gentle Saint Molaisse founded a monastery here in the year 541, and the little stone oratory, popularly known as Saint Molaisse's Kitchen, stands close to the shore on the eastern side of the island. Until it was destroyed by vandals in the eighteenth century, this little Hiberno-Romanesque building had one of those charming steeply-raked stone roofs typical of the native style, but because it is at least five hundred years later in architectural style than the lifetime of the saint, it is impossible that this was ever his oratory. Not that the holy man would not have loved this small hermitage had he seen it, for his affection for such structures is enshrined in many a song:

And for Molaisse of the Lake, Molaisse the Gentle,
'Twas in a small house of hard stone he loved to dwell.

The Round Tower of this settlement is one of the most perfect in Ireland, and it is especially notable because of its unusual sculptured cornice, elaborately carved with four human heads, one over each of the four windows of the ringing-loft, and with some other fine decorative details. The masonry of this tower, which is more than eighty-one feet high and which was built between the ninth and eleventh centuries, is superb, and each stone is cut and dressed to conform precisely with the arc of the circular plan. An internal stairway has been provided, so that you may now ascend the tower and enjoy the view like any monk of old. Beside the Round Tower is the ruin of *Teampall mor, the Big Church*—with little of interest save one lovely window and the tomb of the Maguires of Tempo. This was a Priory of the Culdees, and the Parish Church of Devenish, and it was built in the Romanesque style in the twelfth century.

On the summit of Devenish stands the ruin of Saint Mary's Abbey, a foundation of the Canons Regular of Saint Augustine, who came to Ireland in the twelfth century. We do not know when this Gothic church was built, but that it was restored, and probably enlarged, in 1449, is clear from the Latin inscription on a tablet which is fixed in the wall at the entrance to the tower stair, and which, in English, reads: *Matthew O Dugan did this work for Bartholomew O Flanagan, Prior of Devenish, A.D. 1449.* The groining of the vault of the square Bell Tower is very fine, and the pretty fancy of a bird pecking at leaves, on the lovely Decorated pointed doorway in the north wall, is one of the many delights of this beautiful structure. There are two graveyards here, one perchance for men and one for women in a manner common to some of our island monasteries, and, in addition to some interesting cross slabs, you will see a seven-feet-high Sculptured Cross of most unusual type. The head of this cross is formed of four quarter-circles, placed back to back, the Crucifixion is depicted on the eastern side, and on the shaft is a shaven face set in the repose of death.

Another island you should visit, if you have time, is Inishmacsaint—*(Inis-maige-samh), the Island of the Plain of Sorrel*—where Saint Ninny founded a Celtic monastery in the sixth century. Fragments of a later church stand there to-day, as well as a roughly-hewn fourteen-feet-high Cross, entirely devoid of decoration and belonging to the seventh century. This is a good prototype of the splendid Decorated Celtic High Crosses of which we have already seen examples at Ardboe, in Tyrone, and elsewhere.

Other places of interest in the Enniskillen district are the Plantation castles of Tully, Hume and Monea, the last-named being the best preserved of all the Fermanagh castles. This is a remarkable building, with its two great circular bastions pushed out by corbels to square at the top, in the manner of the Scots baronial castles of the time. And you should certainly try to visit *the Lettered Cave of Knockmore*, wherein you will find the walls decorated with scribings dating from Neolithic times to the early Celtic Christian era.

So we take leave of lovely Fermanagh, with the beauty of the place in our hearts and minds and all around and about us, and perhaps with a stave of the old song in our mouths as we go our ways:

> Fare ye well, Enniskillen, I leave you awhile,
> And all your fair waters and every green isle.
> When the wars they are over we'll return in full bloom.
> And they'll all welcome home their Inniskilling Dragoon.

Monea Castle, Fermanagh

The County of Derry — Contae Doire

ERRY is always Derry to the Irishman, North or South, and you may at once know the stranger by his use of the official name of Londonderry. Of old the City of Derry was known as *Daire/Doire,—the Oakwood of Calgach*—a warrior who appears in the pages of Tacitus and who led the Caledonians at the Battle of the Grampians. *Daire Calgach* continued, as the name of the little settlement about the oak grove that crowned the small hill, well into the tenth century, when the form *Daire Columcille* came into use in memory of the beloved saint who was the Christian patron of the old pagan stronghold. And of course it was not until the days of James the First of England that the alien name of London was tacked on to this most Irish of towns, when the place was sold to the City of London, after being written up in a veritable auctioneer's circular by Chichester, who excelled himself as an auctioneer's tout.

To the majority of Ulster people Derry is, in its own way, a kind of Holy City, a remembrancer, a rallying-place, and anything but a collection of bricks and mortar. For, as Donn Byrne said: *The Walls of Derry will make your heart beat faster, for no gallantry in Froissart rivals that of the thirteen Apprentice Boys who locked the gates against James of the Fleeing, and held the city for eight long months, not only against James but against pestilence and famine as well.* And even those whose faith and historical background might beget a different set of emotions, could never find it in their hearts to grudge the grand old Maiden City its well-earned and most glorious fame. Derry of Calgach, Derry of Columcille, Derry of the Siege—there is fame enough and to spare in these names—the fame of a great siege gallantly withstood to mould the future history of Europe and the world—the fame of piety and mighty Christian works. No need here to borrow a spurious fame of that great and fair city on the English Thames.

> Were the tribute of all Alba mine,
> From the centre to the border,
> I would rather the site of one house
> And it in the midst of Derry.

Thus the noble Columcille, Dove of the Church, away in Iona, off the coast of Alba, or Scotland as we now call that place, whither he had gone in exile after he had been censured by a Synod of the Celtic Church. This censure arose from Columcille's unauthorised transcription of Saint Finnian's copy of the Vulgate of Saint Jerome, and it is likely that the proud spirit of this Dove of the Church, always more Eagle than Dove, was better fitted to the government of Iona than to submission to the autocratic fathers of the Early Celtic Church. For in the veins of Columcille flowed the blood of princes, of the mighty O Donnels, kings of Tirconnail, or Donegal as we now call that region of lakes and mountains and savage coast.

It was in the year 546 that Columcille set up his *dark cell* in the oak grove of Calgach, and we know that the church of this foundation, which was under the austere rule of Columcille himself, *the Columban rule*, was orientated north and south after the manner of Saint Patrick's first church in Saul. And such was his love for this place that it seems never to have been absent from his heart of hearts during the long and lonely years of his exile. But of this foundation no traces remain to-day, for the Foyle was a haven very much to the taste of the fierce Vikings, and the annals record raid after raid by these sea-robbers from the year 812 onwards. After the Norsemen came the Anglo-Norman invaders, de Courcy and Peyton, to plunder the religious houses of Derry, nor were the Irish chieftains behindhand in the same hell-bent work themselves. In 1164 the abbot of the successor of Columcille's monastery erected a great church on the old site, and near this church stood a Round Tower; but whilst the Round Tower has disappeared, its name is still preserved in the present Long Tower Street, and the near-by modern Roman Catholic Church is locally known as the Long Tower Chapel.

In 1566 came the Rebellion of Shane O Neill, and with it the presence of an English garrison in Derry for the first time in history; but not till 1600 was the stubborn place really subdued. Then, under Sir Henry Docwra, most likeable and human of all the Ehzabethans, was achieved the successful issue of a plan worked out by Mountjoy, which included the erection of strong forts at Culmore, Derry and Dunnalong. But with the departure of the diplomatic and popular Docwra in 1604, and the scurvy treatment of his loyal ally, Cahir O Doherty, by the overbearing Paulett, the new Governor of Derry, more trouble came on the place; O Doherty rose in rebellion, as well he might, took the forts of Derry and Culmore, put Paulett and his garrison to the sword, and was not quelled until the old town was once more a place of ruins. Now came the Plantation, with the selling of Derry, like a sack of corn, to the Corporation of the City of London, and in 1613 this ancient place became Londonderry; officially, anyway, for no Irishman ever uses that uncouth form. Now, too, the whole territory was shired, after the English fashion, and the lands to the east and south of the town were formed into the County of Londonderry and divided amongst the various London guilds and companies.

In 1619 The Honourable Society of the Governor and Assistants of London of the New Plantation in Ulster within the Realm of Ireland, a tremendous mouthful of a title which is usually quoted as *The Irish Society*, perhaps because there is nothing Irish about it, built the famous Walls of Derry, and in 1633 the same society erected Saint Columb's Cathedral. This cathedral was used as a battery during the siege, when the lead from its roof was turned into bullets, and it was from this commanding spot that watch was kept on the movements of the Jacobite besiegers. I think you should make a point of climbing to the top of that tower for a wide and most interesting view of the old city and its surroundings, and you should certainly devote some time to an examination of the church itself, for it is full of historical interest and contains many mementoes of the stirring and gallant part which it played in the great siege.

To-day Derry has overflowed its ancient bounds, but from the cathedral tower the formation of the old city-within-the-walls may clearly be seen. The City of York in England attracts thousands of visitors with the fame of its walls, and in lesser degree Chester and Canterbury do the same, but in none of these places is the circumvallation anything like complete. The walls of Derry, in contrast, remain intact to this day, and you may walk entirely round the old city without ever leaving the pathway which runs along the top of them. That walk will provide you with a circular mile of interest and enjoyment, during which you will see several of the original nine bastions, and two half-bastions, which made up the defences of the city, as well as the seven gates known as Bishop's, Shipquay, Butcher's, Ferryquay, New, Castle and Magazine, the first four of which belong to the original scheme of fortification, the other three having been added in 1627 and subsequent years. In the Royal Bastion stands a lofty column, erected in 1826 to the memory of that heroic clergyman, Walker, who was Governor of the City during the siege and whose grave we saw in Donaghmore in far-away Tyrone. If you climb to the top of this column, by means of its internal stairway, the view will fully reward you for your labour. In the Double Bastion is that grand old cannon, Roaring Meg, which played such an important part during the siege, and on a platform of the walls, facing the Guildhall, is a row of five guns, the oldest of which bears the date of gift, 1595, and the monogram of Queen Elizabeth with the emblem of the Tudor rose. The other four were presented, in 1642, by the Vintners', Mercers', Grocers' and Merchant Taylors' Guilds, and all five, with the associated section of the wall, appear in Raymond Piper's accompanying sketch.

The first *Towne House of Derry* was erected in the Diamond in 1616, by the London Companies, and was destroyed and refashioned at various intervals, but the Guildhall which you see to-day, and which stands outside the walls, was built by the Corporation in 1912. In it are preserved the ancient Corporation plate, the Mayor's Medal and Chain of Office, the Mace presented by William the Third, the Sword of State, and the Sword of Sir Cahir O Doherty.

The City of Derry was besieged on three occasions, but when we refer to *the Siege* we mean the third and greatest of these, when Derry moved right out of the circumscribed theatre of local conflicts into the vast arena of European politics. Ireland was then the battleground on which must be decided a titanic issue between Louis the Fourteenth of France and William and Mary of England. James the Second, *James of the Fleeing*, was a shiftless creature whose lack of tact lost him the English throne, and whose foolish machinations had turned the Ulster Protestants against him, to a man, several years before. The French plan was clear enough—the war for the English Throne would be diverted to Ireland, Franee would gain control of the seas, block William's supplies and beat him to his knees, and James would remain what he always was, a puppet in the hands of Louis. But things become somewhat complicated by the deep enmity between

Louis and the Vatican, so that we find the Dutch William fighting in Ireland for the security of the Protestant succession in England, and with funds largely promoted by the Pope of Rome. This tangled tale, which is clear as crystal to the average son of Ulster because it never occurs to him that there is anything tangled about it, has been neatly analysed by some unknown versifier with the detached vision of a visitor to our shores:

> King William was a Dutchman, same as Kruger I suppose.
> He was married to a Papist and he had a Roman nose;
> Yet in yearly jubilation many simple people join,
> 'Cause a Dutchman beat a Scotsman at the Irish River Boyne:
> And we're told to keep the mem'ry green, or
> Orange fierce and hot.
> Of this darling little hooley 'twixt a Dutchman and a Scot.

The story of the great siege is too well known for me to recount it here, and you can turn to any history book for details which are entirely outside the scope and province of this present survey. That the most dreadful privations were endured by the citizens with high and shining courage is not in doubt, nor that several thousand people perished within the walls, from plague, starvation and the accidents of war, rather than submit to the Jacobite besiegers. Water was worth a king's ransom, a quarter of a dog fattened on dead bodies was a luxury only within the reach of the wealthier citizens, and even the addition of a lean mouse to the menu made serious inroads on the housekeeping budget. The Jacobites had thrown a great boom across the Foyle to prevent the arrival of food and relief ships, and not until the famous Mountjoy rammed and broke that boom, under heavy bombardment from the forts at either end of it, was the siege lifted. And the European importance of all this lay in the simple fact that the stubborn heroism of the people of Derry so delayed the plans of James the Second, which were really the plans of Louis the Fourteenth, that the Protestant succession to the throne of England became as much beyond question as was the triumph of the Vatican over the intrigues of France. Truly the history of Europe, and consequently of much of the world, was moulded and set within the stout walls of this small Ulster city, and even more surely within the stout hearts of those Ulster men and women who held the place fast even unto death.

Derry is the second city of Ulster and it is almost entirely dependent on the shirt and collar industry. A severe blow was dealt to the distributing trade of the city by the establishment of the Border, for before that dividing line was set up Derry was the virtual capital of Donegal, and at one swoop a vast volume of trade was cut off when that wide region was removed behind an impassable tariff wall.

The business of shirt-making is not without its romance, for not until William Scott, a Derry weaver, had conceived the revolutionary idea of marketing professionally-made shirts and collars, could such articles be bought over the counter. Until about 1810 such a thing as a ready-made shirt was

Section of Wall and five London cannon, City of Derry.

unknown, and the housewives of those days had to buy the material and make the garments themselves. Scott tried his new idea first on a Glasgow draper, and with such success that he soon found himself at the head of a great and expanding industry, so that soon Australia, a land of many womenless men at that time, was buying Derry shirts as greedily as Scotland and England. Scott cut his shirts in Derry and sent them to the cottage women of Donegal and Tyrone for stitching, but, after the invention of the sewing-machine, one William Tillie set up a machine shirt factory in Derry in 1850, and the Maiden City has never lost its grip on this great industry which it virtually created.

The situation of Derry is one of striking beauty, lying as it does at a noble curve of the lovely River Foyle. And in the old city there is much to dream about, so that when the sun is setting and the soft shadows of evening are working their magic with trees and houses and memory-laden walls, you may be moved to spare a thought for Columcille who loved this place, and who professed the belief that God's angels sang from every leaf of Derry's long-vanished oak grove:

> My Derry, my treasure, my sweet beaming oak grove,
> The house of my heart, my little dark cell,
> 'Tis the ridges of all the wide world I'll be going
> And my heart to be here and in no other place.

One of the finest cashels in Ireland, and the most splendid in Ulster, stands on a hill about five miles north-west of Derry City. It is really in the County Donegal, but as it is more convenient to approach it from Derry than from anywhere else, I will deal with it here. It is popularly known as the Greenan Fort, but its real name is *Grianán Ailigh, the Sunny Parlour of the Stone Fort*, and it was already several hundred years old when Ptolemy showed it on his famous *Map of Ireland* in A.D. 55. This was the residence of the Northern O Neills, kings of Ulster, until the year 1101, when O Brien, king of Munster, destroyed it to avenge the sacking of his own Palace of Kincora by the O Neills. The main fortifications of *An Grianán Ailigh* consist of three concentric ramparts of earth and uncemented stones, which can still easily be traced, and within these the cashel stands and encloses an area seventy-seven feet in diameter, with a wall thirteen feet thick and now about eighteen feet high. This splendid monument of antiquity lay in ruins for many years and was restored in 1878, though with what degree of conformity with the original structure it is impossible to say, for that was not an age of scientific archaeology. The view from the cashel wall is superb, with Inch Island and Loch Swilly almost at your feet, the Foyle just behind you, and the glorious tumble of the Donegal and Derry mountains all about you. And if you are lucky enough to see a sunset from this place, with Loch Swilly, and the mighty Atlantic beyond it, one heaving mass of burnished bronze and gold, you'll never forget it.

For the angler the County Derry is important, though the Foyle, being tidal throughout its length, will only interest the seeker after coarse fish. The upper reaches of the Faughan yield good brown trout, with white trout and salmon lower down towards the end of June, and the Dennet is not unworthy of attention.

Off the main road to Limavady is the pretty village of Eglinton, with the lovely Glen of Muff about four miles south of it, and there, in a fairy like fold of countryside, is the picturesque Ness Waterfall. There also is the Burntollet, free to anglers like almost all the Derry streams, with no mean store of good trout, and an occasional salmon. Farther along, the main road passes through Ballykelly, a neat place belonging to the Fishmongers' Company, who built a fortified mansion for its protection in 1619, and almost everywhere we go now we shall come upon these old holdings of the London Companies.

In Limavady—*(Léim a' Mhadaidh), the Leap of the Dog*—you may seek out the wee pub in Ballyclose Street where Thackeray wrote *Peg of Limavady*:

> Beauty is not rare
> In the land of Paddy,
> Fair beyond compare
> Is Peg of Limavady.

Maybe he was inspired by the good liquor here, though the legend goes that he heard someone singing *Kitty of Coleraine* in the street outside, and wanted to do the right thing by Limavady! Anciently this was O Cahan territory, but Sir Thomas Phillips built a castle here in 1608 when the lands were granted to him, and he and Staples were the only individuals to receive estates in this County otherwise bestowed exclusively upon the London Companies. The town is beautifully placed in the valley of the Roe—**Ruad** (Ró), *Red*—a river which is a rough and convenient line of demarcation between the Antrim and Derry basalts and the incomparably older schistose rocks of Donegal and the western lands. For the angler the Roe is a grand stream, and, with its three main tributaries, it offers splendid sport with salmon and trout.

In Limavady was collected, by a Miss Ross, in 1851, that now-hackneyed but enchantingly lovely *Londonderry Air* which is commonly known to-day as *Danny Boy*. Miss Ross took it down from a country fiddler of the name of MacCormick, and we have to thank her loving industry for the preservation of what must be one of the purest and loveliest melodies ever conceived in the mind of man.

Kane's Rock—Kane, like O Cahan, is an anglicisation of the name of the ancient chieftains here—overhanging the River Roe about two miles from the town, is worth a visit for its scenic splendour, and in near-by Drumrammer—*(Druim Ceata), the Thick Ridge*—was born Saint Canice, who gave his name to Kilkenny and founded Saint Andrews in Scotland. Here, too, a rocky defile, through which the Roe rushes with much vigour and spirit, is pointed out as the scene of that great leap by a faithful dog which gave Limavady its name. It is a grand long trek up the Roe Valley to Dungiven, Maghera and Draperstown, with charming and unusual scenery at your elbows for every mile of it.

In Roe Park is the Ridge of Mullagh, anciently known as *goirtin anama, the Little Garden of the Soul,* and beside this is *Ceata, Ceat's Ridge,* where, in the year 574, a great convention was held, presided over by Columcille who broke a dozen years of exile to attend it. Two findings of this convention are on record, one which regulated the number of accredited bards, and the other which decided that the Irish colony so long settled in south-western Scotland must now be recognised as quite independent of Ireland. Thus was the Plague of the Bards brought to an end, and thus was the future of the Kingdom of Scotland decided.

The road from Limavady to Downhill—*(Dun Faille), the Fort of the Cliff*[1]— runs between a great level plain, which stretches to the sea and to the mouth of the Roe, and the bold basaltic escarpments of Benevenagh—*(Binn Fhoibhne),*[2] *the Happy Peak*—and the Downhill cliffs. Benevenagh, like Garron Point in Antrim, owes its striking appearance to the slippery grey lias which underlies the chalk and the basalt, for much of this lias never hardened into rock and was quite unable to withstand the weight of the deposits and outpourings which were imposed upon it. As a result, chalk and basalt have come down in ruin, and are still coming down to this day, and to this circumstance we owe the singularly handsome outline of these rugged mountainsides. Benevenagh descends, in a series of great steps or terraces, from eleven hundred feet almost to sea-level, and each of these terraces is simply a mass of basalt and underlying chalk which, unseated by the treacherous slippery lias, has detached itself from the mountain and fallen to a lower level. From the summit of this mountain, the escarpments of which are especially rich in such Alpine plants as Dryas or Mountain Avens, Cushion Pink and Purple Saxifrage, you may enjoy a splendid view of the Dutch-like flatlands below you, as well as of the great strand of Magilligan, a post-Glacial growth which is still a puzzle to the geologist. On the slopes of Benevenagh is Duncrun, the Fort of the Cruithni, those early Ulstermen who were pushed back by the Three Collas far behind the *Black Pig's Dyke,* and who, overcrowded in their now contracted territory, crossed to Scotland in search of *lebensraum,* founded a great colony there, and soon commenced to harass the Roman legions on the border. Columcille founded a monastery here in Duncrun, and in the graveyard of the present Roman Catholic Church, according to tradition, lie the remains of Saint Aidan, great Irish missionary to Northumbria, brought here, in 664, by Saint Colman after his disagreement with King Aldfred.

At Downhill ask your way to the Battery or Bishop's Road and enjoy one of the thrills of your life, either afoot or in your car. Through Hell's Hole you'll go, along an unbelievable highway which skirts the edge of the Downhill cliffs, and from which you will look down upon the Atlantic as you would from an aeroplane.

---

[1] Formerly called Dunbo, derived from the Irish *Dún Bó,* (Clachan ed.).
[2] *Foibhne's peak,* (Clachan ed.).

Kane's Rock, River Roe, near Limavady, County Derry.

This road was built by the eccentric and almost fabulous Earl of Bristol, Bishop of Derry, for the entertainment of himself and of the great house-parties which he was wont to assemble at his near-by mansion, and Macaulay said that it was *more like the work of a Roman emperor than of an Irish bishop*. This district was granted to the Clothworkers' Company, but it will ever be associated with the *Volunteer Earl* who constructed this unique highway, built the immense Downhill mansion in 1776, eight years after he became Bishop of Derry, and on the continent of Europe became equally famous for his residence in gaol there for a spell, and for the number of Hotels Bristol which were named after him and which still keep open doors. The most popular figure in the Ireland of his day, this broad-minded but eccentric Protestant prelate fought manfully for Roman Catholic emancipation, led a party of Volunteers into the Dublin parliament to protest against certain English abuses, stood squarely behind Grattan for the complete independence of the Irish legislature, and actually discussed Irish affairs with the Pope and blessed the monks of Saint Bernard.

Downhill, with its excellent hotel and magnificent strand, is a grand place for a quiet holiday, and the eight-mile walk, beside the Atlantic rollers, to Magilligan Point, is worth more than all the nostrums in the drug stores. From Downhill the road ascends the steep Lion's Brae, runs past the once-magnificent but now demolished mansion of the Earl-Bishop, and goes on to Coleraine. But you should turn left at the signpost for Castlerock and enjoy a game of golf on the fine links there, or a walk along the strand to the mouth of the River Bann. The adjacent territory around Articlave—*(Ard a' Chléibh), the Height of the Leper's House*[1]—is rich in souterrains, and you should seek out some of these, and in this district too is *Dun ceitirn, the Fort of the Warrior or Kern*—popularly known as *the Giant's Sconce* and in its heyday a stronghold of the Cruithni. In the vicinity, in 1854, was found a great hoard of Roman silver coins, dated from A.D. 337 to 433, probably part of the spoils of a raid into Roman Britain by those small dark men of Ulster who appear so often in the pages of Roman history.

From Limavady there is a shorter road to Coleraine, and a fine main road at that, which climbs over Ready Mountain and many another mountain forbye. You'll find scenery on this grand elevated highway very much to your taste, with splendid views of Loch Foyle and the Atlantic, and of the wide heathery moors of the rolling mountain-tops.

Coleraine—*(Cúil Rathain), the Ferny Corner*—is a pretty town which enjoys the unusual distinction of having been named by Saint Patrick himself, as you may read in the *Book of Armagh*, though centuries before Patrick came to Ireland as a slave, this place was the capital of a powerful, and possibly Pictish, kingdom. The royal palace was at *dun da beann, the Fort of the Two Peaks*, now known as Mountsandel, and you should walk along the Bann, to the Cutts, for a sight of the

---

[1] Also interpretted as *height of the basket*, (Clachan ed.).

Benevenagh and Mouth of Lock Foyle, from Limavady Road, County Derry.

great earthen mound and ramparts which are all that is left of its former glory. John de Courcy built a mote-and-bailey on the ancient fortress, and the later castle of Kilsanctan was erected on the same site, but the Norman power in this remote part of Ulster only lasted for a brief period. Near this old stronghold is the celebrated Salmon Leap, and the associated and extensive fishery works are most interesting.

In 1248 the Lord Deputy Butler built the first stone bridge at Coleraine, with a castle to protect it, and years before the shiring of Derry there was a County of Coleraine. But the English foothold weakened in Ulster in the fifteenth century, and the Mac-Quillans, Normans themselves turned Irish, became dominant and renamed the territory *MacQuillan's Country of the Route*. Then, prior to the Plantation proper, the Lord Deputy Perrott garrisoned Coleraine for Elizabeth, planned a new town, and brought over from England a number of prefabricated house-frames, and one or two of his frame-houses are still in occupation in the main street and can easily be identified. With the Plantation, Coleraine became part of the new County of Londonderry, and the London Company of Skinners became the responsible landlords.

Convenient to Coleraine are the popular seaside resorts of Portstewart and Portrush, the former in Derry, the latter, which we have already visited, in Antrim, within *a beagle's gowl* of each other, but in different Counties and strong in rivalry. Charles Lever, the Irish novelist, lived in Portstewart, and Thackeray, who visited him there, was charmed with the place but amused by its Sabbatarian excesses. The little town is beautifully situated to the east of the Bann estuary, and though it enjoys the most glorious Atlantic sunsets it is pleasantly sheltered from the bitter east and north-east winds. The soft air is heavy with ozone, and the bathing and golf are magnificent, which explains the famous description of the place as *the most sea-bathingest car-drivingest place in the north*. But don't be fooled by the so-called *O'Hara's Castle*, which looks imposing enough on its high rock and is now a convent, for it was never a castle and was only built about a hundred years ago.

It is a pleasant run from Portstewart to Garvagh—*(Garbhach), the Rough Place*—away amongst the Carntogher Mountains—*(Carn Tóchair), the Grave Monument of the Battle*—through which runs the Agivey, the best salmon-spawning stream in the district. From Garvagh a most picturesque road will lead you to Dungiven—*(Dún Geimhin), the Fort of Given*; and this Given was probably a local chieftain, for the surname is still common enough hereabouts. Beside Dungiven rises Benbradagh—*(Binn Bhradach), the Thieving Peak*—and from its easily-gained summit a view of extreme variety and great extent may be enjoyed. You will especially notice, from that pleasant elevation, the contrast between the rocks of the east and the west, the great basaltic plateau lying before you in all its rugged majesty and the older rocks of the west taking its place about the lovely Roe. From here you may see Ulster from coast to coast, and it is likely that Shane Crossagh, the famous highwayman, so saw it, for these hills and glens are full of stories of his deeds and adventures.

The Owenrigh and Owenbeg come to join the Roe at Dungiven, and the fishing for salmon, and white and brown trout, is good between this confluence and Bovevagh—*(Both-medhbha), the Hut of Maeve*—where you will find a picturesque ruined church perched high above the river. In the graveyard there is a remarkable structure known as *The Saint's Tomb*, a miniature stone oratory of seventh-century construction. In Dungiven itself are parts of the bawn walls of the castle built by the Skinners' Company in 1618, and down a grassy lane is the fine ruin of the Augustinian priory founded by the O Cahans in the twelfth century, and restored and altered in succeeding years. The splendid canopied tomb of *The O Cahan* is the finest sculptured funerary monument in Ulster, and surprisingly enough the chieftain is clad in most un-Irish mail, which perhaps explains his nickname of Cooey-na-gall, Cooey of the Strangers or Englishmen. The great Irish name of the O Cahans still survives in this district as Kane or O Kane. Not far from Dunvigen you may see the Tirkane sweathouse—the name Tirkane means O Cahan's Land—a form of Irish Turkish Bath which is often encountered in our countryside.

From Dungiven to Maghera—*(Machaire Rátha), the Plain of the Fort*—you will travel through the celebrated Glenshane Pass, between the Carntoghers and the White Mountain, and amidst a glory of heather and hills and wide sweeping vistas. You will find this mountain highway smooth as the palm of your hand, for this is the main road from Belfast to Derry, and it is one of the best-kept highways in Ireland. From the highest point on this road the panorama is grand indeed, with Loch Neagh and Loch Beg away beneath you, and the Mountains of Mourne, over seventy miles away, throwing their familiar shapes against the sky to make up a majestic background; there are the hills amongst which rises the River Roe, and there the twin giants of a dozen or more glens of endearing beauty, like Glenedra, *the Central Glen*; Finglen, *the Whitish Glen*; and Alt, *the Ravine*.

In Maghera was born Charles Thompson, in whose handwriting the American Declaration of Independence first existed, and from this neighbourhood went thousands of Ulstermen to put their hands to the founding of the great democracy of the West. In the town is the ruin of a remarkable church, with a west doorway which belongs to an early period of Irish architecture when decoration was unknown, and yet whose massive lintel-stone is carved with a splendid representation of the Crucifixion.

There is much else to see in Derry, but nothing that you cannot easily reach from the places to which I have conducted you. No County in Ireland is much richer in the grand heritage of pre-Celtic and Celtic lore, nor seems better to have withstood the impact of English and other foreign influences. For if, for a time, the County was largely in the hands of the London Companies, a generation had scarcely passed before the people of Donegal flocked into it, driven from their own lands by the rapaciousness of the absentee landlords, and the worse-than-rapaciousness of their agents and stewards. And soon Derry was almost as Irish as it had been before *The Flight of the Earls*.

WE CROSS THE BORDER ...

The Eire Customs frontier post at Muff, which is in the County of Donegal.

... through the Northern Ireland Customs frontier post at Culmore, in the outskirts of the City of Derry, and enter Eire by way of the Eire *Custom Frontier post at Muff, which is in the County of Donegal.*

History repeats itself, for whilst the Black Pig's Dyke, which anciently divided the Irish peoples of the North and the South, is now nothing but an interesting old earthwork, a new Border has been established between Northern Ireland and Eire .

The County of Donegal — Contae Tír Conaill

P to this point we have dealt with those Six Counties of the age-old Province of Ulster which are now known as Northern Ireland, and since the whole area of those Six Counties is one with Great Britain, there are no Customs regulations of any kind to claim the attention of the visitor who travels to Northern Ireland by way of England, Scotland or Wales. But Donegal, Monaghan and Cavan, which are very much a part of Ulster, are not within the political boundaries of *Northern Ireland* but are in *Eire,* and to reach any of them, or any other part of Eire, either from Northern Ireland or Great Britain, certain Customs formalities must be observed; though these formalities will give you little trouble, for the good nature of the officials on both sides of the Border is proverbial. If you travel with your own motor car, either of the two great motoring organisations, the R.A.C. or the A.A., will provide you with the necessary documents, known as triptyques, and with all essential touring information, such as the position of the Frontier Posts most convenient to the places in Eire which you intend to visit.

I use the word *Eire,* which is pronounced AIR-AH with the accent on the first syllable, as a convenient form to designate those *Twenty-six Counties of Ireland* which were known as *The Irish Free State—(Saorstát Éireann),—*until the 1938 Constitution, devised under Mr. De Valera's Government, abolished that title without proclaiming any official substitute for the area.

Properly speaking, Eire means the whole of Ireland, and its use as a designation of the *Twenty-six Counties* of the extinct Irish Free State is inaccurate, but popular use and convenience will undoubtedly establish this erroneous form beyond all the arguments of historical and geographical rectitude. It is doubtful whether *The Republic of Ireland—(Poblacht na hÉireann),* —set up, in 1949, by Mr. Costello's administration, will succeed in amending this popular but inaccurate usage, if indeed it ever desires to do so.

Donegal is known in Irish *Dhún na nGall,* the *Fort of the Foreigners*—more properly applies to the town of that name which in due time we shall be visiting. Conal and Owen Gulban were the historic heads of the two great branches of the Hy Neill, the Kinel Conal and the Kinel Owen, and Conal's name is preserved in the Irish title of this great County of Donegal, just as Owen's name survives in the great Donegal peninsula of Inishowen—*(Inis Eoghain), Owen's Island*—and in the County of Tyrone—*(Tir Eogain), the Land of Owen*—for this warrior was the founder of Ireland's greatest clan, the O Neills.

There are three frontier posts in the immediate neighbourhood of Derry, the posts of Muff, Bridgend and Carrigans, and we will make for the first of these to enjoy the anomaly of travelling from Northern Ireland in a *northerly direction* into Southern Ireland! And where else in all the wide world could you do the like of that? I tell you, this is a great country! As you leave Derry City by the Strand Road, past the docks which were the Headquarters of the United States Navy and the United States Marine Corps during the Hitler War, the first private entrance with a gate-lodge which you pass on the right is that of *Boom Hall*, where the Jacobite boom was placed during the great siege, and a little farther along is the field in which Amelia Earhart landed after her first solo transatlantic flight. Farther still, down beside the Foyle, is the neat little early-nineteenth-century fort of Culmore, successor of the 1609 structure of which only near-by fragments remain, and away on the right is Magilligan Point, stretching across until it almost touches this place, with the splendid mass of Benevenagh towering behind it. But that is in Derry, and we are in Donegal this blessed minute, and if it's mountains we're looking for, isn't that Slieve Snacht ahead of us to the left—*(Sliabh Sneachta), the Mountain of the Snows*—which keeps its white cap till the May Fair of Carndonagh is past and gone: or so the Inishowen people say!

Inishowen can best be considered as a separate part of Donegal, a triangular peninsula with Derry City at its inverted apex, Loch Swilly and Loch Foyle at its opposite sides, and Inishowen Head at one point of its base, with Malin Head, the most northerly point of Ireland, at the other. It is a region of rocky headlands and splendid Atlantic strands, of sweet valleys and rugged mountains, and right in the midst of this holidaymakers' paradise rises the lofty Slieve Snacht, which has already taken our eye. I can recommend two books which deal especially with this entrancing countryside—*Romantic Inishowen* and *Twixt Foyle and Swilly*; both are by my good friend, Harry Swan of Buncrana, and both are little treasure-houses of topographical delights.

The first town on our road is Moville, known in Irish as *Bun an Phobail*, the Foot *of the Foyle*, but obviously derived from *Maigh Bhile, the Plain of the Ancient Tree*. Donegal as a whole is vastly important to the angler, and Moville is the centre for salmon, and white and brown trout, in the Culdaff River, and for trout and char in Lochs Inn and Fad. Climb one of the hills behind the little town for a superb view of the whole of the Foyle region, of the Atlantic beyond Inishowen Head and the adjacent coast, and of many of the mountains and headlands of Derry and Antrim which we have already visited; and thereafter trek two miles to the west, to the ruin of old Cooley Church, beside which is a rare monolithic type of Celtic High Cross with pierced ring, rare because the upper portion of the shaft is holed.

Out towards Inishowen Head is Greencastle, where the nineteenth-century British fort has been converted into a pleasant and well-managed hotel which might well be your headquarters in this region; but the place takes its name from a much older fortress, the grim stronghold of Northburg, now in a state of extreme dilapidation, built in 1305 by Richard de Burgo, the Red Earl of Ulster, in an unsuccessful attempt to subdue the fierce and proud O Donnels and O Dohertys. The ramble from Greencastle, past Shrove with its picturesque lighthouse, to Inishowen Head, and thence to Malin Head by the coastal margin of Culdaff Bay, is something which I cannot too highly recommend, for that indeed is Donegal at its wildest and most inspiring.

Eight-and-a-half miles inland from Ireland's most northerly tip is Malin village—*(Mhálann), a Hill Brow*—which even English-speaking people in the district pronounce in the Irish way—MOLLIN. The village is a charming place, with a bridge of ten arches, a triangular green, and a handful of friendly Donegal people full of good songs and good stories. The road to the Head runs along the margin of Trawbreaga Bay—*(Thrá Bhréige), the Treacherous Strand*—where the suddenly-rising tides bring colour to the place-name, and to your left you will soon see Glashedy Island and the Fifteen Rocks, as well as that ruined stronghold of the O Dohertys, the Castle of Carrickabraghy, t*he Rock of the Maltster.* Malin Head is of no great height, but the coast here is especially grand and the views away over to the Scottish shore are very fine. A mighty chasm in the cliffs is known as *Hell's Hole*, and the Garvan Islands lie out to sea, this side of the Torr Rocks and Inishtrahull—*(Inis Trá Tholl), the Island of Yonder Strand*—and if you have time you should arrange a trip out there, to prove the aptitude of the place-name and to enjoy an unbelievable prospect of the rock-bound Donegal coast. There is a lighthouse on the island, a familiar landmark to travellers on American liners using the northern route.

Carndonagh—*(Carn Domhnach), the Carn of Donagh*—is the chief marketing centre for the agricultural products of the peninsula, but shirt-making, and the manufacture of commercial alcohol, also provide good employment and make this place a particularly compact and thriving little town. Beside the Buncrana road stands *Saint Patrick's,* or *the Donagh Cros*s, between two decorated guard or pillar stones, and these three objects are covered with low-relief carving which seems to be derived from the La Tene styles. The cross, which dates from the seventh century, must be one of the oldest of its type in Ireland, and it marks the climax of a lengthy artistic process which sought to make of the earlier slabs, which for a long time exhibited little more than vestigial arms, definite free-standing crosses in their own right. The outline and contours of this cross are irregular, and exemplify that well-known dislike of straight lines which was characteristic of the Irish artists of that age, and the figures are rendered with a formalism and unreality in keeping with that same tradition. In the near-by churchyard is the so-called *Marigold Stone,* a complicated and rather confused decorated slab of extreme interest, and high above the little town stands the handsome Roman Catholic *Church of the Sacred Heart,* built between 1942 and 1945. If you quailed before that very long ramble I prescribed for you from Greencastle to Malin, you can now reach a fine part of that trek by journeying six miles north-east to the secluded hamlet of Culdaff—*(Cúil Dabhcha), the Corner of the Flax-dam*—from which place a series of superb strands stretches for another six miles to the east, ending in the Queen of the Inishowen Glens, lovely Glenagivney.

Along the Moville Road, from Culdaff, just beyond Bocan—*(Bòcan), a male goat, or a goblin*—Roman Catholic church, the dilapidated Bocan Stone Circle stands in a field above the highway, and about two hundred yards farther on, up a rough pathway on the opposite side of the road, is the so-called *Temple of Deen*. This was the first-recorded Horned Cairn in Donegal, and it is of especial interest because of the lobster-claw horns which relate it to the Clyde/Solway series. Preserved in Bocan church is the celebrated *Bell of Saint Buadan*, a most attractive little hand-bell of cast bronze which marks a transition from the earlier Patrician types made of riveted sheet metal.

From Bocan church a road running at right angles, on the same side as the *Temple of Deen*, leads to Cloncha or Cloncaw—*(Cluain Catha), the Meadow of the Battle*—where an old church, disused since 1827, marks the site of an ancient Celtic monastery probably founded by Saint Buadan. Within this ruin is an elaborately carved grave-slab which bears two inscriptions in archaic Gaelic, of which this is a translation:

> Fergus Mac Alian made this stone:
> Magnus Mac Orriston of the Isles under this mound.

Mac Orriston was a Christianised Scandinavian chieftain from the Norse Kingdom of the Isles, and his sword is splendidly portrayed beside his comaun, or hurling-stick, and ball, whilst the central cross, elaborately foliated at its base, and with arms which expand into twined serpents' heads, is carved with great skill and feeling. Built into the church wall, near the doorway, is an inscribed stone bearing the device of a mallet and chisel. The inscription on this stone may be translated:

> Brian O Dubdagan made this stone
> for Domnall O Neill.

In the adjacent graveyard is the High Cross of Saint Buadan, an excellent example of the type which I described at some length in my Leinster volume. It lacks its arms, parts of which are lying in a field a few yards away. Farther along the road, where it abuts on to the Carndonagh highway, is Carrowmore—*(Ceathrú Móire), the Big Quarter*. The place-name reminds us of the ancient Irish system of land division, when townlands were sub-divided into quarters. In this place are remnants of buildings which succeeded the Celtic monastery founded here in the seventh century, and four very ancient crosses will claim your attention, one entirely plain, monolithic and extremely primitive, and another with a circle, marginal carvings and a key pattern incised upon it. Beside one of the crosses is a bullaun decorated with a cross.

We travel to Buncrana by way of Ballyliffin—*(Baile Lifin), the Town of the White Stone*—a small quiet village lying at the base of that Trawbreaga Bay which we have seen before. The bathing here, as in most of Donegal, is magnificent, and the geologist will find interest in the Holocene formations, the calcretes amongst the sand-dunes which are especially fine, and that natural bridge of calcreted shell-sand known as the *Ballyliffin Arch*. The small world of sandhills in this district, rich in the *kitchen middens* of early man, are well worth exploration for

Carndonagh, County Donegal. with St Patrick's Cross.

their archaeological wealth and interest. Clonmany—*(Cluain Maine), the Meadow of the Monk*—comes next on our road, a typical Donegal village, completely surrounded by mountains, and a grand spot for a quiet sojourn. Not far from Clonmany are a fine strand and a picturesque glen and waterfall. The main road now runs, beside the shoulder of Slieve Snacht, straight into Buncrana, but a smaller road to the west takes you close to Dunaff Head, the eastern guardian of Loch Swilly, which you should not miss. The cliff scenery is truly grand, and the views of Fanad Head, at the other side of the Swilly entrance, are memorable things you will be glad to have enjoyed. From here the Gap of Mamore—*(Mháim Mhóir), the Great Mountain-pass*—one of the steepest passes in Ireland, leads back to the Buncrana Road, but if you are motoring you will have to return to Clonmany to reach that highway. Not that the gap road, reaching an altitude of 700 feet between Croaghcarragh and Mamore mountains, is impassable by car, for one visitor, unaware of its hazards, drove to the top, and, unable to turn, had perforce to go on, a much-shaken man; and I have heard of an unladen lorry, and a tractor, that did no less, but I advise you against any such foolhardy undertaking. Mamore Gap is a hiker's road, pure and not so simple, and a gloriously rewarding one at that. I recommend you to tramp its rugged way, or to climb any of the hills here, great masses of glittering schistose rocks, to enjoy a panorama the equal of which you will not easily find. The Urris Mountains run south-west to Dunree Head, with the valley of the Dunerk River beside them, and over Loch Swilly you will observe that the Dunalla Mountains form a natural continuation, which was broken in remote times by that great irruption of the Atlantic which we know to-day as Loch Swilly. Swilly itself, named from the Irish word *Súilí*, which means *a Place abounding in Eyes* or *Whirlpools*, is big enough to hold the navies of the world, and it now shows up in all the unending variety of its great surface, bemargined with cliffs and mountains of surpassing majesty. This whole region is an absolute paradise for the walker and climber, and if you are seeking something very special in mountainy remoteness, just walk back to Owenerk Bridge and cut up a gorgeous wee road that will lead you through a twisting fairyland to the main Buncrana road. There you will find Donegal in all its glory, the greatest and most rewarding County in Ireland for those who prefer to take their pleasures afoot.

Buncrana—*(Bun Cranncha), the Foot of the Crana River*—is more of a typical holiday resort than any other town in Inishowen, and it deserves the popularity which it enjoys. It has fair hotels, good golf, good fishing and a good situation, and, like most places east of Loch Swilly, it has magical sunsets. Not so far away is Fahan—*(Fathain), a Level Greensward*—close to Derry City, and greatly favoured, during the summer months, by the citizens of that place, to whom the intervening Border must be an infernal nuisance. Columcille founded a church at Fahan, and Saint Mura became the first abbot of the succeeding monastic establishment. *The Cross of Saint Mura* still stands in the graveyard, a fine interlaced example with vestigial arms, and near-by tombstones include those of Horatio Nelson, nephew of the great sailor, and Agnes Jones, who was a colleague of

Florence Nightingale. Built into the wall by the roadside is an interesting Greek Cross, most likely a relic of the ancient monastery, and beside it is a curious cavitated stone which is reputed to be the old monastic message, or letter, box.

As we leave Fahan for Inch—*Inis, an island*—we enjoy a fine distant prospect of the Grianan, and later on our journey, near Burt, we shall be almost beside the hill on which that grand old cashel stands. Inch is no longer an island, for silting sand has connected it with the mainland and we reach it over a fine causeway road: but this O Doherty territory was very much an island in Elizabethan and Jacobean times, and it figures prominently in the English wars, and in the letters of Chichester, to whom it was finally granted. The sixteenth-century castle, one of the famous *O Doherty Four*, still stands in interesting ruin near the water's edge, and in the townland of Carnaghan is the *King's Grave*, much dilapidated. It is usually described as a dolmen, but looks more like the remains of a gallery grave, or a Horned Cairn. The restorer of the Grianan, Doctor Bernard, found a Bronze Age food vessel when he excavated this monument in the nineteenth century, and this seems to dispose of the legend that King Fergus MacRoy was buried here and so brought the popular name on the site.

Back to the mainland we go, to Burnfoot, south-west to Speenoge—*(Spionog), a Place of Gooseberries*—and south-west still to Burt Castle, without ever crossing that imminent border into Northern Ireland. The little ruined castle, another of *O Doherty's Four*, stands pleasantly due west of our road, on the brow of the gentle Castle Hill, and we must cross the intervening fields, or follow the boreen through the near-by farm, to enjoy more closely its picturesque outlines. It is a late sixteenth-century building, a small oblong tower with two round turrets at opposite corners, and in one of these turrets is the winding stair and in the other the usual garderobes and smaller apartments. Traces of the surrounding bawn and external ditch are still visible, and this stronghold of the native O Dohertys was taken by the English Docwra in 1601, was subsequently returned to its owners by that diplomatic and likeable soldier, but was retaken in 1608 and remained an important English strong-point for many years thereafter.

Just before we reach Letterkenny—*(Leitir Ceanainn), the Wet Hillside of the O Cannons*—we take our final leave of the peninsula of Inishowen. Since the Border robbed the City of Derry of its function of virtual commercial capital of the County of Donegal, Letterkenny has enjoyed that distinction and has prospered and expanded enormously. The actual County Town is Lifford, but that place, as we have seen, is little more than a suburb of Strabane, in the County Tyrone. Letterkenny is well placed on high ground above the spot where the River Swilly flows into the great sea-loch to which it gives its name, and the splendid and boldly-executed Roman Catholic Cathedral of Saint Eunan, which was ten years abuilding, proclaims the fact that the town has added to its commercial importance the honour of being the ecclesiastical capital of its great County. The main building is carried out in Donegal sandstone from Mountcharles, cut, dressed and carved by Donegal craftsmen, and *The Four Masters,* the famous Donegal annalists, are appropriately prominent in the decorative scheme. About a mile from the town, at Conwal Glebe, is the dun of the O Cannons, ancient chieftains of this district who were overthrown in 1350 by the redoubtable Godfrey O Donnel, who became Prince of all Tirconnail. Beside the dun is *Cloc na Riog—the Stone of the Kings*—at which the O Cannon chieftains were inaugurated.

On we go to Ramelton—*(Ráth Mealtain), the Fort of Meltan*—a neat village so nicely situated along a stretch of the Leannan River that its picturesque appearance will at once arrest your attention. The Leannan is a noted salmon and trout stream, and The Pool here is reckoned to be one of the finest salmon casts in the country. Killydonnel Friary, a Franciscan house founded by the O Donnels, is in ruins in the vicinity, and a variant of the Cornish legend of Tintagel is associated with the bell of this sixteenth-century establishment. Running alongside the western shores of Loch Swilly, a finely-timbered road leads into Rathmullan, which you could also have reached by ferry from Fahan on the opposite shore. A neat and lengthy promenade fronts the fine *Strand of Rathmullan*, and half-way along this strand stands the ruined Priory of Carmelite Friars, with a curiously attenuated and mean-looking tower, striking enough in its coat of ivy. The eastern portion of this ruin, built by the MacSweeneys, is about two hundred years older than the western portion, which is of Elizabethan age, as its typical brick chimneys proclaim, but Rathmullan's chief fame lies not in this sacred foundation but in the fact that from here, in 1607, O Neill and O Donnel, and many another Ulster chieftain, set sail in that major event of Irish history known as *The Flight of the Earls*. The earls died in Rome and lie asleep there in the Franciscan Church of Montorio, and with their passing the nasty work of the Plantation was made easier for its tortuously-minded architects. Nearly two hundred years after The *Flight of the Earls* Rathmullan again stepped into history, for hereabouts, in 1798, the prisoners of the ill-fated French man-o'-war Hoche stepped ashore, and one of them, Theobald Wolfe Tone, passed from here through Dublin into immortality.

With Rathmullan to the east of its base, and Milford to the west, the wild peninsula of Fanad—*(Fánaid), sloping ground*—stretches most gloriously ahead of you to the north, and as far as Fanad Head it forms the western shore of Loch Swilly. This is MacSweeney country, and of such surpassing grandeur that I need say little about it beyond recommending it most pressingly to your exploring feet. You have everything here from mountains and valleys, from smooth strands and rugged cliffs, from sea caves and stacks and arches, to bathing and fishing and climbing and golfing, that will fill you with wonder and delight, and there is even a most excellent hotel amidst all this remote magnificence, a hospitable house at Portsalon, set above a superb crescent of golden sand, that will not disappoint you. And from Fanad Head, which you can reach along excellent motoring roads, the view is so tremendous that you will find it hard to take it all in, and the memory of this terrible iron-bound coast, torn and contorted by the mighty Atlantic, will abide with you for many a long day. Nor will you find the less titanic delights of the region west of Fanad Head easy to forget, from a fine prospect of the entrance of Mulroy Bay to the sweet sight of the opalescent waters of that quiet arm of the ocean, with many fairylike islands afloat on its calm breast. Here and there a rocky promontory thrusts its black mass into the tender colour of the picture, and everywhere is that peculiar breathless quality of the brooding attendant mountains which is the essence and spirit of the Donegal landscape. Perhaps you will find that the finest things on the Fanad peninsula are the views of Dunree and Lenan Heads across Loch Swilly, and the prospect of Mulroy Bay from the summit above the adorable little village of Tirlayden—*(Tir Leadan), the Land of Burdocks*—along the road which turns south-west for Carrowkeel beside the massive barrier of the Knockalla mountains. The corkscrew roads and the little hillside farms in this region are sheer delight. Carrowkeel—*(An Cheathrú Chaol), the Narrow Quarter*—appears as Kerrykeel on the A.A. signposts hereabouts, but you wouldn't mind a wee thing like that amidst scenery of this quality.

Southwards goes our road to Milford, by way of Kindrum this time for variety—*(Ceann drum), the Head of the Ridge*—and at Milford there is golf and fishing and the much-esteemed MacCreedy's Hotel, and glens and waterfalls as numerous as they are lovely; and then we journey northwards to Carrigart—*(Carraig Airt), the Rock of Art or Arthur*—past Cratlagh Wood, where the third Lord Leitrim, his agent and his driver, were ambushed and shot dead by some outraged peasants. This unpopular landlord was noted, amongst other things, for his extreme punctuality, and the story is told that on the night of his assassination he was ten or fifteen minutes behind his wonted time in reaching Cratlagh; whereat one of the men lying in ambush, with his gun at the ready, was heard to say: His lordship's very late on it. I hope to God nothing's happened the poor gentleman. But dark deeds are out of place in this lovely countryside, and ahead of you is the wild and picturesque peninsula of Rosguill with its magnificent Atlantic Drive, the wide beauty of Sheephaven Bay, properly Shiphaven—*(Cuan na gCaorach),* —and the fine natural golf links of Rosapenna, where every tee brings a fresh eyeful of loveliness and where the hotel is famous. The Lackagh and Owencarrow Rivers are good for salmon in this region, and dozens of neighbouring lakes are stiff with sporting brown trout, whilst the six-mile-long golden strand will bring delight to the bather and walker. Griffin's shop in Carrigart is celebrated for those lovely Donegal tweeds and rugs which are made by hand, in the slow traditional manner, in the weavers' cottages which abound in this district, and other products of ancient crafts will be found on sale in different parts of the County. Opposite Griffin's shop, which you must surely visit, is the excellent Carrigart Hotel.

From Carrigart we go to Creesloch—*(An Craoslach), the Greedy Place*—by way of the hamlet of Glen, which is situated at the head of the pretty lake of that name. There is a fine group of lakelets hereabouts—Greenan, Salt, Reelan, Donnel, More and Natooey—and I recommend you to explore them for their own remote beauty as much as for the extraordinary solitude and grandeur of the countryside in which they lie like a lapful of shining jewels. This is quartzite terrain, composed of rocks so old that little of the present face of Ireland existed when they were formed, and the ancient north-east and southwest foldings of the country are very clearly evident hereabouts, geological features impressed upon Ireland millions of years ago and still imposing their will on the country to-day. Roads and railways, rivers and lakes, all follow the old crumpled valleys, and roads and railways which defy these foldings, in order to achieve a north-westerly direction, have to undertake extraordinary feats of twisting and turning amongst the resistant ridges. There is nothing to detain you in Creesloch, but seawards is the sixteenth-century stronghold of the MacSweeneys, Doe Castle, and near-by is the sweet waterfall of Duntally. *Doe* is an English corruption of the eclipsed Irish word *Tuath (Caisleán na dTuath)*, which means *lands*, and these were MacSweeney lands of such importance that they were much contested and heavily defended. The keep of Doe Castle is lofty and massive, and it stands on a fine elevation, which commands splendid views, within a bawn and a rock-cut fosse, but the whole building was modernised and altered to such an extent that the present ruin is confused and without any great charm or interest. It was used as a residence until 1920 or even later. There is no trace of the Franciscan Friary which adjoined the castle, but in the eastern wall of the graveyard is preserved the remarkable grave-slab of the MacSweeney, carved in low-relief with an elaborate cross and the family coat-of-arms. There are only two slabs like this in Ireland, the other being in Killybegs, not so far away, where it marks the grave of another MacSweeney, Niall Mor.

Creesloch is the place from which you may best ascend Muckish—*(Mucais / an Mhucais), the Back of the Pig*—so called from its resemblance to our friend of the breakfast-table. This mountain, perhaps the most familiar to all visitors to Donegal, is a great hump of quartzite 2197 feet high, and, from the boldness of its escarped face, looking much higher. A nice little road runs from Creesloch to Muckish Gap, and from there the way goes mostly by long grassy slopes to the lengthy plateau at the summit. From the south-western cairn there is a grand view of Errigal and Dooish, with the grey slabby ridge of Slieve Snacht stretching seawards between the two, and from this cairn to its northeastern fellow it is a slow scramble over about a mile of boulder-strewn plateau, but the sweeping grandeur of the panorama will repay you for all your labour. There are many ways up and down Muckish, but if you want the view with a minimum of hard work, keep to the southern grassy slopes and leave the north-eastern heights alone, or drive your car as high as you can up the recently constructed lorry road. But be always on the lookout for mists, and especially that dreadful Donegal smir which is no man's friend. Going now the fine road to Dunfanaghy—*(Dún Fionnachaidh), the Fort of the Fair Warrior*[1] — we find the peninsula of Ards on our right, a most

---

[1] Also interpreted as *fort of the fair field*, (Clachan ed.).

Horn Head, from Atlantic Drive, County Donegal.

picturesque region where the Capuchin Fathers have converted the ancient home of the Stewarts, Ards House, into a monastery, and from whom you should seek permission to ramble through the old demesne. Dunfanaghy is a neat village much favoured by holidaymakers, and there, and in the neighbourhood, there are many good hotels. There is tine golf there too, a splendid three-mile-long strand, and a sea-coast around Horn Head that will awe you with its sheer magnificence. There are seastacks and caves on that magical coast, upon which fanciful names have been bestowed, and the view from Horn Head, a precipitous cliff, rising more than six hundred feet from the Atlantic, which you can reach by a passable road with room to turn a car at the top, is utterly superb. Almost at your feet lie the Islands of Inishbeg, Inisdooey, Inisbofin and Tory, and the next land beyond those rocky outposts is America itself. If you have time, and the weather serves, hire a boat to take you around the Head. Your man will steer you to within a few yards of the sheer mural height of the tremendous cliffs, and any loud noise you can create will bring battalions of seabirds wheeling into the air above you—sea parrots, guillemots, shelldrakes, cormorants, terns, kittiwakes, oyster catchers, shearwaters, gannets, stormy petrels, speckled divers, shags and many more besides—and this will be one of the most memorable experiences in your journey around Ireland. Neighbouring Falcarragh—*(An Fál Carrach), the Rough Hedge or Wall*—and Cloghaneely—*(Cloch Cheann Fhaola), the Stone of MacKineely*—are busy places in the summer months, when students of the Irish language flock there to attend the famous Irish college, and from this district, or from Meenlaragh or Bunbeg, you may take passage to that strange and primitive world which is Tory Island; though you must look upon this as the adventure it is, and be prepared to remain on Tory for a few days if the weather worsens—which it usually does! And please make the O of *Tory* short and pronounce the name *Torrie*, for this place has nothing to do with the English Conservatives at all but is called in Irish *Toraigh,—a Place of Towers*—and for reasons now before your eyes; for aren't those jutting rocks on the island's top for all the world like small little towers and nothing else at all?

Tory is a rather desolate place, treeless, rocky and with the shallowest covering of soil, and its principal revenue has long come from wrecks, for the island lies right in the track of the North Atlantic shipping. Wreckage runs like an economic thread through the fabric of Tory existence, and you will hardly find a farmhouse there that doesn't sport some part of a dismembered ship—a harrow improvised from an old firebox, a hencoop that was once a deckhouse, or a water-trough contrived from the half of a battered funnel. But there is much of interest on the island, and the people are civil and kindly, and, of course, Irish-speaking, but bilingual from their habit of seasonal migration to Scotland for agricultural labour. The cliff and rock scenery on the thither side of the island is splendid, with a great abundance of seabird life, and in the cottages at night there is music and dancing and story-telling galore. And above and beyond all is a deep and abiding peace, surely a most precious thing in this harried, nerve-racked, frantic world of ours. The absence of noise on Tory is like a blessed balm that falls softly on the senses and sinks beneficently into one's very being, and this single quality makes a sojourn amongst the little island community something very much worth while. You will find the flail of Biblical times still in use on Tory, as well as slide-carts, which possibly persist from an age when the wheel was yet unknown; harness is mostly made from plaited straw, known in Irish as SugAn, and the whole agricultural method is pleasantly primitive and unhurried. In the West Village you will find some gathered antiquities grouped around the stump of a shattered Round Tower of unusually crude masonry, the most interesting of these being a Tau Cross, of which the only other specimen extant in Ireland stands in Kilnaboy, in the County Clare. This type of Cross, known as *Saint Anthony's*, is of Egyptian origin, a circumstance which need not surprise us when we reflect on the close connection between the early Coptic and Celtic churches. The original Christian foundation on Tory is ascribed to that beloved Donegal Saint, Columcille, whose name is intimately associated with many of the island folk-tales, and the ruins of the *Seven Churches of Tory*, which are still pointed out, indicate that a monastic establishment of considerable size once flourished there.

Tory men still stick to their canvas currachs, or canoes, despite many Government attempts to woo them to the use of wooden yawls of the drontheim type, and the reason is not far to seek. A currach is light and cheap and easy to work, and a man, looking like a gigantic black beetle, can easily carry a short currach on his back. The islanders vow that the canvas canoes are much safer in their mountainous seas than any wooden boat, and in a treeless country they are much more easily kept in repair. A piece of canvas, a needle and thread, some tar or pitch, and a hot turf, and a currach can be kept tight as easily as a bicycle tyre and in much the same way. The most primitive form of Irish canvas boat is the circular corracle of the River Boyne, which I discussed in my Leinster pages, and between this form and the long currachs of Arran and Kerry with their upturned prows, comes the short currach of Tory. These boats used to be made on a framework of sally rods fastened with horse-hair, but nowadays oak laths and copper fastenings are in almost universal use. There are no seats in the Tory currachs, but on the adjacent mainland you will find a transitional type, longer than the customary eight feet of the island canoe, of graceful sweeping lines and with several seats or thwarts. Tory is about seven hundred and eighty acres in extent, has a population of about two hundred and fifty souls, and lies something more than seven miles north-west of Horn Head. If it lay seven hundred miles away it could not be more remote and primitive, nor more compact of all those qualities of peace and simplicity and kindliness which spring from a deep regard for the real and enduring fundamental things of life.

At Gortahork—*(Gort an Choirce), the Field of Oats*—in the parish of Cloghaneely, is MacFadden's hotel, a small hospitable house which I cannot too highly recommend for plain good comfort and excellent food. It stands on the very threshold of the magical region of the Bloody Foreland—*(Cnoc Fola), the Mountain of Blood*—and the remote glory and grandeur of the splendid road which runs round this iron-bound coast, through the tiny villages of Meenlaragh, Meenclady, Knockfola, Brinlack and Derrybeg, to Gweedore, is something that must be seen rather than described. The very spirit of Donegal is in this place, from the quaint beauty of the little cottages that face the Atlantic gales so gallantly, their comely thatches tied firmly down about their ears against the roaring winds, to the small farms so hardly laboured in this rocky wonderland, their minute fields embraced within deftly-wrought stone hedges that are themselves part of the scant crop that has been so laboriously won from that very land which they enclose. For indeed Donegal is a terrible place for stones, and a stranger is apt to wonder at the spirit which sustains these people in their struggle, for no more than the merest subsistence, in this coastal fringe of undoubted grandeur but equally undoubted exposure and niggardly agricultural yield. And what a people they are, polite, friendly and full of humour and a practical philosophy of life that shines through all their works. Standing above Knockfola, about the spot where Raymond Piper made the accompanying sketch, the patchwork-quilt of the small, little fields shows up in all its endearing testimony to generations of patient labour, whilst farther back towards Gortahork, in the neighbourhood of Meenlaragh—*(Mín Lárach), the gentle spot*—where you may conveniently hire a boat to take you out to Tory, that storied island can be seen to great advantage behind the three islands of the Inishbofin group—*(Inis Bó Finne), the Island of the White Cow*—its rocky towered extremity making it look for all the world like some gigantic sphinx, inscrutable above the restless ocean. The villages on the islands are plainly visible, and you may care to observe the long fields of Inisbofm, cultivated in great stripes which run with the grain of the land in a most striking manner. From this same spot the fantastic cock's-comb of Horn Head shows up superbly beyond Crockaclogher; the sandy wastes of Dooey—*(Dumhaigh), a sandbank*—shine palely beneath the immense skies; and the great masses of Muckish and Errigal fill up the opposite prospect.

Travelling south, and ignoring the left fork for Gweedore, we run into Bunbeg—*(An Bun Beag), the small Foot of the River*—a pleasant long village which stands where the River Clady enters the sea. There are several neat little hotels and guesthouses here, and here you may fish, play golf, walk in entrancing hill country or coastal fairylands, or make delightful trips to the cluster of small islands that lies just off the mainland—Gola and Inishinny, Inishmaine and Inishirrer, Umfin and Inishfree, Owey and the larger Cruit. I can think of only a few places as pleasant as this in which you may tarry a space for a quiet holiday of varied simple delights.

From Bunbeg the road runs south-east along the northern margin of the Gweedore River, and soon turns sharp to the left for Gweedore itself—*(Gaoth Dobhair), the Inlet of Doir*, who was the son of a king of Ireland. There was a fine hotel at Gweedore, but it has been closed for some years now and the loss of its friendly hospitality is still felt in this region where good hotels are not numerous. The district is famous for angling, the Clady and Crolly Rivers, the smaller

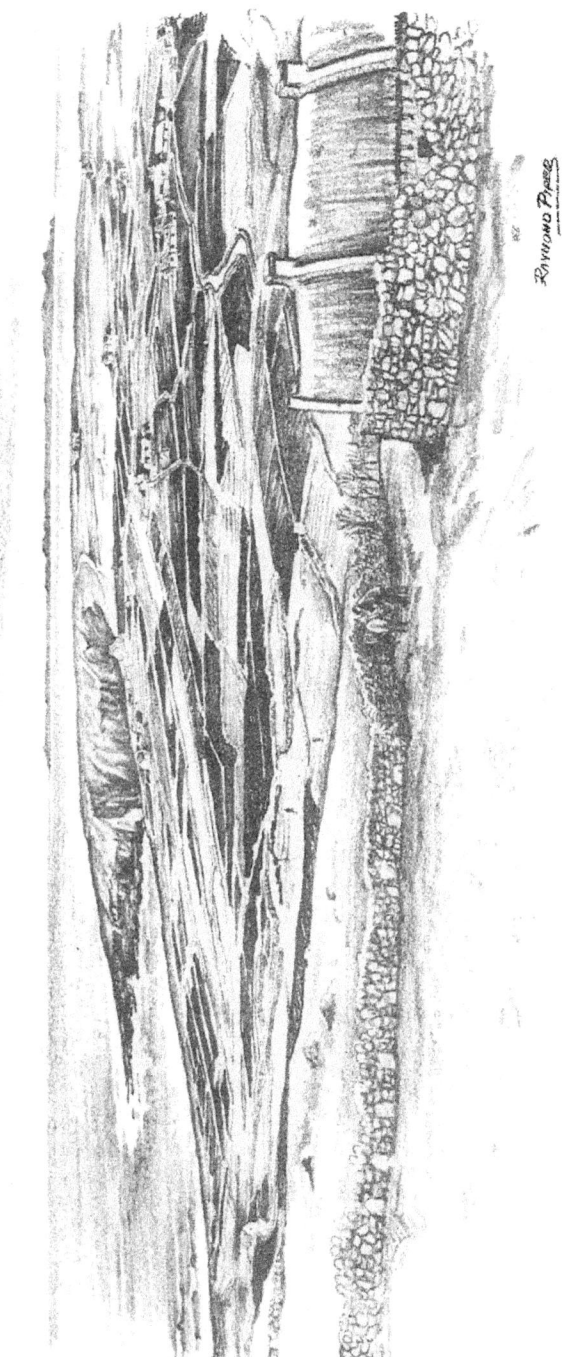

Bloody Foreland, County Donegal, with Tory Island out to sea.

Strancoragh, and the numerous lakes of Nacung, Anure, Glentornan, Corneen, Altan and Nagreenan, all being rich in sporting fish, and this is also the point from which the manifold delights of the Errigal country and the Donegal midlands may best be approached. But Gortahork is only six miles away, and MacFadden's hotel there should be your headquarters.

Errigal means, in Irish, *a habitation*, and in its more usual secondary sense *a small church or oratory*, and it is likely that this great Donegal mountain took its name from some eremite cell which formerly stood near it or on its summit. Errigal, graceful and unusual, whose cone of dreamy, dove-grey quartzite stands out so singularly in the landscape, is the highest of the Donegal mountains, and its 2466 feet are best climbed from near-by Dunlewy—*(Dún Lúiche), the Fort of Lugh of the Long Arms*—a townland which is easily identified by its modern Romanesque church of grey stone with white mouldings, with a campanile built in the guise of an ancient Round Tower. You will have almost a mile of moorland to cross as you approach the col between Errigal and its smaller brother, Wee Errigal, but once on the shoulder ridge you'll find the way clear and easy enough. The ridge becomes rougher and stonier as you ascend, but a number of guiding cairns will keep you right, and you'll find the view, unspeakably wide and varied from either of the twin *Pinnacles of Errigal*, worth all your labour. A *one-man-path* will confront you along the quarter-mile which separates the pinnacles, and it depends on your head whether you walk across this or negotiate it straddle-wise; though you needn't cross it at all if it daunts you, but just go back the way you came. If you make for the col you can easily reach the summit of Wee Errigal, which rises superbly from the savage mountain tarn of Loch Altan and has a fierce grandeur all its own.

Down to earth again, one of the wildest bits of Donegal should attract your attention, though why it is called *the Poisoned Glen* is not at all clear. The Irish Spurge used to grow there, and that is a poisonous plant, but there is no recent record of it, though I have been told of cases of severe sickness caused by drinking the waters of the numerous glen streams; but how much of this is fact and how much folk-lore I would not care to decide. This savage valley was carved out of the granite hills by the ice of long ago, and the result of this natural sculpture is not unlike that other gloomy but picturesque valley of Glendaloch, in the County Wicklow. As you look down from the high road beyond Dunlewy, to the mouth of the glen, you will enjoy a most charming picture of Dunlewy House, of the River Devlin as it twists around sudden meanderings amongst some clumps of trees, and of the lovely Loch Nacung as it points an elongated finger to the north-west. The scramble, for it is more than a walk, up the Poisoned Glen, is heavy going, but I would conjure you not to miss it, for there is nothing quite so fine in the whole of Ireland. If you are persistent you will eventually reach the desolate road that leads through Glen Veagh to Loch Veagh—*(Loch Ghleann Bheatha), the Glen of the Birch Trees*—and if you go astray you'll always have the church at Dunlewy to guide you back again. Loch Veagh is one of the most beautiful lakes in Ireland, approaching the loveliness of Killarney in its lower parts, and perchance surpassing anything in that Kerry paradise in the utterly savage grandeur and magnificence of its upper reaches. Here the hills rise in steep slopes from the very edge of the lake, and the splendid fall of Astellion is embowered in scenery of unspeakable loveliness; but much of this ground is private property and you had best seek permission to enjoy the tramping of it.

From Dunlewy a wonderful mountainy road runs north-east to Calabber Bridge, where you turn left for Muckish Gap and another means of reaching the summit of that fine mountain, or right for Kilmacrenan. On the way to Calabber Bridge the long line of Donegal's greatest mountains, Errigal, Aghla More, Aghla Beg and Muckish, lies stretched to your left in a splendid chain of beshadowed magnificence, and your eye will never weary as these great masses take ever-changing shapes as you move along their foothills. Since you have already been to Muckish, and the farther Creesloch, you will turn right at the bridge and head for Kilmacrenan—(*Cill Mhic nÉanáin or Cill Mhic Réanáin), the Church of the Sons of Enan*, who were relatives and contemporaries of Saint Columcille. The road crosses the northern tip of Loch Veagh, down which a most delectable view will compel you to stop in wondering admiration, but two miles farther on, at Drumfin, be careful to bear right for Church Hill, instead of taking the shorter northern road to Kilmacrenan. You will soon be skirting the eastern shore of the charming and fishful little Loch Akibbin—*(At an cipín), the Ford of the Little Stick*—and a small road to the right, at the foot of this lake, and between it and the larger Loch Gartan—*(Gartán), the little field*—will take you across to Loch Nacally—*(Loc na Caillige), the Lake of the Hag*—which is so intimately associated with the holy Columcille. High above the western shore of the little lake is a ruined church, with added doorways of much later date than the rest of the build-ing, which is reputed to be the successor of a monastery built on the site of the actual birthplace of that princely O Donnel who became one of Ireland's greatest and most beloved Saints. This church is so dilapidated and architecturally nondescript that it is of little interest, but in front of it is an ancient and most primitive monolithic cross, whilst on the hill behind is another cross of the same type. In the adjacent old graveyard are some confused walls which were obviously associated with the later settlement here, and below this is the Holy Well of Columcille, to which pilgrimages still take place. The fiatteran runs round stations which include the church, the two crosses, the graveyard and the well, and, on the Saint's day especially, considerable gatherings of pilgrims carry out their sacred duties. In a near-by townland, known only to the O Friels, who were charged with its keeping, is *Columcille's Clay*, a sure charm against drowning and shipwreck, and a no less certain enemy of rats. There are cases on record of sober Dublin merchants who sought this *Columcille's Clay* to rid their warehouses of destructive rodents, and who were not dissatisfied with the result.

Down the road from the ruined church, and within the Glenveagh Castle demesne, is Lacknacoo—*(Leac na con), the Flagstone of the Hound*—to reach which you must ask permission at the gate-lodge on the road. Here, beside a modem

High Cross, is *Columcille's Bed*, a great slab with cup-markings and incised circles, and legend has it that whoever sleeps a night on this hard couch will never know homesickness or shipwreck. In the days of emigration many a poor peasant spent his last night in Ireland on this cold bed, and it is said that when the lordly MacSweeneys were evicted from Derryveagh they similarly kept vigil here the night before they sailed for America, nor failed to take with them a great lump of *Columcille's Clay*. Another legend relates this stone to the Saint's birthplace, and the church to the place of his baptism, but in this countryside every rock and bush seems to have some connection with the great missionary. To me *Columcille's Bed* looks uncommonly like the covering slab of a Bronze Age grave, a notion in which I am encouraged by the obvious signs of related cairn material. Apart from these ancient associations this district is one of much beauty, with the Glendowan Mountains rising finely in the vicinity, and with sweet tree-clad slopes climbing with charm and loveliness from the many sheets of water which are scattered over the countryside like a handful of jewels.

Church Hill is a neat little village standing on a near-by hill, and you will find MacClafferty's guest-house there both clean and friendly. You may stay the night there if there is room, or you may wish only for food. And food you'll get, fresh and plentiful, nor will you want for an appetite after the good Gartan air.

From Church Hill to Kilmacrenan it is a pleasant run beside the Leannan River, and on a little hill near the village is the ruined Franciscan Friary which an O Donnel built on the site of an old foundation of Columcille's. Sir Cahir O Doherty was killed in this vicinity after his destructive raid on Derry in 1608, and in the churchyard sleeps Dr. Anthony Hastings, of the same family as the celebrated Warren Hastings. Along the road to Creesloch, just short of Kilmacrenan Railway Station, the first turn to the left leads over a bog to the renowned *Rock of Doon*, where the O Donnel chieftains were inaugurated in days of old. You may read a good contemporary description of this interesting ceremony in Edmund Spenser's: *The State of Ireland*, and I would recommend you to do no less. Just beyond the Rock is *The Holy Well of Doon*, famous for its miraculous cures of the halt and the blind, and there you will see not only the usual rag and pin tokens left by the hopeful devout, but also the sticks and crutches discarded by pilgrims who have been made whole. In the neighbourhood is a most exciting little road, good enough for the average car, which leads to Loch Salt and Loch Salt Mountain. There is good fishing there, just as there is in the boisterous Leannan and in the near-by Lochs Keel and Fern.

How you get back to Gweedore, or to Gortahork, if, as I do, you make the comfortable hotel there your headquarters in this region, is a matter of little account. Donegal is all grandeur or loveliness, or both, and you will have no regrets whichever way you travel. Our road runs south from either of those places, through the much-sung, endearing Rosses—*(Na Rosa), the peninsulas or small headlands*—a place-name which you will find confirmed on every hand, to Dungloe, and the first small place we shall meet, after Gweedore, is Crolly—

(*Croithlí* or *Croichshlí*), *a shaking bog*—with its sparkling river, its grand series of miniature waterfalls, its company of ice-borne granite boulders, and its small intimate beauty so much beloved by poet and painter and tourist alike:

> Nor a wee small town like Crolly,
> At the foot of Croghan mountain,
> Where the rivers meet each other
> And go laughing to the sea.

And the rivers are those which come down from Loch Anure and Loch Keel, and mingle their smaller loveliness to create the larger beauty of the Gweedore River itself. This is a wild region of acid intrusive rocks, and as you travel on you will feel the impact of a granite countryside as surely as you will recognise it by the great boulders of that hard rock which lie around in such tremendous confusion. The longer and more picturesque seaward route from Crolly to Dungloe is worth your time for the very wildness of its qualities, for the innumerable small lakes and ocean inlets which beset it on every hand, for its maze of islands and its iron-bound coast which knew the proud ships of the Spanish Armada and them in their distress, and for the sight of Burtonport with its neat harbour and granite quarries. Arranmore lies off Burtonport, largest of the Donegal islands, and you should take a trip out there for a taste of life similar to that which I have described on Tory: but don't confuse this island with its more famous namesakes in Galway Bay. The shorter route from Crolly affords many a pretty eyeful of Loch Anure, and, in about half the mileage of the seaward journey but with less than half its interest and variety, leads us into Dungloe—(*Dun gleo*), *the Fort of Contention*—which is pronounced without the g, as though it were written Dunloe, and with the accent on the second syllable. The real Dungloe lies some distance away, for the ancient name of this present town was *An Clochán Liath,—the little grey village*; but the Fair of Dungloe was transferred to Clochanlee, as a more convenient centre, some centuries ago, and the name followed the fair. The chief fame of Dungloe to-day stems from the romantic story of Paddy Gallagher, affectionately known all over Ireland and Irish-America as *Paddy the Cope*, a poor Rosses boy who dreamed of co-operation as the salvation of the struggling farmers of his homeland, and who, by perseverance and hard work, made his dreams come true. You can read of his success in his absorbing book: *My Story*, which is soon to be made into a film, and I never go near Dungloe without calling for a share of his good talk and jolly company.

Five miles west of Dungloe is the quaint fishing village of Maghery—*(an Machaire), a plain*—which was once a centre of the soapstone and kelp industry, and where they still collect the great sea-rods which you will find stacked in piles beside the road or draped to dry on the walls. Opposite the village is the island of Illancrone, and the old kelp-house still stands there in ruins. An adventurous road, quite good enough for a car, climbs from the village to Crohy Head, and from the schoolhouse there a path leads across the fields to a ruined signal-tower, from which a superb panorama of the wild and rugged coast may be enjoyed.

You will find these towers along the west coast from here to Kerry, and you should not confuse them with the circular martellos of the eastern seaboard. They were only slightly defensible, of an oblong plan with pointed gables, and they originally carried large semaphores on their flat roofs. The coast here has been torn into fantastic shapes by the mighty Atlantic, and a curiously bifurcated seastack near the tower is known as *an Briste,—the breeches*—which is a name of great aptitude, as you will perceive. Beyond this place a singular landslip is known as *talam briste,—broken earth*—which seems a good name for a great chasm nearly a quarter of a mile long and about twelve feet across at its widest part. This whole region is a wonderland for exploring feet and eyes, and all the wild glory and grandeur of the Rosses lies between this place and the coast to the north which we have already enjoyed.

South of Gweebara Bay—*(Gaoth Beara), the Inlet of the Judge*—the peninsula of Dawros—*(Dam-ros), the Peninsula of the Oxen*—flings itself into the Atlantic right to the tip of Dawros Head, from which point the views north and south are most splendid and attractive. The peninsula is full of charm, with small heathery hills and sweet little lakelets, and the coast alternates most unexpectedly between rugged cliffs and smooth golden strands. The road runs from Dungloe to Doochary for a mile, and then turns to the right at the signpost for Lettermacaward, from which place the A.A. sign will direct you to Maas, along the Glenties road, and then to Dawros itself. In Maas—*(Más), a thigh, and thus a long low hill*—Molloy's Hotel is an excellent house with a growing reputation, and the presence of this hotel, as well as those at near-by Narin, Portnoo and Rosbeg, indicates the popularity of this region with visiting holidaymakers. It is indeed ideal country for leisurely enjoyment, and farther on, at Narin and Portnoo, the great tawny strand runs for miles, and the outlying island of Inishkeel—*(Inis Caoil), the Narrow Island*—can be visited dryshod at low tide, and is worth the exploration for its two early ruined churches and interesting incised crosses. The rocks in this vicinity are most varied, black crystalline limestones and contorted slates with great veins of yellow granite visibly squeezed into them, whilst the quaint rock pools with undercut drainage channels, worn and dissolved by sea and rain, are well worth a little study. On Dunmore Head, near Portnoo, are two ancient forts, and in the neighbourhood are eight others, whilst in Loch Doon—*(Loc duin), the Lake of the Fort*—is the second finest cashel in Donegal, sufficient indication of the importance of this territory in early times. To reach Loch Doon you must take the first turn to your left on the road from Portnoo to Dawros Head, and one mile along that by-road you will find the cashel over the fields to the right, beyond the cottage of the genial MacHugh, farmer, wheelwright, boatbuilder, fiddle-maker and traditional fiddler. This good man will act as your guide if you need one, and from him you may hire a boat, of his own manufacture, to take you out to the island on which the cashel stands. And if you leave him without enjoying a few staves of his grand music, well, that will be your own loss. The massive cashel, which might almost be considered as the stone

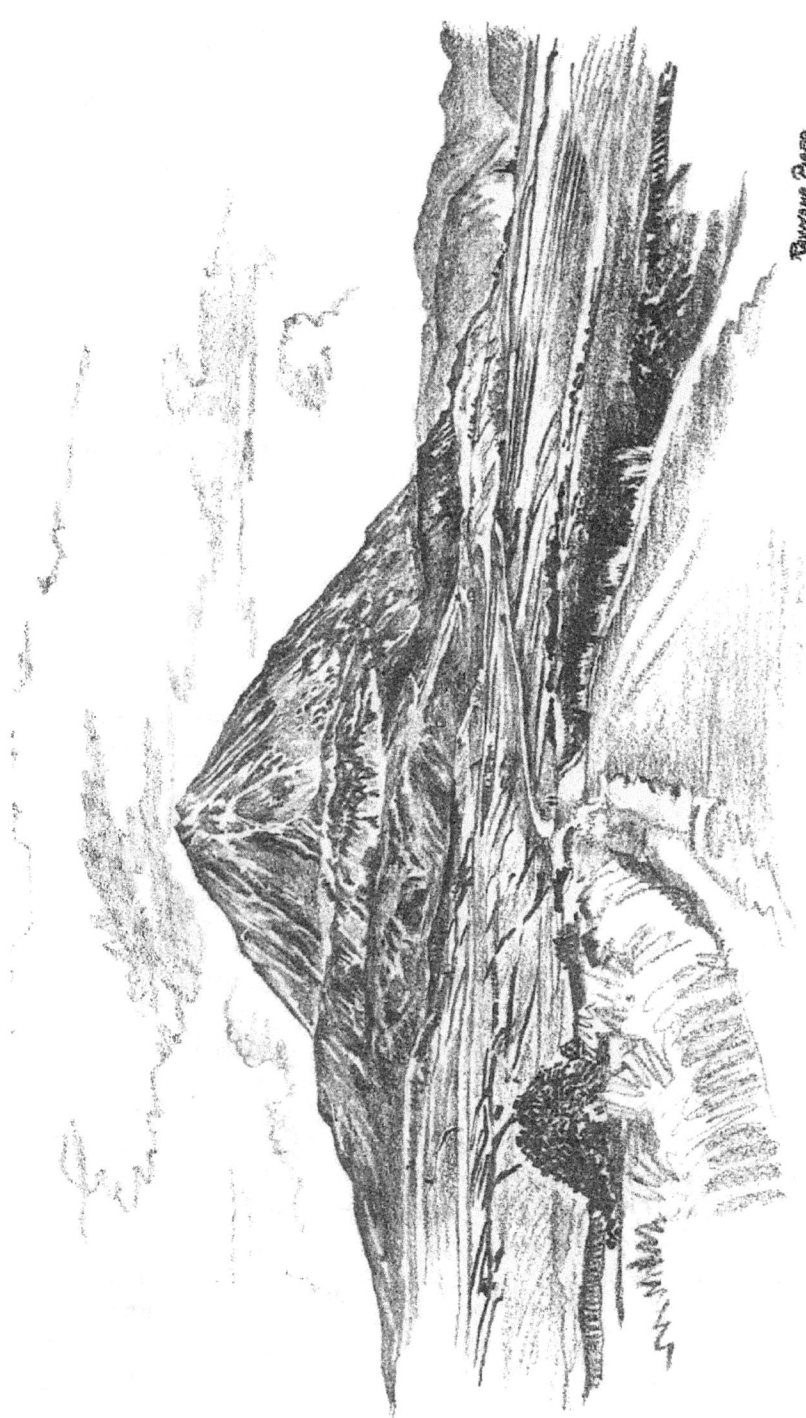

Errigal, County Donegal.

counterpart of a crannog, occupies the whole of the little island on which it is built, and, unlike its more famous fellow, Grianan Aileach, it has not been restored. It stands, apart from its sad dilapidation, much as its Iron Age builders left it, a magnificent example of mortarless building out of the local slaty rock. Perhaps Larminie had it in mind when he wrote his celebrated poem: *The Nameless Doon*:

> Who were the builders? Question not the silence
> That settles on the lake for evermore;
> Save when the seabirds scream, and to the islands
> The echo answers from the steep-cliffed shore.

Near Loch Doon is Loch Birroge— *the reedy lake*—with traces of a similar cashel, and a little to the south is the larger Loch Kiltooris, with scant remains of an O Boyle castle on the little island at its tip. From the hillock behind MacHugh's cottage, which was the spot chosen by Raymond Piper for his sketch of Loch Doon Cashel, there is an inspiring view right across Lochrosmore Bay— *(Loc Ros Mór), the Lake of the Great Peninsula*—to the splendid Slievetooey—*(Sliabh Tuaidh), the northern mountain*—and the adjacent small islands and most fantastic seastacks, and I consider this one of the finest vistas of its kind in all Donegal. In certain conditions of light it takes on a magical quality that defies adequate description. The road from Loch Doon continues round Loch Kiltooris to Rosbeg and Dawros Head, which should not be missed, and you have then but to retrace your way back to the main road for Ardara, the surface of which will be a welcome change from the rather rough by-roads which we have just travers*-6ed. The bathing in this Dawros area is superb, there is a nice little nine-hole golf 0course within easy distance of the hotels, and for fishing the Rosses offers about a hundred lakes and many rivers, variously good for salmon and trout, whilst the sea-angling is quite notable.

Ardara—*(Ard an Rátha), the Height of the Fort*—is one of the chief towns of Donegal, well graced for the angler and golfer, and prettily situated in a deep valley where the Owentocher River flows into Lochrosmore Bay. This district is celebrated for the manufacture of Donegal homespun tweeds, rugs, knitwear and hosiery, and you will be welcome at any of the cottages, or cottage workshops, where you may watch the men and girls pursuing their ancient craft. From Ardara a marvellous road runs through Glencolumcille to Glen Head, but the wild and extensive region to the north of this road can only be explored on foot. There is indeed a road from Ardara as far as Maghera, a road which you should not miss, but generally speaking this whole section of the southern margin of Lochrosmore Bay, from Maghera to Glen Head, twenty-five square miles of roadless wonderland, is one for the foot-slogger. And what a section it is, surpassing almost anything in Ireland in the sheer magic of its desolate beauty, the grandeur of its far-flung vistas, and the atmospheric colours of its prospects by land and sea.

Loch Gartan, County Donegal

Another road, leading you in the opposite direction from Ardara, would take you to Glenties—*(Na Gleannta), the Glens*—which stands at the head of two superb glens, the Glen of Stracashel, *the River-holm of the Stone Fort,* and that other glen with the Irish name which sounds like a little song—*Gleann Fada na sealga,— the Long Glen of the Hunting.* We are well off our track here, but the pleasant woods and glens of this place will bring you a sweet contrast with the rugged majesty of that walk along the Lochrosmore shore. Even farther off our route is the run from Glenties to Ballingrath Hill, where, half-way down that hill, a rough road to the right will lead you into one of the wildest and most splendid mountainy defiles you have ever seen. This is the district of Croaghs, an Irish word meaning *stacks* or *ricks* but mostly applied to a territory of crowding mountains, and out of the great conclave of mountains here you will easily recognise the lovely Croaghgorms to the south, for once correctly anglicised as *The Blue Stacks,* by which name they are best known. And blue they are, blue as any of the blue hills of Ireland, till the setting sun turns them to a tawny prune, and then throws even that dark shade into contrast with the deeper purple with which it fills every hollow and defile of their riven sides.

Back in Ardara you should make for Maghera, a place-name which is here, quite unusually, pronounced with the accent entirely on the first syllable, along a most picturesque little road that hugs the southern margin of the great river-fretted sandy inlet of Lochrosbeg Bay. You will reach the quiet little village in about five miles, a place of thatched cottages where the villagers themselves, scorning the professional craftsman, thatch their own houses with the bent which grows so abundantly in the adjacent dunes. Even their thatching-ropes are made on the spot, hand-twisted from straw or bent and known in Irish as *súgán,— soogawn*—and against decay and infestation they often spray their thatches with a solution of sulphate of copper, a substance known throughout Ireland as *bluestone.*

Westwards from the village a superb strand runs to the mouth of Lochrosbeg Bay, and at low-water this is indeed a sight of the utmost magnificence. The walk along this strand round the splendid quartzite cliffs is something you will remember all the days of your life, the many fine caves, full of deep pools where lobsters, crabs and shrimps abound, and the distant roar of the great rollers at the entrance to the bay, bringing added delights to a joy already full beyond measure. The caves, for the most part, owe their existence to geological faults, and to jointing, but two of the ten display narrow dykes which run in the direction of their cavities, one transformed into serpentine and the other into hornblende. The contrast between the light grays of the quartzite and the dark greens of the intrusive hornblendes is charming beyond words, and this is a region of varied beauty and delight from which you will not willingly depart.

From Maghera a road, not marked on the half-inch O.S. maps, now runs south-west up Granny Glen to Strabby, and there joins the chief road to Glencolumcille, but if you are daunted by this rough track that runs beside the

Doon Cashel, Loch Doon, County Donegal.

Owenwee River up a glen once notorious for its stillers, moonlighters and poteen-makers, you had better return to Bracky Bridge, just south of Ardara, and travel to Glencolumcille by the usual route up the celebrated corkscrew road of Glengesh—*(Glean Géis), the Glen of the Swans.* You will soon reach an elevation of almost a thousand feet by means of these twists and curves, which take the sting out of the climb, and you may care to notice how the meandering of the Glengesh River repeats the twisting of the road. By the time you've finished with this corkscrew you'll feel a bit like that useful implement yourself, or maybe you'll only be in the mood to use one on something suitable! The road ahead is now rough, but scenic in a high degree, with a detour to the tiny village of Port, on the coast, if you feel like it, and your way lies amongst elevated bogs and moorland, and descends into that remote glen of quiet beauty which gives its name to our next stopping-place, the village of Glencolumcille.

It was here the *Dove of the Church* loved to dwell for a space, and he tells us, in his writings, how the mists that crept across the sombre valley, and the sound of the great Atlantic rollers on the near-by strand, brought a deep sense of peace and devotion to himself and his followers. Glencolumcille is full of memories of its much-beloved patron, and as you enter the village you will see a curious and most primitive monolithic stone cross beside the roadway opposite the Guards barracks, and another cross of similar type farther down the road, past the Church of Ireland, placed atop of a small mound to your right. The design of these crosses, based on a Greek pattern, is interesting, and it seems to have been intended to suggest a metal cross riveted to a stone background, or, in other words, to be a metal-worker's idea carried out in stone. The angled corner-pieces in the cantons, and the concentric circles squared off to fit into a narrow upright space, are details of much significance. From the mound cross, at midnight on the 9th of June each year, the great *Pilgrimage of Columcille* starts on its *patteran* of something more than three miles, and includes in its circuit most of the crosses and stones which you will find between here and the adjacent Garveros—*(Garbhros), the Rough Point.* In that place is the Station of Prayer, and on the hillside are *Columcille's House, Bed and Well,* all great places of pilgrimage as the pile of stones will testify, for every visiting pilgrim adds a stone to that pile. The so-called House is really one of those small Irish oratories now familiar to you, and its altar is at the north end instead of at the east, a peculiarity which I have already pointed out to you in connection with the original church of Columcille in Derry, and with

Cross at Glencolumcille, County Donegal.

that of Patrick in Saul. *The Eye Stone* set in the east wall of the House, the thirteen stations around which the great *patterans* go, and the *Saint's Well* at Glen Head, are all easy to reach and identify, and a ramble around Glen Head itself will yield much of delight in the way of rock and cliff scenery and glorious seascape. But the best view of this bold projection, which descends to the ocean in a mighty sweep, is to be had from the road to Malinmore, whither we journey next. Properly considered, Glen Head is but the centre of a mountain which has been half eaten away by the ocean.

At Malinmore—*(Mhálanna Mór), the Great Hillbrow*—there is the neat and friendly Glenbay Hotel to take you unawares with its pleasant amenities in such wild countryside, and I recommend you to make this hospitable house your headquarters in this region. Near-by is the Maam Rock, where *Bonny Prince Charlie* is said to have lain in hiding, regularly fed by the faithful Pat Nanny, some of whose descendants live in the neighbourhood, but whose cottage is now in ruins. But unfortunately for this legend, and for many similar stories you will hear around Malinmore, it seems unlikely that Prince Charles Edward Stuart was ever in Donegal, or in Ireland at all. The whole period of his life, from the time of Culloden, 14th April 1746, until he sailed for France on the 20th of the following September, is fully accounted for in the loving itinerary, known as *The Lyon in Mourning*, compiled by the good Blaikie, every day of the tragic five months is precisely documented, and Ireland does not appear in a single entry. Thus are the warm fancies of legend dissolved by the cold logic of history. Beyond Malinmore is Malinbeg, *the Small Hillbrow*, a picturesque village that lies along the length of a steep ocean cliff, with a most quaint and attractive little harbour and several silvery strands that lie most invitingly in the embrace of fine rocky amphitheatres. On the headland is a signal-tower similar to that which we saw at Croghy Head, and from that elevated spot you can get a good view of the outlying fifty-acre island of Rathlin O Beirne, with its lighthouse, holy well, penitential stations and the ruined church of Templecavan. You may reach the island by boat from the small harbour below, and the sight of this terrific coast from that place is worth the journey a dozen times over. From the signal-tower you can also enjoy a superb view, over the top of Slieve League and across the wide Donegal Bay, of Ben Bulbin and Knocknarea in Sligo, of storied Inishmurray, of the Stags of Broadhaven and of the great mountains of Mayo.

But the crowning glory of this superb region is Slieve League—*(Sliabh Liag), the Mountain of the Flagstones*—which, like Glen Head, is really the centre of a mountain eaten away to its very core by the mighty Atlantic. To a height of almost two thousand feet this stupendous mass of contorted quartzite presents a magnificent

Cross at Glencolumcille, County Donegal.

and wellnigh vertical wall to the ocean, and of all the coastal cliffs of Great Britain and Ireland this must stand supreme for sheer grandeur and mural splendour. This grand spectacle can best be enjoyed from two easily-gained places, and since both are conveniently reached from the little town of Carrick, it is to that place we must go, by way of Malinmore and Meenavea, and thence along the northern margin of the fishful Owenwee River—*(Abhain Bhui), the Yellow River.* At the Slieve League Hotel you can get a drink and some advice from the genial Sean Maloney, who knows as much about this district as most people, and if you decide to climb the mountain, rather than look at it, you can take your motor car more than half-way to the summit up a road which the same Sean will point out to you. At the spot where you turn your car and leave it for the foot-slogging part of your journey, stand awhile and enjoy a wide and a colourful panorama: the village of Teelin lies, as it were, at your feet; a little to your right is Carrigan Head, full of shadows and blue delights; and beyond Teelin a narrow spit of land, interesting as an outpost of that Carboniferous Limestone which we have almost forgotten in this territory of more ancient rocks, runs out to Saint John's Point with its terminal lighthouse. To the right of that lighthouse is Bundoran, twenty-five miles away across the dancing opulent beauty of Donegal Bay, and the rest of that distant landscape we have already seen from Malinbeg. In the opposite direction a veritable sea of mountains will be your portion, with our old friends Errigal and Muckish prominent in the tremendous prospect. But now come to the summit and look down below. One mighty escarpment falls in a sheer precipice almost two thousand feet to the Atlantic, and this view must be one of the most tremendous things of its kind in the world. From the summit, the ridge runs to easy walking over grass and scraw, but soon the escarpment cuts off the land-slope and you are confronted with the celebrated *One-man-pass.* Whether you negotiate this dizzy path, or leave it alone, is your own business, but you'll see nothing better from it than the view you have already enjoyed, and you can reach Bunglass on the other side from the lower road; and from that place an even more breath-taking view of Slieve League is to be gained.

For there the great cliff sweeps inwards in a four-mile-long arc, so that you may see the whole of it at once, and the quartzite and gneiss, of which it is composed, set up a kaleidoscope of colours if the sun is shining. Golds and ambers, yellows and greens, whites and reds, gleam and burn in a wondrous symphony, and dance a bizarre measure in the sea-laden atmosphere, and, below, the restless Atlantic beats a rhythm to this age-old dance, itself the deepest of deep blue or anon the jade green of some barbaric idol. To reach Bunglass— *(Bunglas), the End of the Green,* most apt place-name, as you will soon observe—you must run back through Carrick to that fishing village of Teelin—*(Teileann), the House of the Flowing Tide*—which you saw from Slieve League. From Teelin a most adventurous road runs through a pass in Scregeighter Mountain—*(Screagioctar), the Lower Rocky Ground;* lower, that is, than Slieve League—and eventually comes out on the seaward side of that same mountain at a most dizzy altitude. This is no road for nervous or unskilful drivers, and I would warn such people against it;

Glen Head, County Donegal.

as strongly as I would recommend all others not to take a car farther than the lake beside the road, where a cutaway in the right-hand bank makes turning comparatively easy; but every driver, however skilful, should proceed with extreme caution, and keep a sharp look-out for that cutaway, for once beyond it the task of turning the car is perilous and most difficult. This amazing road soon becomes a mere ledge, without any wall or protecting bank on its seaward edge, perched a full thousand feet above the Atlantic, and I know of nothing to compare with it, for rugged majesty and a terrible grandeur, in the whole of Ireland. From the car you must walk the half-mile to Bunglass, at the south-eastern extremity of the great sea-cliff, and there indeed you will agree that I have not overdrawn the wonder and drama of this stupendous spectacle.

We journey now to Muckros Head—*(Mucros), the Peninsula of the Pigs*—mostly for the sake of the celebrated caves which have there been blasted out of the lower Carboniferous Sandstones and Limestones by the tempestuous seas. The road from Carrick passes through some delightful country, over the Ballaghdoo River—*(Bhaile Dhuibh), the Black Pass*—into the nice little town of Kilcar—*(Cill Charthaigh), the Church of Saint Carthach*—and on our way we get many an inspiring view of the changing outline of Slieve League behind us, and of the little-less opulent splendours of Crownarad—*(Cró na Roda) the Valley of the Red Iron-Scum,*—which are soon spread before us as we travel south-eastwards. There is a Donegal tweed factory in Kilcar, into which the famous hand-loom weavers of Shalwy—*(Na Sealbha), possessions*—have been drawn, to the destruction of their leisurely old domestic handcraft, but, apart from that sign of progress which is not at all to my taste, there is nothing about Kilcar that calls for further comment.

The road from Kilcar to Muckros Head is quite good, and you can drive your Car to within a very short distance of the caves, and have plenty of room to turn it there. A clamber over the great dark Carboniferous flags will lead you to the massive clatform-like formations which run out into the sea, and at the landward side of these the splendid caverns await your exploring feet. The rocks are flat as a table, and the only danger is their slippery light covering of weed against which you should continually be on your guard. Without great care you may get a very nasty abrasive fall. The sea has worked magnificent confusion here and the resulting sculpture is savage and superb in the extreme, with terrific effects created by most violent undercutting.

A picturesque road runs round the southern flank of Crownarad through Shalwy, where nearly two dozen cottage weavers worked until recent times, and on round the silvery splendours of the great strand of Fintragh Bay—*(Fionntrá), the White Strand*—into Killybegs. As you journey towards Shalwy the two delectable strands of Trabane and Traloar, the first safe for bathing and the second most dangerous, will take your eye with beauty, and the Irish names of these are *An Trá Bhán, the White Strand,* and *An Trá Laragh, the Strand of the Mare.* In Shalwy one or two of the cottages retain their looms, and a Mr. Curran there, though he now does his weaving in the Kilcar factory, may show you the more gracious leisurely method. All along this superb coastal road the cottages are neat and most comely, and you will not fail to encounter many delightful specimens of the thatcher's ancient craft.

Killybegs—*(Na Cealla Beaga), the little churches*—is a very neat and prosperous town most agreeably situated at the edge of a fine natural harbour, and in this place the renowned Donegal carpets are made in the factory of Messrs. Morton. Mr. Campbell, their most courteous manager, is usually available to show visitors the interesting processes involved in the making of these lovely coverings, which have been sent to most parts of the world. The colour-harmonies employed are most subtle and beautiful, and the carpets themselves seem to wear for ever. Up the hill from the town stands the Roman Catholic Church, and inside this building, set into the south wall, is that MacSweeney grave-slab which is a fellow of the remarkable specimen we saw at Doe Castle graveyard. The road runs north and then east, across the top of Killybegs Harbour, to Dunkineely—*(Dún Cionnaola), the Fort of Kinneely*—and there are some tender bits of scenery on the way, especially memorable being the view down the long, narrow harbour of Killybegs, with Rotten Island and its lighthouse standing in the middle distance, and the long finger of Saint John's Point filling up the colourful background.

Just before you reach Dunkineely you will come upon the road, to your right-hand side, that is signposted Saint John's Point—*(Teach Eóin), John's House*—and the six-mile run down that road, to the lighthouse, will remind you of a similar journey which we made in our Leinster wanderings, down the equally remarkable attenuated finger of land which terminates in Hook Head, where there is also a lighthouse. The similarity does not end there, for this Saint John's Point, like the narrow spit which leads to it, is composed of Carboniferous Limestone, as is Hook Head, and the two long fingers, though separated almost by the length of Ireland, point to the same part of the compass[1]. You will have learnt by now that Carboniferous Limestone and dust are never far apart, and as you motor down this pleasant road beside MacSwyne's Bay, the dust clouds will chase you all the way if the weather is dry. The peninsula is rarely more than half-a-mile wide and fifty feet high, but at its extremities it rises pleasantly to 217 feet at Sentry Hill, and to 151 feet at Ballycroy Hill, where the rock is thickly covered with drift. The views from these points are wide and handsome, especially from the watchtower near the lighthouse, but they are much the same as those we enjoyed from Slieve League, except that they now include that monster itself. There is another Trabane Strand here, with everything about it to tug at the heart of the bather.

From Dunkineely to Inver—*(Inbhear), the River-mouth of Saint Naill or Natalis*—is a charming run through tender country, and you may care to

---

[1] Originally *art of the compass,* (Clachan ed.).

remember that Naill was the Abbot of Devenish on Loch Erne. At Inver is the comfortable and well-managed Drumbeg Hotel, and I have not the slightest hesitation in recommending you to make this hospitable house your headquarters in this district of varied beauty and interest. East of Inver is Mountcharles, really *Tamhnach an tSalainn, the Field of the Salt,* and the stone which built the National Library in Dublin, the cathedral at Letterkenny, and many other great Irish buildings, came from the famous quarries of this small place. The fishing is excellent here, the bathing all that could be desired, the golf small and sporting, but for me the chief delight of the place is the view from the top of the steep little mount which gives the village part of its English name.

Another four miles and we are in Donegal Town—*(Dhún na nGall), the Fort of the Strangers*—the strangers in this case being the Norsemen, for the name is older than the Anglo-Norman invasion and we know that the Norsemen had a settlement here early in their era. This town, for all its name, is not the capital of the County, as we have already observed, but it is an important commercial and agricultural centre, and only the shortcomings of its water approaches have prevented its becoming a busy little port. It is a place rich in historical interest, and a most excellent centre, with several reasonable hotels, for the angler and rambler. Donegal Castle is a fine example of that Jacobean architecture which combined defensive strength with domestic grace, and the ruin to-day displays a tall gabled tower, reminiscent of the Scots baronial style, with two bartizan turrets of which one is perfect. The splendid Jacobean wing is attached to the altered tower built by the O Donnels, in 1474, and said to have been burned by Hugh Roe just before he left Ireland in *The Flight of the Earls*, and thereafter the entire structure was remodelled by the English grantee, Sir Basil Brooke. Fine mullioned windows light the main apartment, and the richly carved fireplace bears the arms of Brooke impaled with those of Leicester of Toft in Cheshire.

At the head of the town is the handsome Roman Catholic *Four Masters Memorial Church of Saint Patrick*, a modern building carried out in granite in the Hiberno-Romanesque style, and including a replica of an Irish Round Tower in its design. It is indeed a fitting memorial to the four scholars who brought undying fame on Donegal, as well as to our Patron Saint.

The remains of Donegal Franciscan Friary stand in the graveyard down beside the little harbour, just off the road for Ballyshannon, and opposite is *the Lovers' Walk*, a shady riverside path with a charm all its own. The Friary is usually described as an Abbey, and quite incorrectly, for the Franciscans have no abbots, and without an abbot there cannot be an abbey. It is commonly stated that the celebrated *Annals of the Four Masters* were compiled in this Friary, but this is by no means certain and the question is still highly controversial. It is known that this house was destroyed by fire before the annals were even commenced, and certain scholars favour the idea that the annalists did their work in the near-by Magherabeg Friary, a small house of the Third Order of Saint Francis, of which some remains are still extant, about a mile to the south on the same side of the

Slieve League, County Donegal.

estuary. Another writer avers that *the Four Masters wrought at Donegal Friary, within a small shelter raised among the ruins*, but he gives no authority for this statement.

And so we must keep an open mind, though the popular idea of the great annalists working within the walls of a considerable monastery, with all the amenities of a well-stocked library and good living, must be discarded, for that particular monastery had long lain in charred ruins when the first record was set down. What is certainly known is that *the Four Masters* were compelled to move from place to place, and that finally they found refuge with Fergal O Gara, Lord of Coolavin, at Moygara Castle on Loch Gar. The original manuscript of their great work is in the library of the Royal Irish Academy in Dublin, one thousand quarto pages, beginning with the year of the world 2242, ending with the year A.D. 1616, and purporting to cover the whole history of Ireland for four-and-a-half-thousand years. But luckily for us, *the Four Masters*—the two brothers O Clery, Fearfeasa O Mulconry, and Cucogry O Duigenan—exercised a wise discretion, and, whilst they only just touched upon remote events, addressed themselves with extreme diligence to the history of the eventful times in which they lived. A handsome obelisk, to the memory of these four scholars, stands in the Diamond of Donegal Town, and a recent postage stamp did honour to their labours.

A very pleasant circular tour of about fourteen miles in all, just north of Donegal Town, will take you round the comely Loch Eske—*Loch Iascaigh* or *Loch Iasc, the Lake of the Fish*—which is seen at its tender best from the southern end, with the colourful Blue-stack Mountains filling up the northerly background beyond the low heathery hills which surround the lake.

A fine road leads us from Donegal Town along the shores of Donegal Bay to Ballyshannon, but we should stop at Ballintra to have a look at *the Pullens—Poillín, Little Caverns*—in the grounds of Brown Hall. Here the Ballintra River has cut itself a mile-long course through the soluble Carboniferous Limestone, a wild and deep ravine through which it tumbles in the most boisterous manner; but this is not all, for Carboniferous terrain is notorious for queer tricks with water, and soon our lively river dives underground into *Sheepskin Cave* with its fantastic formations, reappears in a meadow, dives into the *Piper's Cave* and reappears again, and finally casts itself into a sixty-foot-deep chasm from which it emerges under a lovely natural limestone arch. To reach Brown Hall you must turn left, at the church at the Donegal Town end of Ballintra, and thereafter take the second road to the right. The good Mrs. Wilson, at the gate-lodge there, will do the rest, and what she doesn't know about the Pullens isn't worth knowing. To the west of Ballintra is Rosnowlagh—*(Ros Neamhlach), the Wood of the Apples*[1]—with its superb strand and comfortable hotel, and just before we reach Ballyshannon we come on the sadly dilapidated remains of the Cistercian

---

[1] Also interpreted as *heavenly headland*, (Clachan ed.).

Donegal Castle.

Abbey of Assaroe, founded in 1178 by a colony of monks from Boyle Abbey, and sung into immortality by William Allingham:

> The boor tree and the lightsome ash across the portal grow
> And heaven itself is now the roof of Abbey Assaroe.

The name in Irish is *Es-aeda-ruaid, the Waterfall of Red Hugh*, and this chieftain, who was the father of that Macha who founded Emania in Armagh, was drowned here and lies buried in near-by Mullaghshee, *the Hill of the Fairies*. In a field to the west of Assaroe is an interesting sweathouse, and two bullauns stand in an adjacent cave, above the entrance to which is an ancient cross cut in the rock.

Ballyshannon—(*Béal Átha Seanaidh), the Ford-mouth of Shannagh*—is another example of the persistence of the Irish pronunciation of place-names on the lips of the people. The Anglicised name is most misleading, with its suggestion of some connection with the River Shannon, but the local people disregard this and adhere to the proper Irish form. In this they were long ago confirmed by the great Ballyshannon poet, Allingham, in his celebrated song:

> Farewell to Bellashanny
> And the winding banks of Erne

Truth to tell, the town looks better from a distance than at close quarters, and it is divided into two parts by a bridge of twelve arches, the lower part being known as *the Port*. As you cross the bridge you have the boundless Atlantic on the one hand and the noisy glittering river on the other, and in your ears will be the unceasing sound of roaring waters; but, most remarkable of all, this bridge bears a tablet, not to the usual local *Tomnoddy*, but to William Allingham himself, Poet of Ballyshannon and Provider-in-Chief to the Irish nation at home and abroad of the Race of Fairies:

> Wee folk, good folk, trooping all together,
> Green jacket, red cap, and white owl's feather.

Ballyshannon is justly proud of Allingham, and the house in which he was born is one of the show-places of this wee town on the River Erne. The river itself is one of the most noted salmon streams in Ireland, and the great salmon-leap at the Falls of Assaroe is internationally famous; but I am afraid much of this fame must inevitably fade when the extensive hydro-electric works, now in progress, are completed.

Towards Bundoran—*(Bun Dobhráin), the Foot of the Doran River*—we come upon sandhills and a magnificent strand, but we do not come upon that Doran River from which the town takes its name. Rivers there are in plenty, to be sure, such as the Braddoge and the Duff, but not a Doran in the wide world, and I'm afraid this must remain an unsolved problem in Irish place-names. Not that the town seems to mind, for it is gay as gay can be in the season, rich in good hotels, and more like the typical seaside resort than any other place in Donegal, though the neighbourhood will give you all you want in the less-sophisticated delights. The local rocks are nicely varied, sandstones, shales and limestones of the Lower Carboniferous series, overlain by glacial clays in the form of drumlins. *The Fairy Bridges of Bundoran*, popular with tourists, are the result of the solvent action of water on the thin limestone beds, and before we leave the place I should mention Glenade, though it is over the County border in Leitrim, for you can conveniently reach it from here. Run out to that lovely cliff-lined valley, deeply bitten into the limestone, and enjoy the sight of pretty Loch Glenade that lies in its bosom.

We are now at the southern extremity of Donegal and must make our way back to Ballyshannon, and on to Pettigo by the northern shores of Loch Erne. We are not now concerned with the Fermanagh part of the town, which we have already visited, but with that major section of Pettigo which lies in Donegal, and which is the great place of rendezvous, from the first of June to the fifteenth of August every year, of those devout people who go on the celebrated pilgrimage to Loch Derg, *the Red Lake*, which lies five miles to the north. We are now in a country of mica-slates, and the change from the richly fertile limestone terrain which we have just left is most striking. The road from Pettigo climbs into ever more desolate country, poor pasture gives way to heathery boglands and then abruptly we come upon the great lake surrounded by acres of forbidding turf-covered hills. The pervading bleakness is thrown into extreme contrast by the assemblage of ornate buildings, which wellnigh overflows that narrow strip of rock known as Holy, or Station, Island, rising forlornly in the lake less than a mile from the shore. For almost fifteen hundred years this place has been reverenced by the people of Ireland, and for almost as long it has been famous throughout Europe. Calderon, the national poet of Spain, wrote a drama, *Saint Patrick's Purgatory*, based on the miraculous history of this rocky islet, and Shakespeare made several references to it, whilst Henry, a monk of Saltrey, in Huntingdonshire, wrote, some time early in the twelfth century, a description of *The Vision of Saint Patrick in Purgatory*. In the following century the place really became widely celebrated, and pilgrims from all over Europe came to visit it; in 1397 Richard the Second of England granted to the Chamberlain of France, and his entourage, a safe conduct to Loch Derg, and for a hundred years from that time great numbers of people made the pilgrimage, but on Saint Patrick's Day in 1497 the Purgatory was destroyed by order of the Pope, Alexander the Sixth, on account of excesses committed there. Pope Pius the Third revoked this order, and the place flourished more prodigiously than ever for the next hundred years and more. Then, in 1632, the pilgrimage was again suppressed, but in spite of all obstacles the Purgatory continued to attract the faithful, and to-day it is more fully attended than ever. The original cave of *Saint Patrick's Vision* was destroyed, as I have recounted, and in the eighteenth century another cave was chosen in its stead, but to-day *the Minor Basilica of Saint Patrick* takes the place of this cave, and it is in this sacred building on the rocky islet that the penitents keep their prescribed nightly vigil, the counterpart of Saint Patrick's vigil in the original cave. The penitential devotions commence with several circuits of the church, with visits to rock and earthen beds named in honour of Saints Brigid, Brendan, Catherine and Columcille, and continue with stations performed every day. Several thousand pilgrims present themselves every year, carry out the prescribed exercises in bare feet, and observe a black fast for the entire period of their penance. One meal a day is allowed, of oaten bread without butter and tea without milk, but the pilgrim is permitted to drink of the water of the lake, boiled and sweetened with sugar, if the desire is on him. The pilgrimage occupies three days, and may be extended to six or even nine, but longer than nine days no penitent is allowed to remain on the island without the special permission of the Prior.

From the black featureless hills of Loch Derg it will be a relief to get back to Donegal Town, and from there to pursue a magnificently scenic road through the renowned Barnesmore Gap to the twin villages of Stranorlar and Ballybofey. Beauty and interest will be at your elbows all the way, and it will not be long before you are back in Derry, back in that old city so well-beloved of Donegal's own royal Saint, Columcille, the Dove of the Church.

Man and Turf-donkeys, Horn Head.

The County of Monaghan — Contae Muineacáin

HE Irish name of this County means *The Little Shrubbery*, and for a district which has long been famed for its small little hills and spreading woods, it is apt enough. The same fate which befell the noble covering of trees that once almost clothed Ireland from end to end has overtaken most of the Monaghan woods, but the small little hills are still there; so much so, indeed, that you would have to search for miles to find a field level enough for a hurling match! Monaghan of the Small Little Hills! Monaghan of the Songs!

My good friend Padraic Colum, in his *The Road round Ireland*, has committed himself to the statement that the Monaghan people care little for song or dance, but in my childhood one of the servants in our home came from Ballybay, which is in the County Monaghan, and it was from her that I learnt most of the Irish ballads that first whetted my appetite for folk-song. This girl would sing from morning till night, and judging the Monaghan people from her, who must have learnt her vast repertoire around her own home, I can only conclude that Padraic is guilty of a base calumny against a song-loving tribe.

Monaghan of the Songs! But, alas, the ballad singer is fast disappearing from her roads, as he is disappearing from the roads of our other Irish counties. At one time a familiar figure, with his handful of narrow, ill-printed ballad-sheets, or his store of brightly-coloured song books, he is now only occasionally seen. The coming of the cinema to even the smallest of our Irish villages is completing his extermination, which was already begun with the advent of national education and the cheap newspaper. Not so long ago every event of local and national importance was put into a ballad, and sung on the roads or streets to a crowd eager alike for musical entertainment and the latest titbit of news. But if those days are passing we have still a few ballad singers and *Men of the Roads*; and the older people of the countryside, and some of the younger ones too, may yet be persuaded to sing their ancient songs. But they become fewer and fewer, and that is why I have long been active in taking down as many of these songs as I can discover, and in committing them to the comparative safety of the gramophone record. About a hundred-and-fifty of these old songs, sung by me in the authentic manner of the roads, are now available in music shops all over the world.

The Monaghan country.

The authentic Irish ballad singer is more concerned with the words of his song than with the melody, for almost always he has a story to tell. He is a direct descendant of the ancient bards, and it was the bards who kept the history of our country in an unbroken memory-succession through the hurrying years. History was not committed to writing, for writing did not then exist in Ireland, but it was preserved in an enduring body of song and story handed down orally from one generation to another. The *Men of the Roads* thus became, in due time, the virtual history books and newspapers of the main body of the Irish people.

Monaghan is a county of small, well-tilled fields and trim thorn hedges, with never a level space at all, and with here and there the gleam of a lovely wee lake, Tke people, are rauch given, to thrift and comfort, and the sturdy qualities of the Ulster folk are much in evidence. The County was planted with extreme thoroughness, as I have already pointed out, and many of the place-names reflect this circumstance, such as Ballinagall, the *Town of the Stranger*, and Ballyalbany, the *Town of the Scotsmen*. The great demesnes of Rossmore, Glasloch and Castleshane in the north of the County, and of Castleblayney, Dartrey and Carrickmacross in the south, are as fine as anything of the kind in Ireland, and if Monaghan lacks the opulent beauty of Armagh, or the rugged magnificence of Donegal or the Antrim coast, it has its own small kind of loveliness which is at once highly individual and most attractive. You will find the Monaghan folk pleasant to talk to, cordial, friendly and humorous, and always ready for *a bit of a crack*. Enquire for the road to Clones, and instead of the usual *wheel straight and turn left at the first cross*, you'll more than likely be treated to a wee piece of a discourse. You'll hear all about the roads for miles around, about the hills of them and the surface of them, about the people who live along them and the people who used to live along them, *God be with the ould days*, and about the fields that border them and the kind of crops that come off those fields. And you may also be told how to get to Clones, which seems fair enough!

Monaghan Town is the capital of the County, and if you go there from Northern Ireland the City of Armagh is the nearest point; and you travel through Middletown by way of the Tyholland frontier post. Nearing Monaghan Town you will notice, on your right hand, a considerable stretch of the old Ulster Canal, now a weed-grown ditch of mournful appearance, which should remind you of the near-madness of the early nineteenth century in the haphazard construction of inland waterways. Monaghan Town is a thriving business place with little interest for the tourist, though the Georgian houses in Dublin Street, with quaint top-storey windows, are worth looking at. It was already an ancient town when James the First granted its charter, there was a Celtic monastery there which was plundered in the ninth century, and in 1462 Sir Phelim MacMahon founded a Franciscan Friary. The Roman Catholic cathedral is a handsome modern building standing on a commanding elevation on the outskirts of the town, and near-by is the Saint Louis Convent, one of the best-known educational establishments in Ireland. Sir Charles Gavan Duffy, leader of *the Young Ireland Party*, and later Prime Minister of Victoria, was born in the town.

Five miles to the north is Glasloch—*(Béal Glas Loch), the Town of the Green Lake*—with the magnificently timbered demesne of Sir Shane Leslie, the noted Irish writer, delightfully situated beside the picturesque lake. I can recommend the excellent Patton's Hotel there. From Glasloch a road runs to Emyvale—*(Lomda), a Bed*—a place-name which tells us that some saint or holy man once made his resting place there. Loch Emy is famous for its wild swans, and in this old country of the MacKennas, *The Green Woods of Truagh*, you will find some of the best timbered stretches in Ireland. In a house in Emyvale, which will be pointed out to you, Wolfe Tone was lodged for the night on his way to Dublin and immortality.

A few miles south-west of Emyvale is Tedavnet—*(Tigh Damhnata), the House of Downat*, a name better known in its Latinised form of *Dympna*. This lady became a Christian at a very early age, and, to avoid a Pagan marriage which her father tried to force upon her, fled to Gheel in Belgium. Thither her father pursued her, and, finding her obdurate in her decision to oppose his will, beheaded her on the spot. Dympna thus became one of the earliest martyrs of the Celtic Church, as well as the patroness of the celebrated establishment at Gheel for the care of the mentally diseased.

Back through Monaghan Town, and over to the south-east near the Armagh border, is Clontibret—*(Cluain Tiobrad), the Meadow of the Spring or Well*—where the little river ran red with blood on the day the great Earl of Tyrone led his Irish warriors against the might of the Elizabethan English. The gigantic Segrave was in command of the English, and as soon as he saw Tyrone he galloped full tilt at him. Both broke their lances against each other's armour, and then grappled and swayed until the O Neill was unseated. The hope of Ireland seemed dead, but Tyrone contrived to draw his short Irish sword, and, using his own body as a hammer, to drive it into the giant's groin. With Segrave slain, the English forces broke and fled, leaving their standard behind them.

Travelling south we reach Ballybay—*(Béal Átha Beithe), the Ford-Mouth of the Birch*—the prettily situated home of the singing maid-servant who taught me my first songs, and a place once famous for linen manufacture and bleach greens. To the east, Sliev, monarch of Armagh and most storied mountain in Ireland, shows up clearly in a glory of blue-shadowed magnificence, and associated with this little town is that fine poem: *He came from the North*, which breathes a gentle plea for the unity of Ireland:

> He came from the North, so his words were few.
> But his voice was kind and his heart was true,
> And I knew by his eyes that no guile had he
> So I married my man from the North country.
>
> Oh Garryowen may be more gay
> Than this quiet street of Ballybay,
> And I know that the sun shines softly down

On the river that runs through my native town.
But there's not—and I say it with joy and pride—
A better man in all Munster wide.
And Limerick Town has no happier hearth
Than mine has been with my man from the North.

I wish that in Munster they only knew
The kind kind neighbours I came unto:
Small hate or scorn would there ever be
Between the South and the North country.[1]

A most picturesque road runs south for about six miles to Bellatrain—*(Bel-atha-irtin), the Ford Mouth of the Hero*—and here the County narrows to a corridor, only about twelve miles wide, between Cavan and Armagh . The little village of two houses and two pubs lies in country bejewelled with charming small lakes and streams, and in days gone by it boasted its own tanneries, breweries and flour mills, as well as a strong castle that stood at the Famey border of the hamlet. This renowned territory of Farney—*(Fearnaigh), the Plain of the Alders*—was thickly wooded with alders until the beginning of the eighteenth century.

Eleven miles away, and close to the Louth border, is Inishkeen—*Inis Caoin, the Beautiful Island or River Holm*—where there are slight remains of an ancient monastery, the stump of one of the only two Round Towers that exist in Monaghan, and a curious old stone cross embedded in a wall. And there is excellent trout fishing in the River Fane in this very pretty countryside.

Ten miles to the north-west is Castleblayney, founded by Sir Edward Blayney, who was Governor of the County Monaghan under James the First. The town is very English in appearance and is an important centre of the flax-growing industry. Within the fine demesne of Hope Castle, which is now a convent, is Loch Muckno—*(Mucnamh), the Lake of the Swimming-place of the Pigs*—the most beautiful lake in the County. With its many tree-clad islands and charming little bays it is an ideal place for a picnic, but the angler will not find much interest in its too-plentiful pike and perch.

Carrickmacross—*(Carraig Mhachaire Rois), the Rock of the Plain* of the Woods—is famous for its lace, which was first made here in the year 1820, and you may see some fine specimens of it, and of the almost equally celebrated Guipure, at the Saint Louis Convent. Elizabeth granted a large tract of land in this region to Essex, and some remains of the castle built by the third Earl still exist; but most of the cut stones of this stronghold were looted for the building of the Market House in 1780. From Carrickmacross went Monaghan's famous Gentleman Bandit, James MacClean, to take the drawing-rooms of London by storm in 1750. Arrested for the bare-faced hold-up of a stagecoach at Turnham Green, he

---

[1] By Thomas D'Arcy McGee (1825-1868), (Clachan ed.).

pleaded from the dock that he had certificates from four Members of Parliament, as well as from several Monaghan justices; but London had no need of a Carrickmacross clergyman's son turned highwayman, and they strung him up despite his credentials.

Across the County to the west, and close to the Fermanagh border, we find Clones, and on the way to that place, before we reach the neat village of Newbliss—*(Lios Darach or Cúil Darach), the Fort of the Place of Oaks*—(you'll see the fort itself on the Clones road beside the village) we are bound to notice three gallauns, or standing-stones, rising boldly against the skyline. These are known as the *Fir breige*, which means the False Men, and which is also the native term for a scarecrow. On the other side of Newbliss, and midway between that place and Clones, a fine avenue of lime trees leads from the Bridge of Annalore into the demesne of Ballynure, an avenue known as the Shades of Annalore. This place-name—*(Áth an Lobhair), the Ford of the Leper*—reminds us that leprosy must at one time have been fairly prevalent in Ireland, for there are many place-names in the country of like significance.

Clones—*(Cluain Eois), the Meadow of Eos*—is a well-known pronunciation-trap for the unwary stranger, for the name is pronounced *Cloh-nes*, with the stress entirely on the first syllable, as its Irish form indeed indicates. The celebrated Saint Tighernach was the first Christian prelate of Clones, and his death here, of the plague, in 548, speaks for the very early ecclesiastical importance of the place. The monastery which followed the original foundation of Saint Tighernach was burned in 1095, but was rebuilt, and perhaps the ruined nave of a once-splendid twelfth-century church is a remnant of this reconstruction. On the north wall is preserved a curiously-wrought Celtic cross, and between this spot and the Round Tower is a shrine made from a single block of red sandstone. The Round Tower, one of the only two in the County, is of very rude masonry of undressed stones, but the inner lining of limestone blocks is smooth enough. The tower lacks its conical cap, which was destroyed by lightning, but the doorway is intact and stands eight feet above the ground. The splendid tenth-century *High Cross of Clones* is in the Market Square, the shaft, which is eight feet high, being divided into three panels. The entire cross is beautifully decorated with the typical interlaced ornament derived from La Tene importations[1], as well as with the familiar carved representations of Biblical stories. Behind the parish church, which stands on a fine eminence beside the High Cross, is a fairly good example of an Anglo-Norman mote-and-bailey.

---

[1] La tène culture is a culture of Protohistory which develops in Europe between about 450 BC and 25 BC. Regarded as the apogee of the Celtic civilisation, (Clachan ed.).

Dublin Street, Monaghan

The High Cross, Clones, County Monaghan.

Monaghan of the Songs! Monaghan of the Small Little Hills! We come to the end of your delights too quickly. But it would never do to dally too long over them, for we might grow dizzy travelling the ever-winding roads round the maze of small hills, in and out amongst the adorable wee lakes with the islands floating on them. As we move along, the little hills seem to spin about us over the neat thorn hedges, so that we begin to think that here, and not in bleak Ballyshannon at all, is the country of the fairies and leprechauns where the poet Allingham should have been born.

For the County Monaghan is a place where everything is in little, and the small little hills and lakes and rivers, and the diminutive sweet fields, seem indeed to belong to *the Land of Heart's Desire* and the never-never country of the *Wee People*.

Tyrladen Village, County Donegal.

The County of Cavan — Contae an Cabáin

OST people seem to think of Cavan as a dull inland County, and even the majority of Irish people know singularly little of this glorious region of lakes and streams, woods and valleys, and hills and mountains, which, taken as a whole, is a place of much charm and loveliness. It is like the County Monaghan on a larger scale, and whilst it is one of *the Nine Counties of Ulster* its people are only half Northern. There is an historical reason for this, for the County Cavan anciently formed that great Irish district known as East Breffni, or Breffni-O Reilly from the O Reilly family which ruled it as princes from remote times. The whole of Breffni covered the present counties of Cavan and Leitrim, but over Leitrim, which was West Breffni, the O Rourkes held sway. This territory was shired by Sir John Perrott, but before the Elizabethans formed the present County of Cavan and included it in the Province of Ulster, Breffni as a whole was part of Connacht. Perrott cunningly divided the new County amongst the O Reillys, so as to set up jealousies amongst the rival factions of that great house and thus reduce their power, and so well did his scheme work that James the First was able to take over the whole County, as the property of the Crown of England, on the pretext of unrest and rebellion. But though the County of Cavan was then thoroughly planted in accordance with the great scheme with which we are now familiar, much of the O Reilly and other native Irish blood remained, and, by intermarriage, became mingled with the blood of the planted interlopers, with the result that the Cavan people of to-day are largely a mixture of the folk of Ulster and the folk of the west.

This two-coloured strand in the fabric of Cavan life is reflected in literature in a most interesting manner. Of the purely Celtic writers, the bard Fargail Dalean was a Cavan man who flourished in the sixth century, who was known as *the arch master and supreme professor of the antiquities of Ireland*, and whose master-piece was a long elegy on Columcille. Next came Saint Killian, an Irish poet greatly esteemed by Douglas Hyde, who sang mostly the glory and wonder of Ireland and the sorrow and degradation that was to come with usurping strangers. The Anglo-Norman invasion, which occurred long after Saint Killian's death, was foretold by him even to the details of its origin in the faithlessness of Dervorgilla. Much later came Tadhg Dali O Higgin, chief bard to the Maguires of Fermanagh, whose *White-walled Rampart among the Blue Hillocks*, the very title of which is almost a poem itself, is a glowing panegyric of that Maguire stronghold at Enniskillen which we have already considered. In the eighteenth century, Fiachra MacBrady, known as *The Stradone Schoolmaster,* was an honoured exponent of verse in his native tongue, whilst the Reverend Philip MacBrady, better known as Philip Ministeir and as the friend of Carolan, was not only a good poet but enjoyed a great reputation as a wit. This is part of what we may call *the green strand*, and even if we dub the other strand *orange* we shall find it no less nationally noteworthy. It was spun by those descendants of the Jacobean Planters who promptly and incurably fell in love with Ireland, and who did the greatest honour to the country of their adoption.

The Brookes and the Sheridans are by far the most distinguished of the Anglo-Irish writers belonging to the County Cavan. The Reverend Thomas Sheridan was born at Quilca in 1687 and ran a school in Dublin. As a translator of the classics he became celebrated, and he was generally reckoned to be *poor but gay, and the best scholar in the three kingdoms*. Sheridan and Swift were inseparable friends, and it was during a visit to Quilca that the great Dean got his inspiration for *Gulliver's Travels*, after he had seen a giant of a man walking the Cavan roads. Sheridan's illustrious grandson, Richard Brinsley Sheridan, belongs not to Cavan but to the world, and if he was born in Dublin itself there's a power of Cavan blood in him. Henry Brooke was born at Rantavan in 1706, but his literary work was done in London where he became the great friend of Pope. He translated Tasso's *Jerusalem Delivered*, wrote several successful plays, and in 1766 published his gigantic masterpiece, *The Fool of Quality*, which Wesley said was the most beautiful thing he had ever read. Like his masterpiece, his family also was gigantic, and when he died in Cavan in the year 1783 he was the father of twenty-two children. Of this immense family Charlotte Brooke carried on the tradition of her father, and, in 1789, published that invaluable work: *Relics of Irish Poetry*. Without this collection many gems of Irish culture would be lost for ever, and scholars are eternally grateful for the fact that alongside her translations Charlotte printed the Irish originals. As a kind of commentary on this racial dichotomy of the County Cavan, it is significant that the only newspaper printed in the County is the weekly Anglo-Celt. The only bad thing I know about that paper is the execrable local pronunciation of the word *Celt* with a soft C. It does violence to my ear every time a Cavan man uses such an un-Irish sound.

But before we leave our loom, what is that other thread sticking out of the fabric? American, as I live. For Edgar Allan Poe, inventor of the tale of horror, came from Cavan stock, and the ancestral home of the Poes was pointed out, near Kildallan, until it was demolished some years ago.

The capital of the County is Cavan Town—(*an Cabhán*), *the hollow*—and it is aptly named, for the place is encircled with the green hills which rise steeply on every hand. The slight ruins of a Franciscan Friary, founded in the fourteenth century by Giolla Iosa Roe O Reilly, may still be seen in the centre of the town, but the fate of this house was so stormy that very little of it remains. It started its history as a Dominican monastery, but passed to the rule of Saint Francis in the fifteenth century, and Ua O Reilly, Prince of all Breffni, was laid to rest there in 1491. Owen Roe O Neill, hero of the Confederate Wars, was also buried there, after he had been poisoned in Cloughoughter Castle in 1649, or so the story goes, and that famous O Reilly, *Myles the Slasher*, another great Confederate warrior, came here for his long rest after his death-blow at Finea. From the time of the Reformation until the eighteenth century the now-ruinous church was used for public worship, and within the chancel you may still see the tomb of Primate Hugh O Reilly. Just outside the town is Tullymongan Hill, sometimes known as *Gallows Hill*, and there stood the principal O Reilly stronghold and the famous *Mint House* of the clan. On Tullymongan the O Reilly chieftains were crowned, and on Shanthoman Mountain, a few miles away, they were inaugurated, and you may still see the *Inauguration Stones* there to-day, though they were used for the last time as long ago as 1585. From the *Mint House* came the celebrated *O Reilly Coin*, which was legal tender, even in Europe, until the Parliament of the Pale, at Trim in 1447 and at Naas in 1449, forbade its currency.

Four miles south-west of Cavan Town is Kilmore—*(Cill Mhór), the Big Church*—which is the seat of an ancient bishopric. The first regular bishop was Andrew MacBrady, appointed in 1454, but for centuries before that date there were prelates here known as *Bishops of Breffni*. The most illustrious Bishop of Kilmore was Bedell, who first translated the Bible into Irish, and he lies asleep in a special section of the graveyard, under a tombstone of 1642, beside a contemporary and gigantic sycamore. Opposite his grave is a fine Anglo-Norman mote-and-bailey of the usual type, and a church of some kind was undoubtedly erected on that neighbouring hill soon after the builders of this temporary fortification had more securely established themselves. The present cathedral was built between 1858 and 1860, on the site of several older structures, but there is really little of interest about it except the marvellous Hiberno-Romanesque doorway which serves as a vestry door. This was brought from the remains of a thirteenth-century Premonstratensian Abbey on Trinity Island, in Loch Oughter, the graveyard and ruins of which still survive and are worth a little pleasant delving, and this doorway is one of the only two Hiberno-Romanesque specimens now standing in Ulster. The other we have already examined on White Island, in Loch Erne, and it is a strange coincidence that our only two extant Ulster specimens of this lovely style belong to small island foundations not so very far apart. It is a pity that this superb piece of architectural carving, more expressive of Scandinavian influence than anything in the whole of Ireland, is not better maintained, for even an annual cleaning would greatly enhance its beauty and clarify its astonishing detail; but lichen, which attacks everything here and is making sad work of the embowering noble trees, is permitted to have its will of this remarkable specimen of our one native architectural style. It is a further pity that when the architect was planning the re-erection of this portal he did not place it inside the church, in the manner of a similar translation at Killaloe, in the County Limerick, where it would have been protected from further dilapidation. In its journeyings this wonderful doorway has suffered some confusion, and whilst many of the stones have been set upside down in their present location there is also an obvious mixture of styles and ages; but none of these blemishes

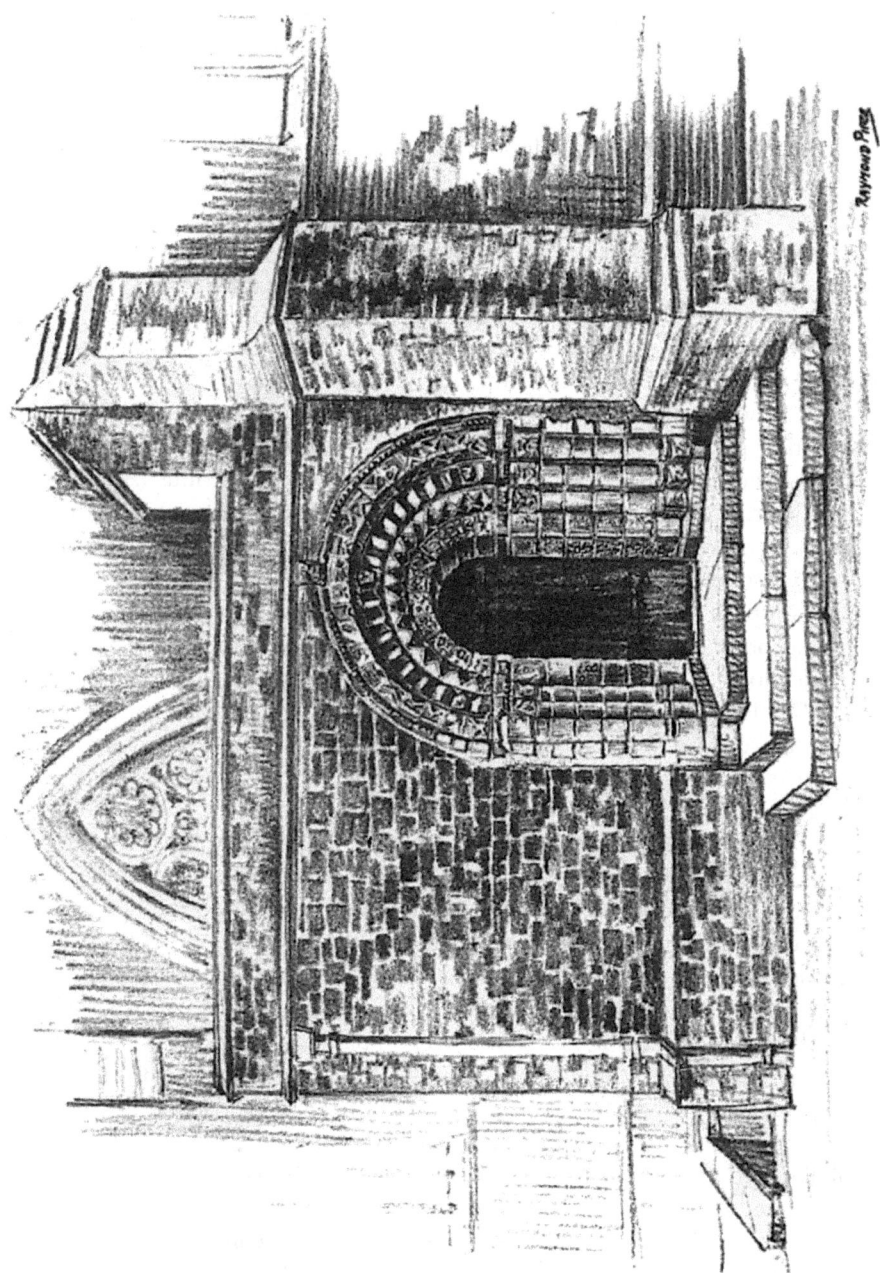

Hiberno-Romanesque Doorway, Kilmore, County Cavan.

can take away from the inherent beauty of this priceless relic of the finest period of native Irish building.

Close at hand is Loch Oughter—*(Loch Uachtair), the Upper Lake*—which is really an expansion of the River Erne, as I have already pointed out. Over an area of seventy-six square miles, the labyrinthine windings of spreading water present the appearance which was familiar to us when we examined Upper Loch Erne, and, of course, the complex configuration of both areas is due to the same causes—the formation of basins by solution of the Carboniferous Limestone in those parts where it is exposed, and its protection from such solution by the frequent overlying banks of drift material.

A road round the southern end of Loch Oughter will lead us to the pretty lakeside village of Killeshandra—*(Cill na Seanrátha), the Church of the Old Rath*—and you may still see the ruins of the early church, within the circumference of an old rath beside the lake, which gave this place its name. Here, surely, is another example of the significance of our usually melodious place-names.

We now follow the main road for Belturbet, making sure that we travel the eastern road to that place: for a mile from Killeshandra this highway splits into two and we must be certain to take the right-hand or easterly route. Almost precisely two miles from Killeshandra another fork occurs, and again we take the right-hand way, up an ascending narrow road which actually faces us, and thus we leave the Belturbet road on our left. For a further mile-and-a-half we follow this narrow road to Corglass Lake—*(Loch corr Glas), the Lake of the Little Rounded Green Hills*—and at that point we leave the car and take to our feet. We shall have to walk a good mile along a cart-track to reach that part of Loch Oughter in which Cloughoughter Castle stands, for though it would be possible to drive a car along this narrow way there is no possibility of turning it anywhere, nor of passing any agricultural vehicle which might be coming or going. At the end of the track a hilly field confronts us, and from the summit of this field there is a wide and splendid view of both the lake and the island fortress. This countryside is a glory of golden whins, and I know of no better spot from which to enjoy the opulent lacustrine loveliness of the County Cavan, or from which the mazy windings and convolutions of this singular lake may more easily be contemplated.

Cloughoughter Castle—*(Cloch Uachtair), the Upper Stone*—is a thirteenth-century circular keep, obviously built to conform with the crannog, or artificial island, on which it stands, and it was a most formidable stronghold of the O Reillys until the Elizabethans took it from them and fitted it as a prison for priests of the proscribed Roman Catholic Church. It was garrisoned by the English in 1601, was retaken by O Reilly, for Lord Delvin who was *on the run,* in 1607, but fell again to the English a year later, when Chichester decided that it must be strengthened both structurally and in the number of its garrison and the store of its munitions. Nevertheless, Phillip MacHugh O Reilly occupied the disputed fortress in 1639 and still held it at the time of the 1641, when he came forward in support of Owen Roe O Neill, the great leader of the national forces.

But in 1653 Cloughoughter came to the end of all its adventures, for in that year it was surrendered to the Cromwellians, who at once slighted it in their usual ruthless manner. The ruin to-day is most picturesque and impressive, and it remains an excellent example of the rather uncommon Irish circular keeps or castles.

During *the 1641* the illustrious Bedell, Protestant Bishop of Kilmore, whose grave we saw not long ago, was a prisoner in the castle, and it was at his dying request that O Reilly had him buried in the graveyard of Kilmore Cathedral. The grand old bishop and scholar was accorded full military honours, for he was greatly beloved by the Irish people of all persuasions. Owen Roe, according to some authorities, died in the castle in 1649, and in 1653 O Reilly made his last stand there, obtained an honourable peace, and went into exile in Flanders, where he died.

We regain the Belturbet road now and travel north along it towards Milltown, but just before we enter that village we turn up a sharp elbow to the right, and, at the end of that cart-track, where there is good room to turn a car, we come upon the ruins of the most important monastic settlement in the County Cavan, one of *O Reilly's Seven Abbeys*, Saint Mary's, or Drumlane as it is more usually known—(*Droim Leathain), the Ridge of the Men of Leinster.*[1] The situation beside Derrybrick Lake—*(Doire Bhroic), the Oakwood of the Badger*—which only just misses being part of Loch Oughter by a narrow neck of land, is most charming, and the ruins stand on the spot where Columcille founded a Celtic monastery, as a daughter-house of Kells, in the year 555. The present church is much confused, the west door being composed of thirteenth-century fragments re-erected in the seventeenth century, to which latter date probably most of the western part of the church belongs; but the many sculptured heads are of fifteenth-century style. The Round Tower, the only one in the County Cavan, is peculiar in displaying two distinct types of masonry, the ground and first stories, up to a height of about twenty feet, being built of worked ashlar blocks in fairly regular courses, whilst the remaining twenty feet of the incomplete tower is constructed of rough masonry. The internal wall of the tower is recessed at the point of demarcation; but the belfry stage and conical cap are entirely missing, having fallen many years ago. The round-headed doorway of the tower, with inclined jambs, belongs to the middle period of building, and on the opposite side from this doorway, about six feet from the ground, are two weathered blocks with a sculptured bird, possibly a hen and a cock, on each. Not much is known about Drumlane, which most likely fell into ruin, or was destroyed, soon after the Dissolution, but by 1586 the lands were already leased by the Crown to the Dillons, who also held Trinity Island where the Kilmore doorway originally

---

[1] Also interpreted as *The Broad Ridge*. (Clachan ed.).

stood, on a similar rent. It seems likely that the foundation, following that of Columcille, was one of Augustinian Canons from Kells.

More than two miles west of Milltown is Kildallan—*(Cill Dalláin), Dalean's Church*—an ancient parish taking its name from that Fargail Dalean who wrote the *Amra Choluim Chille* that great elegy on Columcille to which I have already referred, and the so-called Relic here is a hill-top circular graveyard in which stands an ancient stone inscribed with a cross in low relief. Near Kildallan stood the house of the ancestors of Edgar Allan Poe, in a row of mud-walled cabins in Ardlougher—*(Ard Luachra), the Height of the Rushes*—but such is thesmall regard of the Irish people for monuments of this repute that not a trace of this memorable house survived the fairly recent demolition.

Our road to the west takes us, by way of Ballyconnell, to Swanlinbar, and we soon pass Loch Brackley—*(Loc Bhreaclaigh), the Lake of the Wolf-field*—in which is the island where Saint Mogue was born. Mogue was the patron saint of Drumlane and his holy well can still be seen there. We are now in the anciently celebrated region of Moy Sleacht, *the Plain of Prostrations*, where the Pagan Irish set up their chief god, the terrible *Cromm Cruaicli*, referred to by Sir Samuel Ferguson in his well-known poem, *The Burial of King Cormac*:

> Cromm Cruaicli and his sub-gods twelve,
> Said Cormac, are but carven treene;
> The athat made them, haft or helve.
> Had worthier of our worship been:
> But He who made the tree to grow
> And hid in earth the iron-stone.
> And made the man with mind to know
> The axe's use is God alone.

The Cormac referred to is King Cormac MacAirt, who was king of Ireland from A.D. 213 for forty years, a long reign for any king, but more especially for an Irish king who; according to legend, is reputed to have earned the enmity of his subjects by his denunciation of Cromm. In the midst of a circle of twelve other golden idols Cromm was said to stand, and in sifting fact from legend we may assume that here was a stone circle with a dolmen at its centre, and we must believe that the place was one held in very special fear and reverence. As such it was bound to claim the attention of Saint Patrick, and we read in *The Tripartite Life*:

> When Patrick saw the idol ... he raised his arm to lay the Staff of Jesus on him, and it did not reach him. Cromm stepped back from the attempt upon his right side, for it was to the south his face was, and the mark of the Staff lives in his left side still ... and the earth swallowed the other twelve gods to their heads.

Cloughoughter Castle, County Cavan.

That human sacrifice to Cromm was part of the ritual associated with his worship is likely enough, though I do not look kindly on unfounded speculation of this kind, which, for too long, has beset Irish archaeology with much arrant nonsense. All that seems reasonably probable is that until Saint Patrick's advent Cromm was the chief god of the Pagan Irish, and that, cruel as he was, his end was for long regretted by the people; so much so that Saint Patrick, in his great wisdom and diplomatic understanding, and with all that tolerance which leaves the history of the early Celtic Church without the blemish of a single instance of religious persecution, found it good to declare: *Cromm is gone, but his charities and good works are more than a balance for all his sins.*

Swanlinbar is the border town between the Counties of Cavan and Fermanagh, but you would scarcely think that it was once known as the *Harrogate of Ireland*. Yet it was indeed a famous spa, and *The Postchaise Companion of 1786 says: Large concourses of the best families frequent the Swanlinbar wells, and the place has become a resort of fashion.* But if the village is a poor enough place to-day the scenery is grand, for we are now in the midst of the rugged wonderland of the North-western Highlands of Cavan. And you may still see the old Sulphur Well, at the roadside near the Eire frontier post, though it is now neglected and unattended and covered with a simple stone canopy. Gone are the tastefully arranged walks and pleasure-gardens, the handsome pump room, and the other elegant adornments about which we read in eighteenth-century journals of fashion; gone so utterly that not even an expected hump in the green field remains to tell us of their vanished splendours. Swanlinbar is situated on the Claddagh River, which rises in a fine gorge in the neighbouring mountains, and which pursues an underground course for some three miles before it emerges into the light of day. If you have time to explore parts of this subterranean stream you will not be surprised to know that you are only four miles from the Marble Arch, at Florencecourt, near Enniskillen, for this is part of that same region of Carboniferous Limestone with all the tricks and pranks which we expect of it. The name of the town is interesting, for whilst Joyce makes no reference to it, and other authorities hold that it is not Irish at all, the form seems to be of respectable age. The fancy that four engineers, who started an ironworks here, named the place from the beginning letters of their surnames, has the authority of Dean Swift behind it, but the accepted Irish place-name has nothing to do with *Swanlinbar*, but is *An Muileann Iarainn, the Iron Mill.* And iron was indeed worked here on a large scale, until the year 1765, from ore deposited on the east side of Loch Allen by the torrents which swept it down from Slieve Anieran—*(Sliabh an Iarainn), the Mountain of Iron.* Smelting was done by charcoal, to the destruction of the extensive forests which then flourished in this district, but in 1788 coal was used for this purpose for the first time in Ireland, and this coal was raised from the near-by Arigna coal mines, which are still in active production. But iron is no longer made in any part of Ireland.

Drumlane, County Cavan.

The view from the summit of Slieve Anieran, or of Cuilcagh, is well worth all the labour of an easy-going climb, and from your lofty perch you will look down on the ancient Kingdom of Gian, ruled by the Magaurans until the eighteenth century was no longer young. These lands were the last part of Cavan upon which the invading English set their feet, and until a very late date Irish laws and Irish systems of inheritance and tenure held unchallenged sway in this territory.

Seven miles from Swanlinbar is Lugnashinna—(Log na Sionainne), The Shannon Pot—a small reedy pool of peaty water around which the bog myrtle flourishes in the limestone soil. This is the traditional source of the lordly Shannon, the longest river in Ireland, and longer too than any river in England, Scotland or Wales. This great waterway washes the soil of ten Irish counties, and is navigable for almost the whole of its journey of two hundred miles to the Atlantic, away beyond Limerick. But, strictly speaking, *The Shannon Pot* is not the source of the Shannon, any more than it is the spring-well it is reputed to be in all the old tales and legends. For about a mile away, up on the slopes of Tiltinbane, is a small lake without any apparent outlet; but if you cast a handful of grass on the surface of this lakelet, it will, in due course, appear in *The Shannon Pot*. Which is just another way of saying that the bubbling, singing waters of *the Pot* are but the quiet waters of this and other small lakes, after their mysterious journey through the many subterranean channels which abound in this region of Carboniferous Limestone.

There are many legends which seek to explain the name of our greatest Irish river, but this is the one I like best:

It was long ago, in the childhood of the world, that Sionnain, the daughter of Lodon, the son of the great Lir, became filled with an unholy desire for knowledge, which at that time was the proper possession of man alone. It was in *The-Land-under-the-Wave* she dwelt, and in that fair land was Connla's Well, with the Nine Sacred Streams running from it and the Nine Sacred Hazels growing about its margin. These were the Hazels of Science and Poetry, the Many-melodied Hazels of Knowledge, and it was in the same hour that their fruit and their blossoms and their foliage would break forth and fall upon the well in one shower; and they would raise upon the water a royal surge of crimson. In the well the Salmon of Knowledge lived, and it fed upon the rich crimson nuts of the Sacred Hazels, so that whoever would eat of this salmon would have all the knowledge and wisdom of the world at him. But few men were ever permitted even to prepare themselves for such a feast, and no woman at all on the Seven Wide Ridges of the World. Not without due preparation and solemn rite did any man dare to approach the Sacred Well of Connla, and it was an impious and wicked desire which set the feet of Sionnain towards the margin of the well, and guided her hand towards the Sacred Salmon as it lay in the crimson flood. Swiftly the salmon flashed beyond the reach of the bold intruder. Outraged by the sudden assault upon its immemorial sancity, the Sacred Fish lashed its tail in a frenzy of rage, and the boiling waters of Connla's Well overflowed and swept in

Kilgolagh Horse-fair, County Cavan.

nine roaring cataracts along the Nine Streams that ran beside the Nine Sacred Hazels. Flying, wild-eyed, from the scene of her impiety, the hapless daughter of Lodon was quickly overtaken by the waters which she herself had stirred from peace to fury, and her lifeless body was swept into the Land of Mortals through a hole in the earth which was for ever to be associated with her name and to be known as Lugnashinna, *The Shannon Pot.*

This north-western part of the County Cavan pushes itself in a long finger for about thirty miles from Loch Oughter to Upper Loch Macnean, and, never more than seven miles in breadth, marches with the County Fermanagh in the east over the lofty summit of Cuilcagh—*(Binn Chuilceach), chalky*—and with the County Leitrim in the west over Slieve Nakilla, *the Mountain of the Church.* It is a region unknown to the tourist, and little enough known to the general run of Irish people, and for this reason, as well as for the grandeur of its scenery and the interest of its legendary and historical associations, I would commend it whole-heartedly to your wandering feet, for there indeed is Cavan and there indeed is wild, unspoiled Ireland. But now we must work our way down the valley of the Owenmore, *the Big River,* to Scrabby—*(Scrabaige), Rough or Bad Land*—which lies close to the Longford border. Here is Loch Gowna—*(Loch Gamhna), the Lake of the Calf*—which is the source of the River Erne and really a piece of partially submerged drumlin country, a veritable network of land and water. In a region of Silurian rocks such as this, for we are away from the Carboniferous Limestone now, drumlins are especially common, great mounds of glacial drift deposited by the ice of long ago. This district is picturesquely Irish in landscape, manners and customs, but it is mostly known only to anglers, who greatly prize the big Loch Gowna trout.

We visited Finea, over the Westmeath border, in my Leinster volume, and close to Finea is Kilgolagh—*(Choill Ghabhlach), the Wood of the Fork*—where the most singular horse-fair in Ireland is held. If you want to see this fair, and there's nothing like it anywhere else in the wide world, you'll have to be at Finea on either the 17th of January or the 27th of November, for it is only held twice a year and only on those two days. There is no fair ground, no square, no fair hill or field, but along half-a-mile of narrow Irish road the animals are lined up, nose to hedge on either side, and through a contracted lane of swishing tails and kicking heels the sellers and buyers make their way and transact their business. If you are unused to horses you'll contemplate this busy noisy scene from a distance, for I can imagine nothing more terrifying to the uninitiated than that long aisle of restless plunging animals.

Finea, as I have already pointed out, was immortalised by Percy French in that grand song which all the world sings—*Come back, Paddy Reilly, to Ballyjamesduff*—in which we are most melodiously directed to:

> Turn to the left at the Bridge of Finea
> And stop when half-way to Cootehill.

Mulroy Bay, County Donegal

So, following that direction, we soon reach Ballyjamesduff itself, with its good hotel, sitting most prettily in the region of our fairy lake, Loch Sheelin, and move on to Virginia, a neat little town born of the inconclusive Plantation of Elizabeth, and named after that red-headed harridan of England. Virginia! It will make some of you think of America, but for some reason it always reminds me of the schoolboy howler: *Elizabeth was known as the Virgin Queen. As a Queen she was a great success.* The town is situated most charmingly on the northern shore of Loch Ramor—*(Loch Ramhar), the Lake of the Fat Neck*—and amongst the pretty woods which almost surround that fine sheet of water is an attractive holiday hotel which was once the sporting residence of the Marquess of Headfort. You will find it compact of all the desirable qualities of peace and comfort.

Two miles north-east of Virginia is Quilca, the old home of the Sheridans, and there is pointed out *Stella's Bower*, a pleasant circle of greensward surrounded by eighteen beautiful lime trees, where Dean Swift is reputed to have written much of *Gulliver*. There, too, Richard Brinsley Sheridan worked on *The School for Scandal*, gone thither from Shercock where he lived at the time.

At near-by Killinkere—*(Cillín Chéir), the Small Church of the Bernes[1]*—where Henry Brooke's father was rector, stands the cottage where Phil Sheridan was born in 1830. Unrelated to the family of the great dramatist, this poor boy set out with his ass and cart for Drogheda, joined shipping there for the New World, and, in the fullness of time, became General Phil Sheridan, Commander-in-Chief of the United States Army. To reach Killinkere the best plan is to follow the road through Virginia for Bailieborough for four miles and there turn left. Soon you will see Killinkere Church ahead of you, and soon, by the roadside, you will find Phil Sheridan's little cottage, still neatly and lovingly preserved by the good Gillicks who own and farm the land. Into the gable of the historic little house, one Father Joseph Meehan, to whom God be good, set a marble tablet in 1925, and on this tablet appears this inscription:

Here was born
1830
Phil Sheridan
Comm.-in-Chief
U.S. Army.

J. M.   1925.

We are now in the Barony of Clankee—*Clann-an-chaoich\Clann-an-kee, the Clan of the One-eyed Man*—and this one-eyed man was the celebrated O Reilly chieftain, Niall Caoch O Reilly. The district is littered with ruined castles and more ancient remains, and you should seek out the

---

[1] Also interpreted as *Little Black Church*, (Clachan ed.).

moated burial-mound of Moybolgue, the largest in all Breffni and the last resting-place of Fiacha, High King of Ireland when he died in A.D. 56; the Castle of Tonragee—*Backside to the Wind*—which was the O Reillys' chief fortress in this region; and the Castle of Muff, which was another great stronghold of this powerful clan. Near the castle is the *Rock of Muff*, notorious for those faction fights which are so magnificently described by Carleton. Along the Monaghan border we go to Shercock—*(Searcóg), sweetheart*—a pretty wee place perched above Loch Sillan—*Loch Sailéan, the Lake of the Willow Grove*—where Richard Brinsley Sheridan lived for a time. And ten miles more will bring us to the end of our Cavan journey, and to Cootehill, once a stronghold of the O Reillys, who knew the place as *Muincille, a Sleeve of Land*. This is the second-largest town in the County Cavan, exceeded in size only by Cavan Town itself, and it got its present name early in the seventeenth century, when Sir Charles Coote, by force of arms, took it from its rightful owners. These Cootes, not now represented in the town, became the Earls of Bellamont, and the Forest of Bellamont perpetuates their name. Mrs. Sadlier, the celebrated Irish-American authoress, was born in Cootehill.

And now, at the end of our sojourn amongst the manifold beauties of this old and storied Ulster county, and indeed at the end of our journey through all the Nine Counties of the age-old Province itself, we may fittingly take a drink, hard or soft according to our tastes, or maybe a wee tint of both, and, in one of Cootehill's hospitable houses, raise our glasses to the good old Ulster toast with the friendly ring about it— *na sláinte de bhradán, croí láidir folláin, agus gob fliuch,*—*the health of a salmon, a strong wholesome heart, and a wet beak.*

General Phil Sheridan's Birthplace, County Cavan.

Loch Sheeling, The Fairy Pool

Maghery, County Donegal, with sea-rods drying on the wall.

INDEX

Agricultural methods, 5
Antrim town, 39
Ardara, 158, 160
Ardboe High Cross, 100
Ardglass, 59, 61, 62
Armagh, 4, 9, 10, 40, 58, 66, 67, 78, 80, 82, 83, 84, 85, 86, 88, 90, 92, 94, 96, 97, 99, 102, 104, 107, 132, 172, 177, 178, 179
Armagh City, 15, 85
Armagh, County, 43
Augher, 104
Ballintoy, 46
Ballycarry, 52
Ballycastle, 49, 50, 209
Ballygally, 51
Ballymena, 24, 43
Ballymoney, 44
Ballynahinch, 42, 71
Ballyshannon, 112, 168, 170, 172, 173, 183
Banbridge, 12, 67, 68
Bangor, 5, 61, 74
Baronscourt, 107
Battle of the Diamond, 16
Belfast, 1, 12, 13, 14, 15, 17, 19, 20, 22, 24, 26, 27, 28, 30, 32, 34, 36, 37, 38, 39, 43, 44, 46, 52, 54, 55, 57, 63, 67, 69, 72, 74, 76, 77, 106, 120, 135, 208
Belfast City Hall, 26

Belfast Museum, 27
Belleek, 114, 117, 118
Belmore Mountain, 114
Benburb, 102
Bessbrook, 90, 107
Black Pig's Dyke, 4, 66, 69, 82, 91, 117, 130, 136
Blackwatertown, 88
Bocan Stone Circle, 139
Broughshane, 43
Bunbeg, 148, 150
Buncrana, 138, 139, 140, 142
Bundoran, 4, 164, 172
Bushmills, 45, 46
Caledon, 104
Camloch, 90
Carleton, William, novelist, 104
Carndonagh, 138, 139, 140
Carrick-a-rede, 49
Carrickfergus, 6, 20, 39, 52, 54, 55, 56, 83
Carrickmacross, 94, 177, 179
Carrigart, 145
Castle Coole, 116
Castleblayney, 177, 179
Castlecaulfeild, 98
Cavan Town, 185, 186, 199
Cave Hill, 15, 20, 26, 34
Charlemont, 85, 98, 102

201

Charlemont, village of, 88
Clones, 177, 180
Cloughoughter Castle, 186, 188
Coagh, 100
Coalisland, 100
Coast Road, 50
Coleraine, 9, 12, 129, 132, 134
Comber, 71
Cookstown, 99
Creesloch, 145, 146, 153, 154
Crossmaglen, 94
Cullybackey, 42, 43
Cushendall, 49, 50, 52
Cushendun, 50
Dane's Cast, 4
defenders, 15
Derry City, 24, 123, 138
Donaghadee, 74
Donaghmore, 98, 125
Donegal Town, 168, 170, 174
Downhill, 130, 132
Downpatrick, 55, 57, 59, 82, 97
Dromore, 42, 69
Dundonald, 32, 34
Dundrum, 62
Dunfanaghy, 146
Dungannon, 12, 84, 91, 97, 98, 100
Dungloe, 154, 155, 156
Dunlewy, 152, 153
Dunseverick, 46
Dunseverick Castle, 46
Ecclesville, 105
Eire, 1, 3, 13, 14, 16, 17, 64, 66, 67, 92, 104, 106, 110, 117, 136, 137, 192
Eisenhower, 17
Emania, 4, 69, 82, 83, 92, 172
Emigrants to teh USA, 11
Enniskillen, 112, 113, 114, 117, 118, 120, 121, 122, 184, 192
Entrys, 37
Fair Head, 49, 50
Fathom Mountain, 66
Fintona, 105, 106
Flagstaff Road, 66
Forkhill, 94
Gap of the North, 1, 92, 96
Garvagh, 134
Giant's Causeway, 45, 91
Giant's Ring, 19
Glasloch, 177, 178
Glencolumcille, 158, 160, 162
Glengesh, 162
Glens of Antrim, 50

Glenshane Pass, 135
Glenties, 156, 160
Gortahork, 149, 152, 154
Gortin Glen, 108
Goward Horned Cairn, 67
Grianan, 143, 158
Horn Head, 148, 149, 150
Inishkeen, 179
Inishowen, 110, 137, 138, 139, 142, 143
Inver, 167
Kesh, 118
Kilkeel, 63, 67
Killevy, 90, 91, 92
Killinkere, 198
Killybegs, 146, 166, 167
Killyleagh, 71
Kilmacrenan, 153, 154
Kilmore, County Armagh, 85
Kilmore, County Cavan, 186, 189
Kilnasaggart, 92
Knockmany Hill, 104
Larne, 26, 46, 50, 52, 54, 74, 97
Leslie, Sir Shane, 178
Letterkenny, 143, 168
Limavady, 129, 130, 132
Lisburn, 24, 40, 42, 57, 71
Lisnaskea, 116
Loch Erne, 112, 113, 114, 116, 117, 168, 173, 186, 188
Loch Neagh, 1, 39
Loch Oughter, 186, 188, 189, 196
Lochbrickland, 68
Lochgall, 88
Londonderry, 9, 51, 74, 123, 124, 129, 134
Lurgan, 24, 39, 86, 88, 97
MacArt's Fort, 15, 26, 37
MacKelve Frank y, 27
Maghera, 12, 129, 135, 158, 160
Mahee Island, 72
Malin Head, 138, 139
Malinbeg, 163, 164
Malinmore, 163, 164
Marlacoo Lake, 90
Marshall, W. F., 13
May, Andrew MacL., 99
Milford, 144, 145
Milltown, 189, 190
Monaghan, 4, 9, 10, 37, 104, 106, 137, 175, 177, 178, 179, 183, 184, 199
Mountains of Mourne, 62, 63, 67, 135
Moville, 138, 139
Moy, 102, 190
Moyry Castle, 92, 96

Muckros Head, 166
Narrow Water Castle, 66
Newcastle, 62, 63, 67
Newry, 1, 4, 12, 24, 66, 67, 68, 90, 91, 98
Newtownards, 20, 34, 72
Norsemen, 6, 52, 61, 72, 76, 83, 84, 112, 124, 168
O Neill, Hugh, 6, 88
O Neill, Sir, 10, 104, 107
Omagh, 97, 106
Pettigo, 118, 173
Plantation of Ulster, 8
Plumbridge, 108
Pogue's Entry, 39
Pomeroy, 99
Portadown, 1, 24, 28, 70, 84, 85, 86
Portora Royal School, 113
Protestant, 8, 13, 14, 15, 16, 28, 126, 132, 189
Quilca, 185, 198
Raholp, 61
Ramelton, 144
Rathfriland, 67, 68, 84
Rathlin Island, 49, 50

Rosses, 154, 155, 156, 158
Round Tower, 39, 40, 45, 57, 59, 72, 85, 121, 124, 149, 152, 168, 180, 189
Saul, 58, 59, 60, 61, 124, 163
Scarva, 4, 69, 91
Scrabo Tower, 26
Shannon Pot, 194, 196
Shercock, 198, 199
Siege of Derry, 123
Slieve League, 163, 164, 166, 167
Stormont, 32, 34
Strabane, 12, 107, 108, 110, 143
Strangford, 6, 26, 57, 61, 71, 74
Struel Wells, 59
Swanlinbar, 190, 192, 194
Tanderagee, 90
Tory Island, 148
Ulster dialect, 2
Ulster Rising, 14
Ulster Sails West, 13
Ulster Volunteers, 13
Virginia, 8, 12, 198
Waringstown, 70, 71
Warrenpoint, 64

GEOLOGICAL MAP OF ULSTER

DATE B.C.		PERIOD	CLIMATE
8000	Fini-glacial retreat / Pre-boreal	**PALEOLITHIC** Old Stone Age	Warm interglacial land sinks
		no certain evidence of occupation	Climatic fluctuations
7000		**MESOLITHIC** Middle Stone Age	disappearance of ice
			land rises
6000	Boreal		Dry and invigorating temperate species
		Maglemose	Land sinks
		• Larnian Culture	
5000	Post Glacial Time / Atlantic	Island Magee Cushendun Toome Bay Maglemose occupied the dry bed of the North Channel migratory hunters and fishers River Ford Culture mud flats, open country First boats, pottery	temperate moist
4000			
3000		**TARDENOISIAN** River Ford Culture raised beaches, etc.	
		NEOLITHIC AGE	
		• PASSAGE GRAVES First civilised folk pastorals	land rises open pine forests higher than at present
2000	Sub-boreal	• HORNED CAIRNS	
		• **BRONZE AGE** "B" Beaker Folk STONE CIRCLES Neolith 'B' Pottery and Cists Gallery graves Few Raths Late Bronze Crannogs	Dry invigorating
1000		**IRON AGE** 1st Celts. Cruitneach IRON AGE 'A' La Tène (Celtic Art) 2nd Celtic invasion IRON AGE 'B' LAGIN IRON AGE 'C' FIR BOLG continued Bronze Age	Sudden deterioration bad peat bogs form
AD	Sub-Atlantic	**CRANNOGS** Black Pigs Dyke OGHAM inscriptions	Land sinks moist warm
		CHRISTIANITY Dál Riada First Monasteries Carndonagh High Cross VIKING INVASIONS, Norse Destruction of Armagh Muredachs Cross 923	
1000		Hiberno-Romanesque Anglo Normans.12th cent. to 1360. Bruce 1315 Plantation of Ulster Irish War of 1641 Cromwell 1651 William of Orange 1689	increase of forests cut for iron smelting
2000			

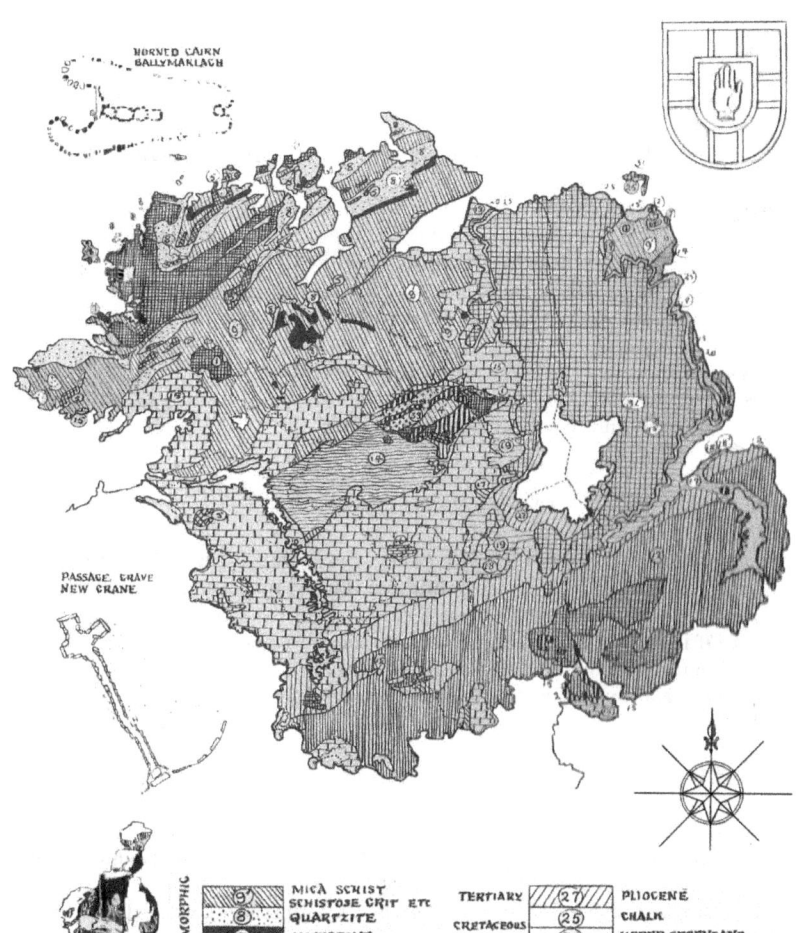

Clachan's 'Historic Irish Journeys' series

Travels In Ireland - J.G. Kohl

This is a very readable account by a German visitor of his tour around Ireland immediately before the Great Famine.

Disturbed Ireland – 1881 - Bernard Becker

A series of letters written as the author travelled around the West of Ireland, visiting key places in the 'Land War'. We meet Captain Boycott and other members of the gentry, as well as a range of small farmers and peasants.

A Journey throughout Ireland, During the Spring, Summer and Autumn of 1834 - Henry D. Inglis

Inglis travels Ireland attempting to answer the question, 'is Ireland and improving country?' using discussion with landlords, manufacturers and tenants plus his own insightful observations.

The West Of Ireland: Its Existing Condition and Prospects - Henry Coulter

This is a collection of letters from *Saunders's News-Letter* relating to the condition and prospects of the people of the West of Ireland after the partial failure of the harvests of the early 1860s.

Highways and Byways in Donegal and Antrim - Stephen Gwynn

Take this book with you as you travel around Donegal and the Glens of Antrim and you will find that you journey not only over land, but also over time.

*   *   *   *   *   *

Clachan 'Local History' Series

Henry Coulter's account has been sub-divided for the convenience of local and family historians.

The West Of Ireland: Its Existing Condition and Prospects, Part 1, by Henry Coulter. This is an extract from the complete edition dealing with Athlone, Co. Clare and Co. Galway.

The West Of Ireland: Its Existing Condition and Prospects, Part 2, by Henry Coulter. This is an extract from the complete edition dealing with Co. Mayo.

The West Of Ireland: Its Existing Condition and Prospects, Part 3, by Henry Coulter. The final extract from the complete edition dealing with Counties Co Sligo, Donegal, Leitrim and Roscommon.

*   *   *   *   *   *

J.G.Kohl's account has been sub-divided for the convenience of local and family historians.

Travels in Ireland – Part 1, takes us through Edgeworthtown, The Shannon, Limerick, Edenvale, Kilrush and Father Mathew.

Travels in Ireland – Part 2, his journey continues through Tarbet, Tralee, Killarney, Bantry, Cork, Kilkenny and Waterford.

Travels in Ireland – Part 3, this section deals with Wexford, Enniscorthy, Avoca, Glendalough and Dublin.

Travels In Ireland - Part 4 – he goes north for the last part of his journey through Dundalk, Newry, Belfast, The Antrim Coast, Rathlin, The Giant's Causeway.

*   *   *   *   *   *

Henry D. Inglis' account has also been sub-divided for the convenience of local and family historians.

A Journey throughout Ireland, During the Spring, Summer and Autumn of 1834, Part 1 takes us from Dublin. Through Wexford, Waterford and Cork.

A Journey throughout Ireland, During the Spring, Summer and Autumn of 1834, Part 2 is an account of Kerry, Clare, Limerick and the Shannon and concludes in Athlone.

Stephen Gwynn's account has also been sub-divided for the convenience of local and family historians.

Highways and Byways in Donegal and Antrim Part One: Donegal

Highways and Byways in Donegal and Antrim Part: Two - Derry & Co. Antrim

*   *   *   *   *   *

Clachan 'Local History' Series

Aghaidh Achadh Mór, The Face of Aghamore – edited by Joe Byrne. This is a reproduction of a title originally published in 1991 and is of enduring interest to local historians and to those with ancestral roots in East Mayo. It covers such topics as Stone Age archaeology, family history, local hedge schools, O'Carolan's connection with the parish, the Civil War and townland surveys.

Lough Corrib, Its Shores and Islands: with Notices of Lough Mask - by William R. Wilde, first published in 1867. In the words of the author: 'A work intended to … rescue from oblivion, or preserve from desecration, some of the historic monuments of the country'.

A Statistical and Agricultural Survey of the Co. of Galway – by Hely Dutton

This is a detailed description of the agricultural conditions and practices of Galway in the early 19C, including detailed chronologies of Galway officials and its governance, senior churchmen and abbeys, monasteries and convents.

A History of Sligo: Town and Country, Vol. I, by Terrence O'Rorke

This classic and well-loved history, first published in 1889, is the work of a man born and bred in Sligo. It remains a work of fascination for anyone with connections to Sligo, and is an important reference for anyone interested in the history of Ireland.

Captain Cuellar's Adventures in Connaught and Ulster, A.D. 1588, by Francisco de Cuellar, Hugh Allingham and Robert Crawford

This is an extraordinary first-hand account of the survival of a captain of the Spanish Armada. Ship-wrecked off the Sligo coast he faces horrors and pursuit to the death. He finds sanctuary among two Irish chieftains before making his way to the North Coast of Antrim and final deliverance.

A Step Up – by Pat Nolan

This is the story of the BIM 56-footers. The book contains details on each boat, and recollections of individuals who owned and/or fished on them.

Valhalla and the Fjörd: A Spiritual Motorcycle Journey through the History of Strangford Lough by Peter moore

As a previously published Director of archaeological excavations, the author has researched the sites with all the available resources, but as well as examining the history of these sites and monuments and their upstanding remains, the book seeks to explore how they make you feel; the tangible aura that some of the sites exude.

* * * * * *

Ballads and Songs

Songs of the Glens of Antrim, Moiré O'Neill

These Songs of the Glens of Antrim were written by a Glenswoman in the dialect of the Glens, and chiefly for the pleasure of other Glens-people.

Away with Words, by Michael Sands

Poems of family, home, place and music in North Antrim

Clachan Publishing, Ballycastle, Glens of Antrim.

www.ingramcontent.com/pod-product-compliance
Lightning Source LLC
Chambersburg PA
CBHW070738160426
43192CB00009B/1485